SOUTH WESTERN VEGETARIAN

SOUTH WESTERN VEGETARIAN

BY STEPHAN PYLES
WITH JOHN HARRISSON

CLARKSON POTTER/PUBLISHERS NEW YORK

Published by Clarkson Potter/Publishers, New York, New York.
Member of the Crown Publishing Group.
Random House, Inc. New York, Toronto, London, Sydney, Auckland
www.randomhouse.com

CLARKSON N. POTTER is a trademark and POTTER and colophon are
registered trademarks of Random House, Inc.

Printed in China

Design by Lauren Monchik

Library of Congress Cataloging-in-Publication Data
Pyles, Stephan.
Southwestern vegetarian/by Stephan Pyles with John Harrisson.—
1st ed.
1. Vegetarian cookery. 2. Cookery, American—Southwestern style.
3. Cookery—Texas.
I. Harrisson, John. II. Title.
TX837.P95   2000
641.5'636'0979—dc21   99-045619

ISBN 0-609-60118-0

10 9 8 7 6 5 4 3 2 1

First Edition

Acknowledgments

Special thanks to Geoffrey Meeker, for all his help in the early stages of this book, and to Katherine Clapner, for her inspiration in developing the desserts chapter.
And to Katie Workman, my more-than-patient editor, who was the only person more excited about this book than I was.

CONTENTS

Introduction

I am a fifth-generation Texan living in my home state,
where the saying goes, "Cattle is king." The very thought of a vegetarian book seemed a bit heretical at first blush, if not downright foolish. After all, when you think of Texas cooking, the first things that come to mind are plump, juicy steaks; barbecued and smoked meats; wonderful Gulf Coast seafood; and spicy Tex-Mex cuisine that relies heavily on pork and beef—all, of course, served in generous "Texas-style" portions.

Things were not always this way in the Southwest. For centuries, Native Americans of the region were an agrarian people, growing corn, beans, squash, and chiles, and gathering wild fruits, nuts, and vegetables. These staples were supplemented by wild game, and trading occurred with the more hunting-oriented cultures of the Plains and South. Still, the diet was primarily vegetarian until the Spanish moved north from Mexico in the sixteenth century.

A book about Southwestern vegetarian cooking is also appropriate because, as in the rest of the country, Texan tastes are changing. An awful lot of top-quality vegetables, fruit, and other produce are grown in the Lone Star State, and Texans are learning to appreciate the fine vegetarian dishes that can be created with this abundance. Over the past decade or more, public awareness of the healthful qualities of vegetarian food has gained momentum, and this style of eating has moved in the United States from the fringe to the culinary mainstream. All kinds of new and interesting vegetables and fruits are popping up on the shelves of supermarket and gourmet store produce sections.

The National Restaurant Association reports that one in five restaurant guests plan on ordering a meatless meal. About one in fifteen Americans describe themselves as "vegetarian"; this term runs a wide spectrum, from vegans, who eat nothing that comes from an animal, including milk and eggs, to "almost vegetarians," who usually enjoy a little chicken or fish now and again with their plant-based diet. For many vegetarians (and would-be vegetarians), the choice is made easier because of health considerations that have become well publicized over recent years. Far from being viewed as dull and uninspiring—typified by the nut burgers and bland lentil cakes of the 1970s—vegetarian cooking is now immensely popular. Talented chefs have shown the way with imaginative and tasty dishes presented with flair. Many upscale restaurants now have complete vegetarian tasting menus. Many others have at least one vegetarian option for a main course, and vegetarian cookbooks are big sellers these days.

Let me state for the record that I am a card-carrying carnivore. Perhaps I should better describe myself as an "omnivore," because I have always loved the color, flavor, and texture that vegetables contribute even to dishes that feature meat. This is a book about great vegetarian cookery as it pertains to my favorite style of cooking: Southwestern. It is about dishes that can be eaten as a meal all by themselves or as accompaniments to everything from grilled fish to roast prime rib. Most are disarmingly easy to prepare. A few recipes in this volume even include seafood, since many people I know are part-time vegetarians who sometimes enjoy a little meat protein on the plate. In most cases here, the meat element in these recipes is optional. The recipes sometimes include dairy products and eggs, so vegans and lacto- and ovo-vegetarians will need to take a more selective approach.

Many times, on a Sunday night off from the restaurant, I have composed entire vegetarian meals for family and friends. They are based on a variety of cooking methods that only reinforce the diversity of vegetarian cooking. Wouldn't most people consider a plate of roasted-garlic mashed potatoes, black bean quesadillas, or marinated grilled asparagus a pretty wonderful element of a filling meal? Dishes such as corn with artichokes or roasted portobello mushrooms are just as likely to whet appetites.

When I opened Star Canyon in Dallas in 1994, I decided to put a vegetarian main course on the menu—something I had never done in my previous ten years of restaurant ownership. I must admit, I was a little surprised at the popularity of the vegetarian special. Soon, I began to experiment with new variations of vegetable recipes, and out of this work and creative process came the idea for this book. After all, ingredients such as fresh herbs; wild mushrooms; toasted spices, nuts, and seeds; and sun-dried tomatoes can excite any palate. Flavored oils and vinegars and other pantry staples can transform good recipes into great meals.

In addition, many of the recipes or their components in this book derive from my fascination with, and love for, foreign ingredients and produce markets, especially in Mexico and points farther south. Finding potatoes in Peru that are almost every color of the rainbow, thirty varieties of corn in Ecuador, or chiles of every shape, size, and degree of heat in Mexico immediately puts my mind in creative overdrive. The same is true of Southeast Asia. The markets of Hong Kong, Bangkok, and Saigon can also put the visitor into sensory overload with their myriad ingredients such as galangal, lemongrass, and choy sum.

When using the recipes in this book, remember that the ingredients are often taking center stage, so take care to choose the very best available or that you can afford. I strongly recommend choosing whatever is in peak season. With the growth of farmers' markets, this task is much easier than it used to be. Wherever possible, support organic farmers because their produce is raised without the chemicals applied by large-scale commercial agriculture. Natural food stores are excellent sources of affordable vegetarian ingredients, and their products will be free of artificial flavors, preservatives, and coloring. Most have bulk food sections with a wide range of whole grains and other nutritious foods. If you are able to, grow whatever you like to eat best in your garden.

I am not yet quite ready to agree with Albert Einstein when he wrote, "Nothing will benefit human health and increase the chances for survival of life on earth as much as evolution to a vegetarian diet." However, increasing numbers of people understand the importance and spiritual significance of redressing the balance in this country that for years has been tilted toward beef, pork, and other meat.

CHAPTER ONE
FROM THE
LONE STAR
PANTRY

JELLIES, JAMS, AND PRESERVES

PREPARING JELLIES, JAMS, AND PRESERVES IS WELL WORTH THE EFFORT BECAUSE OF THE DIFFERENCE IN flavor compared to store-bought items. You can also be assured of the quality of the ingredients.

It is best to use standard-size canning jars with matching lids that ensure an airtight seal. The components, including the rubber rings, should be washed and rinsed, and the jars must be hot when filled. Place them in a large saucepan or stockpot, cover with water, and bring to a boil. Remove from the heat and keep hot until ready to fill.

Fill hot jars to within ¼ inch of the top and seal quickly and securely with the ring and lid. If there is only enough to fill a jar or glass partly, do not seal. Instead, keep refrigerated and use as quickly as possible.

Where using paraffin as a seal to keep the air out, melt the bars in a double boiler; never melt paraffin in a saucepan over direct heat as it is highly flammable. Seal one jar at a time with a thin layer of melted paraffin. (Follow specific canning and sealing instructions on the paraffin box.)

In general, sealed condiments will last for 6 months, while refrigerated and unsealed jars will last up to 2 weeks.

Jalapeño-Cilantro Jelly

Jalapeño jelly has become a great souvenir item from Texas over the years, but this version is much more than a novelty item. Try it mixed with cream cheese or goat cheese spread on fried tortillas or, better yet, on Ancho Focaccia (page 176).

1½ cups cider vinegar
5 cups sugar
7 jalapeño chiles, seeded and minced
2 green New Mexico or Anaheim chiles, seeded and finely diced
½ bunch of cilantro, leaves only, chopped
¾ cup liquid pectin
Paraffin, for sealing

Place the vinegar and sugar in a large saucepan and bring to a boil, stirring until the sugar has dissolved, about 5 minutes. Reduce the heat to low, add the jalapeño and New Mexico chiles, and simmer for 10 minutes, skimming the foam occasionally with a ladle. Add the cilantro, stir in the pectin, and return to a boil. Cook for 1 minute, remove from the heat, and let stand for 20 minutes.

Pour into a hot, sterilized quart jar (page 206) and pint jar and seal with paraffin according to the instructions on the package (if using immediately, you do not need paraffin). The jelly will keep sealed in a cool, dark, dry place for 1 year, or unsealed in the refrigerator for 2 to 3 months.

MAKES 5 CUPS

Cactus Pear Jelly

Cactus pears, or *tunas*, are the fruit of the prickly pear cactus. They have a melonlike aroma and a sweet, earthy flavor, and they are available at Hispanic markets. Visitors to Texas and the Southwest are often surprised that the brightly colored fruit of such an uninviting plant is edible, but more than that, it can be delicious. Although they come in a rainbow of colors (green through yellow and purple), most cactus pears in the United States yield a vivid dark red flesh.

10 ripe cactus pears (about
  2 pounds)
1³/₄ cups sugar
 2 tablespoons freshly squeezed
   lemon juice
 3 tablespoons liquid pectin
 ¹/₂ cup dry red wine
Paraffin, for sealing

Using thick gloves, slice the cactus pears in half lengthwise and scoop out the pulp, discarding the skin. Place in a food processor and blend for 1 minute. Press the pulp and liquid through a food mill to remove the seeds (or press through a medium strainer), and transfer the liquid to a saucepan. Add the sugar and lemon juice and bring to a boil, stirring until the sugar has dissolved. Reduce the heat to medium-low and simmer for 5 minutes. Stir in the pectin and wine and bring to a boil. Cook for 30 seconds, then remove the pan from the heat. Let stand for 30 minutes.

Pour into a hot, sterilized quart jar (page 206) and seal with paraffin according to the instructions on the package (if using immediately, you do not need paraffin). The jelly will keep sealed in a cool, dark, dry place for 1 year, or unsealed in the refrigerator for 2 to 3 months.

MAKES 4 CUPS

Green Mango–Habanero Jam

Mangos are native to India, where they are considered sacred by some. In the Tamil language the fruit is pronounced "mangay," hence the Westernized name. The unripe green fruit is often used in the cuisines of India, Thailand, and the Caribbean, and in this form it contains the same enzyme as papaya—papain—which aids digestion and breaks down the connective tissue in foods. This makes it useful in marinades for tougher cuts of meat. The flavors of mango and the devilishly hot habanero chile were practically created for each other, which makes this jam a terrific pantry item. You can seal it in jars with paraffin if you like.

6 pounds green (unripe) mangos,
  peeled, pitted, and diced
3 red habanero chiles, seeded
  and minced
6 cups sugar
¹/₂ cup premium tequila
¹/₄ cup freshly squeezed lime juice

Combine the mangos, habaneros, sugar, and tequila in a large mixing bowl and refrigerate, covered, overnight.

Place the macerated fruit in a large, heavy-bottomed saucepan and bring to a boil over high heat. Reduce the heat to medium-low, add the lime juice, and simmer for 35 minutes. Cook the jam, stirring almost constantly, until a candy thermometer reads 219°F., about 12 to 15 minutes. (Another sign the jam is cooked is when a small amount poured on a chilled saucer congeals quickly and does not run when tilted.) Spoon into 2 hot, sterilized pint jars (page 206), leaving a ¼-inch headspace, and seal tightly. The jelly will keep sealed in a cool, dark, dry place for 1 year, or unsealed in the refrigerator for 2 to 3 months.

MAKES 4 CUPS

Tomato-Ginger Jam

This jam is certainly a taste treat. The tomato was known as the "apple of love" when it was first taken to Europe from the New World, although by some, it was considered poisonous. Tomato jam may sound a bit odd, but then again, botanically the tomato is a fruit. Travel to L'Arpège restaurant in Paris to see how tomatoes are transformed into a wonderful dessert: Tomatoes are cooked in sweet syrup with raisins, tableside.

5 pounds firm ripe tomatoes, blanched and peeled (page 203)
2 large lemons
1 tablespoon peeled minced fresh ginger
½ teaspoon salt
5 cups sugar
1 teaspoon coriander seeds, toasted and ground (page 211)

Cut the tomatoes in half crosswise and squeeze the seeds into a fine mesh sieve set over a bowl. Discard the seeds, reserving the juice, and chop the tomatoes coarsely. Place the chopped tomatoes and tomato juice in a large stockpot. Grate the zest from the lemons and add to the tomatoes. Cut the lemons in half and squeeze the juice; add ½ cup of the lemon juice to the stockpot. Add the ginger and salt.

Bring the mixture to a boil, stirring occasionally. Reduce the heat to medium-low and simmer, uncovered, until the chopped tomatoes are soft, about 15 minutes. Stir in the sugar. Raise the heat to medium-high and cook the jam, stirring almost constantly, until a candy thermometer reads 219°F., about 12 to 15 minutes. (Another sign the jam is cooked is when a small amount poured on a chilled saucer congeals quickly and does not run when tilted.)

Remove the stockpot from the heat and stir in the coriander. Ladle the jam into 4 hot, sterilized half-pint jars (page 206). Seal tightly and let the jam cool, then store in a cool, dark, dry place. The jam will keep, sealed, for up to 6 months. It can also be refrigerated unsealed for up to 2 weeks.

MAKES 3¾ CUPS

Spicy Peach Preserves

Peaches are native to China, where they have been cultivated for thousands of years. While nothing beats a ripe, juicy peach, this recipe is simply an excellent way to store the best fruit of the season. What better way to get your day started than to awaken your palate with some good coffee and a subtle kick of chile for breakfast?

6 cups peeled and coarsely chopped ripe peaches
2 cups (packed) light brown sugar
6 tablespoons freshly squeezed lemon juice (2 lemons)
1/2 cup dark rum
1/4 teaspoon cayenne
1/2 teaspoon pure red chile powder
1/4 teaspoon ground canela
Pinch of ground cloves
Pinch of ground allspice
2 cups granulated sugar

Combine the peaches, brown sugar, lemon juice, rum, cayenne, chile powder, canela, cloves, and allspice in a large mixing bowl and refrigerate, covered, overnight.

Pour the mixture into a large heavy saucepan. Bring to a boil over medium-high heat, reduce the heat to medium-low, and simmer for 15 to 20 minutes, or until the peaches are tender and begin to turn translucent. Add the granulated sugar and stir constantly for about 10 minutes, until a candy thermometer reads 219°F. (Another sign the jam is cooked is when a small amount poured on a chilled saucer congeals quickly and does not run when tilted.) Pour into 2 hot, sterilized pint jars (page 206) and seal tightly. (Pour the remaining 1 cup into a bottle or 1/2-pint glass container.) The preserves will keep sealed in a cool, dark, dry place for 1 year, or unsealed in the refrigerator for 2 to 3 months.

MAKES 5 CUPS

Ancho Chile Preserves

These thickly textured preserves are similar in style to the Jalapeño-Cilantro Jelly (page 11), and I often use them as a garnish for grilled meat or fish that has a dried chile sauce; they are also wonderful as a spread for good crusty bread. Anchos are dried poblano chiles that have mellow heat and complex flavor tones of dried raisin, coffee, and chocolate. You can seal the jars with paraffin if you wish.

8 ounces dried ancho chiles (12 to 15)
1 cup (packed) light brown sugar
1/4 cup freshly squeezed lemon juice
2 tablespoons grated orange zest
1 tablespoon ground canela
1 dried bay leaf
2 tablespoons chopped fresh cilantro leaves
1/4 cup liquid pectin

Preheat the oven to 450°F.

Place the anchos on a cookie sheet and toast in the oven for 1 or 2 minutes, or until fragrant. Transfer the anchos to a mixing bowl, cover with warm water, and weight down with a plate or pan so the anchos stay submerged. Let soak for 10 to 15 minutes, or until just pliable. Drain the anchos; stem and seed them under running water. Finely dice and set aside.

(continued on next page)

Combine the brown sugar, ½ cup water, the lemon juice, orange zest, canela, and bay leaf in a saucepan and bring to a boil. Cook at a low boil for 10 minutes. Add the reserved anchos, cilantro, and pectin. Return to a vigorous boil and continue to boil for 5 minutes longer, or until the chiles are no longer chewy, stirring frequently. Spoon into 2 hot, sterilized pint jars (page 206) and seal tightly. The preserves will keep sealed in a cool, dark, dry place for 1 year, or unsealed in the refrigerator for 1 month.

MAKES 4 CUPS

Preserved Lemons

Preserved lemon rinds are a staple of Moroccan cookery, and they deliver a distinctive, exotic flavor to dishes. After curing for a few weeks in salt and lemon juice, the lemon rinds develop a certain eucalyptus-like quality that makes an intriguing flavor component.

10 small lemons
½ cup salt
4 cups freshly squeezed lemon juice

In a large mixing bowl, soak the lemons in lukewarm water for 5 days, covered with a towel, changing the water daily.

On the sixth day, partially quarter each lemon by slicing from the top to within ½ inch of the bottom. Open the lemon slightly to sprinkle ¼ teaspoon of salt on the exposed flesh and then close again.

Place 2 tablespoons of salt on the bottom of a sterilized 1½-quart jar (page 206). Pack in the lemons and push them down, adding the remaining salt between each layer. As you pack, press down on the lemons to release their juices and make room for the remaining lemons. Add the lemon juice (or enough to cover the top), leaving ½ inch of air space at the top of the jar. Cover tightly.

Let the lemons ripen in a warm place for 3 weeks, turning the jar upside down each day to redistribute the salt and juice. Remove the lemons to use as needed; rinse under running water, remove and discard the pulp, and use only the rind. There is no need to refrigerate the opened jar. The preserved lemons will keep in a cool, dark, dry place for up to 1 year.

MAKES 1 QUART

PICKLES AND PESTOS

NO SELF-RESPECTING TEXAS PANTRY WOULD BE WITHOUT PICKLES, AND I GREW UP IN A FAMILY FOR whom pickles were a way of life. They were always on the table. The same cannot be said of pestos, but I love them, as they are so simple to make and they provide a wonderful medium for some great flavors.

Bread and Butter Pickles

These pickles are a true Southern treasure. Their pleasantly sweet-and-sour characteristics make them the perfect accompaniment for any of the tortas, sandwiches, or pizzas in Chapter 10. For pickled spears, quarter the cucumbers lengthwise.

2$\frac{1}{2}$ pounds cucumbers (about 5),
      washed and cut into
      $\frac{1}{2}$-inch slices
2 onions, thinly sliced
2 tablespoons salt
2 cups crushed ice
1$\frac{1}{2}$ cups sugar
1$\frac{1}{2}$ cups white wine vinegar
1 teaspoon mustard seeds
$\frac{1}{2}$ tablespoon celery seeds
$\frac{1}{2}$ teaspoon ground turmeric

In a large stainless steel bowl, combine the cucumber and onion slices. Sprinkle with salt and cover with ice. Cover the bowl and refrigerate for 3 to 4 hours. Drain the cucumbers and onions and rinse with cold water.

In a large saucepan, place the cucumbers, onions, sugar, vinegar, mustard seeds, celery seeds, and turmeric. Bring to a boil and remove from the heat. Ladle into 2 hot, sterilized quart jars (page 206) and seal tightly. These pickles will keep sealed in a cool, dark, dry place for 1 year, or unsealed in the refrigerator up to 3 months.

MAKES 2 QUARTS

Pickled Jalapeños

In Texas, pickled jalapeños are considered one of the four major food groups (barbecue is another). A dish of these was always on the table when I was growing up. Because the seeds are left in, these are very hot. They are not only a terrific accompaniment for barbecue, but they also make a good addition to marinades, relishes, and salads.

12 jalapeño chiles
$\frac{1}{2}$ cup olive oil
1 large onion, thinly sliced
4 large garlic cloves, minced
1 carrot, thinly sliced
1 cup cider vinegar
1 teaspoon sugar
2 teaspoons salt
$\frac{1}{4}$ cup chopped fresh cilantro
      leaves
2 dried bay leaves
1 teaspoon cumin seeds

Place the jalapeños in 2 sterilized pint jars (page 206). In a saucepan, heat the oil to lightly smoking and add the onion, garlic, and carrot. Sauté over medium heat for 5 minutes. Add the vinegar, $\frac{1}{2}$ cup water, sugar, and salt and bring to a boil. Remove from the heat. Stir in the cilantro, bay leaves, and cumin seeds.

Pour the liquid over the jalapeños, filling the jars to the top. Seal tightly. These pickles will keep sealed in a cool, dark, dry place for 1 year, or unsealed in the refrigerator up to 3 months.

MAKES 1 QUART

Citrus-Pickled Horseradish

Horseradish, an herb indigenous to eastern Europe, possesses a long history—it is even mentioned in the Book of Exodus. Although most horseradish is bought prepared and bottled, it's readily available in its fresh state. The citrus flavors in this recipe, especially the orange, lend a pleasant, unusual dimension to these "pickles." Try them sliced in Asian-style salads or wherever you might use pickled ginger. *(photograph opposite)*

 1 pound fresh horseradish,
       peeled
1½ tablespoons kosher salt
 1 cup champagne vinegar
 ¼ cup freshly squeezed
       lime juice
 ¼ cup freshly squeezed orange
       juice
 2 tablespoons grated
       lime zest
 2 tablespoons grated
       lemon zest
 3 tablespoons sugar

Using a vegetable peeler, shave strips of horseradish into a bowl. Add the salt and toss to coat. Refrigerate, covered, for 24 hours and toss from time to time.

In a mixing bowl, combine the vinegar, citrus juices and zests, 3 tablespoons water, and sugar and stir until the sugar is fully dissolved. Set aside.

Place the horseradish strips in a colander and let drain for 30 minutes. Place the drained strips into 2 sterilized pint jars (page 206). Pour the reserved citrus mixture evenly into the jars to cover the horseradish, seal tightly, and refrigerate for at least 3 days before using. Keeps sealed in a cool, dark, dry place for 1 year, or unsealed, refrigerated, up to 3 months.

MAKES 4 CUPS

Garlic-Onion Pickles

A member of the lily family, garlic has been used for its healthful and medicinal qualities as well as for its culinary versatility since ancient times. Garlic is believed to stimulate the immune system and is used as an herbal remedy for respiratory and digestive ailments; it is also believed to help prevent heart disease and cancer. In this recipe, the pickling process softens and sweetens the hot, bitter flavor that many (myself included) find offensive in raw garlic. I use these pickles in salads and relishes and with everything from soup to fish.

 3 onions
10 garlic cloves, peeled and
       cut in half
 1 carrot, thinly sliced
 2 tablespoons black
       peppercorns
 1 teaspoon cumin seeds, toasted
       (page 211)
1½ cups champagne vinegar or
       white wine vinegar
 ½ cup sugar
 ¾ cup salt

Slice the onions as thinly as possible, preferably with a mandoline or electric slicer. Place in a mixing bowl and combine with the garlic, carrot, peppercorns, and cumin.

In a saucepan, combine the vinegar, 2 cups water, sugar, and salt and bring to a boil. Remove from the heat and pour the liquid over the onion mixture. Transfer to 4 hot sterilized pint jars (page 206) and seal tightly. These pickles will keep sealed in a cool, dark, dry place for 6 months, or unsealed in the refrigerator up to 3 months.

MAKES 8 CUPS

Pickled Peaches

This recipe brings together a very Southern cooking technique—pickling—and a very Southern ingredient—peaches. Try these pickles in salads or any recipe where you might use pickled cucumbers or other ordinary pickles.

4 cups sugar
2½ cups champagne vinegar
20 whole cloves
12 allspice berries
6 slices peeled fresh ginger (each about the size of a quarter)
2 canela sticks or 1 stick cinnamon
2 tablespoons grated lemon zest
1 teaspoon dried red pepper flakes
4 pounds firm peaches, peeled, halved, and pitted

Combine the sugar and vinegar in a saucepan and heat until the sugar dissolves, 4 to 5 minutes. Combine the cloves, allspice, ginger, canela, lemon zest, and red pepper flakes in a 12-inch square of cheesecloth and tie the top to form a sachet. Place the sachet in the vinegar and sugar mixture and bring to a boil. Remove from the heat and allow to sit for 30 minutes so that the spices can infuse.

Add the peaches to the liquid and bring to a simmer. Simmer for about 30 minutes, or until the peaches are tender but not mushy (the cooking time may vary depending on the ripeness of the fruit). Using a slotted spoon, remove the peaches from the liquid and place in 4 sterilized pint mason jars (page 206). Remove the sachet and bring the remaining syrup to a boil. Boil the syrup for 10 minutes, or until it has reduced by one third. Pour the syrup evenly over the peaches, let cool, and seal tightly. Refrigerate for 2 weeks before using. Keeps sealed in a cool, dark, dry place for 1 year, or unsealed in the refrigerator up to 3 months.

MAKES 8 CUPS

Cilantro-Walnut Pesto

This recipe makes a refreshing variation on the classic basil pesto. You can use it in salad dressings and on grilled vegetables, or with tomatoes and mozzarella. Walnuts can sometimes be bitter tasting, in which case soak them in warm water for 6 to 8 hours or overnight and then place them in a very low oven (200°F) for 20 to 30 minutes to dry them thoroughly. If you wish, you can freeze this pesto.

¼ cup toasted walnuts (page 211)
1 cup fresh cilantro leaves
¼ cup freshly grated Parmesan cheese (about 2 ounces)
3 garlic cloves, peeled and chopped
Juice of ½ lemon
½ cup walnut oil

Place the walnuts, cilantro, Parmesan, garlic, and lemon juice in a food processor and blend until perfectly smooth. With the machine running, slowly add the walnut oil to form a thick paste. Keeps, refrigerated, for up to 1 week or frozen for up to 2 months.

MAKES 2 CUPS

Sun-Dried Tomato–Kalamata Pesto

This pesto is especially good on grilled or roasted eggplant and asparagus. It also makes a great dressing for hors d'oeuvres. Try spreading a little on a crouton and topping it with capers and a grated aged cheese like Parmesan, pecorino, or asadero. As an alternative to sun-dried tomatoes packed in oil, use dried sun-dried tomatoes that have been rehydrated in warm vegetable stock or water.

1 cup dried sun-dried tomatoes, rehydrated in warm water, drained, and chopped
1/3 cup pitted kalamata olives, drained
2 tablespoons chopped fresh oregano leaves
1/4 cup freshly grated Parmesan
3 garlic cloves, peeled and chopped
1/4 cup toasted pine nuts (page 211)
1/2 cup extra-virgin olive oil
Salt to taste

Place the tomatoes, olives, oregano, Parmesan cheese, garlic, and pine nuts in a food processor and blend until smooth. With the motor running, drizzle in the olive oil. Season to taste with salt. Keeps, refrigerated, for up to 1 week or frozen for up to 2 months.

MAKES 2 CUPS

Red Chile–Citrus Zest Pesto

This is a decidedly Southwestern pesto! Try whisking about 2 tablespoons into a cup or so of plain vinaigrette for a flavorful and spicy salad dressing. I also like to brush it on fish or chicken before it goes on the grill.

6 dried ancho chiles
2 tablespoons grated lime zest
2 tablespoons grated lemon zest
3 tablespoons grated orange zest
2 tablespoons chopped fresh cilantro leaves
3 garlic cloves, peeled and chopped
1/4 cup toasted pumpkin seeds (page 211)
1 tablespoon sugar
1/4 cup grated *queso fresco* or crumbled feta cheese
1/2 cup corn oil
Salt to taste

Preheat the oven to 450°F.

Place the anchos on a cookie sheet and toast in the oven for 3 or 4 minutes, or until fragrant. Transfer the anchos to a mixing bowl, cover with warm water, and weight down with a plate or pan so the anchos remain submerged. Let soak for 10 to 15 minutes, or until just pliable. Drain the anchos; stem and seed them under running water. Transfer to a food processor and add the citrus zests, cilantro, garlic, pumpkin seeds, sugar, and cheese. Process until smooth, then drizzle in the oil with the motor running. Season with salt to taste. Keeps, refrigerated, for up to 1 week or frozen for up to 2 months.

MAKES 1 CUP

MUSTARDS, AIOLIS, AND KETCHUPS

ALL THE MUSTARDS IN THIS CHAPTER SHOULD BE KEPT REFRIGERATED FOR TWO WEEKS BEFORE USING, AS the flavors need to marry and the mustard needs to mellow. The aioli recipes will keep, refrigerated, for up to one week and the ketchups will keep for several weeks in the refrigerator.

Ginger-Honey Mustard

This mustard features one of my favorite flavor combinations—sweet and hot. In this condiment, the sweet honey subtly softens the hotness of the ginger. This is the perfect accompaniment for ham sandwiches, but vegetarians will love it with oven-roasted eggplant and mushrooms. This mustard may not form a paste at first, but it will thicken up as it sits.

¼ cup yellow mustard seeds, finely ground
¼ cup Colman's mustard powder
¼ cup cider vinegar
¼ cup honey
2 tablespoons peeled finely grated fresh ginger
1 tablespoon ground turmeric
½ tablespoon salt

Combine the mustard seeds, mustard powder, ½ cup water, vinegar, honey, ginger, turmeric, and salt in a mixing bowl. Stir until well blended and the mixture forms a paste. Transfer to a sterilized ½-pint glass jar and keep refrigerated for 2 weeks before using. Keeps, refrigerated, for up to 1 month. Sealed, keeps up to 6 months.

MAKES ABOUT 1 CUP

Jalapeño-Tarragon Mustard

Tarragon, garlic, and jalapeños may not be an obvious trio of ingredients for a mustard, but they actually complement each other very well. I use this mustard as the main condiment in my favorite potato salad. For a delicious snack, it can be spread on Swiss or provolone cheese, which can then be rolled around blanched asparagus.

¼ cup yellow mustard seeds, finely ground
¼ cup Colman's mustard powder
3 tablespoons cider vinegar
4 teaspoons light brown sugar
1½ tablespoons minced fresh tarragon
1 jalapeño chile, seeded and minced
½ garlic clove, minced
½ tablespoon ground turmeric

Place the mustard seeds, mustard powder, vinegar, 2 tablespoons water, sugar, tarragon, chile, garlic, and turmeric in a food processor and process until smooth. Transfer to a sterilized ½-pint glass jar and keep refrigerated for 2 weeks before using. Keeps, refrigerated, for up to 1 month. Sealed, keeps up to 6 months.

MAKES ABOUT 1 CUP

Star Canyon Whole-Grain Mustard

This is the homemade mustard we use on our lunch sandwiches at Star Canyon in Dallas, Las Vegas, and Austin. It also makes a delicious mustard sauce for shrimp and other shellfish. Not recommended for the faint of heart.

1/4 cup yellow mustard seeds, coarsely ground
1/4 cup brown mustard seeds, coarsely ground
1/4 cup Colman's mustard powder
3 tablespoons cider vinegar
3 tablespoons light brown sugar
2 teaspoons cumin seeds, toasted and ground (page 211)
1 tablespoon pure red chile powder
1 tablespoon paprika
1/2 tablespoon salt

Combine the yellow and brown mustard seeds, mustard powder, 1/2 cup water, vinegar, sugar, cumin, chile powder, paprika, and salt in a mixing bowl. Stir until well blended and the mixture forms a paste. Transfer to a sterilized 1/2-pint glass jar and keep refrigerated for 2 weeks before using. Keeps, refrigerated, for up to 1 month. Sealed, keeps up to 6 months.

MAKES ABOUT 1 CUP

Spicy Tomato Ketchup

This is a recipe I first developed some fifteen years ago when I didn't want to use bottled ketchup in a barbecue sauce that I was making. Since then, I have used it at lunchtime in a number of my different restaurants. If you have never tasted the difference between bottled and fresh ketchup (especially one with a little spicy kick to it), you're in for a real treat.

1/4 cup dried sun-dried tomatoes, rehydrated in warm water and drained
6 pounds very ripe tomatoes, cored and chopped
1 large onion, chopped
2/3 cup cider vinegar
1/2 cup firmly packed light brown sugar
1 cinnamon stick, about 2 inches long
1/2 teaspoon cayenne
1/2 teaspoon ground allspice
1/2 teaspoon ground cloves
Pinch of ground mace
Salt to taste

In a large saucepan, cook the sun-dried tomatoes, ripe tomatoes, and onion over medium-high heat for about 30 minutes. Remove from the heat and press through a mesh strainer or food mill. Return to the pan, add the vinegar, sugar, cinnamon, cayenne, allspice, cloves, mace, and salt, and simmer over low heat until quite thick, 1 to 1 1/2 hours.

Remove the cinnamon stick, transfer the sauce to a blender, and puree until smooth. Pass through a fine-mesh strainer. Let the mixture cool, transfer to a sterilized glass jar with an airtight cover, and refrigerate. Keeps, refrigerated, for up to 1 month. Sealed, keeps up to 6 months.

MAKES ABOUT 3 CUPS

Cranberry-Horseradish Ketchup

Cranberries and horseradish team up here to add a distinctive flavor to an otherwise ordinary condiment. Use this ketchup wherever you would use regular ketchup, for French fries, sandwiches, or burgers. It can also be added to dressings or sauces to enhance the flavors.

1/4 cup dried sun-dried tomatoes, rehydrated in warm water and drained

3 pounds very ripe tomatoes, cored and chopped

1 large onion, chopped

2 pounds fresh cranberries

1/2 cup cider vinegar

2/3 cup firmly packed light brown sugar

1 cinnamon stick, about 2 inches long

1 tablespoon grated fresh horseradish

1/2 teaspoon ground allspice

1/2 teaspoon ground cloves

Pinch of ground mace

Salt to taste

In a large saucepan, cook the sun-dried and ripe tomatoes and the onion over medium-high heat for about 30 minutes. Remove from the heat and press through a mesh strainer. Return to the pan and add the cranberries, vinegar, sugar, cinnamon, horseradish, allspice, cloves, mace, and salt. Simmer until quite thick, 1 to 1 1/2 hours.

Remove the cinnamon stick, transfer the sauce to a blender, and puree until smooth. Pass through a fine-mesh strainer. Let the mixture cool, transfer to a sterilized glass jar with an airtight cover, and refrigerate. Keeps, refrigerated, for up to 1 month. Sealed, keeps up to 6 months.

MAKES ABOUT 1 1/2 CUPS

Chipotle Aioli

Aioli is the classic garlic mayonnaise from the Provence region of southern France. Here is a classic example of "France meets Mexico" when the delicious, smoky chipotle chile enters the fray. Use this aioli on any roasted or grilled vegetables and on any torta or sandwich from Chapter 10. You can also spread it on a crouton and float it in a vegetable or fish stew.

2 cups Mayonnaise (page 212) or store-bought

4 tablespoons roasted garlic puree (page 203)

1 teaspoon chipotle chile puree (page 206)

1 teaspoon paprika

1/2 teaspoon pure red chile powder

1/4 teaspoon cayenne

Place the mayonnaise, garlic and chile purees, paprika, chile powder, and cayenne in a bowl and whisk to combine. Transfer to an airtight container. Keeps, refrigerated, for up to 1 week.

MAKES ABOUT 2 CUPS

Smoked Tomato Aioli

Using smoked tomatoes in this recipe as well as chipotles—smoked jalapeño chiles—results in a distinctively flavored condiment. It makes a good all-purpose dipping sauce for potato chips, tortillas, or cooked shrimp, and it can also be used as a sandwich spread. Ideally, the tomatoes should be smoked over hickory wood.

8 ripe tomatoes, smoked and diced (page 209)
2 tablespoons roasted garlic puree (page 203)
1 cup Mayonnaise (page 212) or store-bought
1 tablespoon chipotle chile puree (page 206) or tomato paste
Salt to taste

In a saucepan, cook the smoked tomatoes over high heat, stirring frequently, until reduced to a thick paste, about 15 minutes. Transfer to a blender and puree with the roasted garlic, mayonnaise, and chipotle puree until very smooth. Season with salt. Transfer to an airtight container. Keeps, refrigerated, for up to 1 week.

MAKES ABOUT 3½ CUPS

INFUSED OILS AND VINEGARS

FLAVORED OILS AND VINEGARS HAVE BECOME INCREASINGLY POPULAR AS THEY WIDEN TASTE HORIZONS in all sorts of dishes. They are highly versatile and healthful, especially when used instead of butter compounds or cream sauces. If you take the time to package them at home in attractive glass bottles, they also make great gifts.

Annatto Oil

The brick-red seeds of the subtropical annatto tree make an intensely beautiful paste or oil. Annatto, also called achiote, is an ingredient commonly used in the Yucatán region of Mexico and parts of the Caribbean. When made into an oil, the seeds lend not only color but also a subtle, earthy flavor—both good reasons why I like to drizzle this oil around the plate. You can also use it to sauté vegetables, and shrimp are particularly attractive when sautéed in annatto oil.

¼ cup annatto seeds
1 cup canola or vegetable oil

In a saucepan, heat the annatto seeds and oil until the oil becomes very hot and is lightly smoking. Remove the pan from the heat and let the oil infuse for 3 hours. Carefully skim off the colored oil, leaving the bottom layer undisturbed. Discard the bottom layer. Pour the oil into a sterilized ½-pint jar or bottle and seal tightly (page 206). Store in the refrigerator for up to 2 months.

MAKES ABOUT 1 CUP

Red Chile–Canela Oil

Canela is a wonderful Mexican cinnamon that is much softer, both in flavor and texture, than the cassia cinnamon we typically use in the United States. Pairing canela with red chile oil reminds me of "red hots," the popular childhood candy. Not to worry, though—this oil is not sweet. Instead, it makes a delicious medium for flavors when used to sauté vegetables such as wild mushrooms or wilted greens. Mix it with champagne vinegar for a great salad dressing.

3 cups grapeseed, canola, or vegetable oil

½ cup dried de arbol, cayenne, or habanero chiles, crushed (with seeds)

5 canela sticks or 3 cinnamon sticks, crushed

Place the oil in a large saucepan and add the chiles and canela. Heat very slowly over medium heat until the oil is hot but not smoking, about 5 minutes. Remove the pan from the heat and let the oil cool completely. Pour into a sterilized quart jar or bottle and seal tightly (page 206). Store in a cool, dark, dry place or refrigerate for 2 weeks; shake the jar or bottle every 2 days or so to blend the flavors.

After 2 weeks, strain the oil through a fine-mesh strainer into a sterilized quart jar or bottle and seal tightly. If you wish (both for flavor and presentation), add some whole dried chiles and a canela stick or two. The oil will keep in a cool, dark, dry place for 2 to 3 months. Refrigerated, the oil will last up to 2 weeks.

MAKES ABOUT 3 CUPS

Cilantro Oil

This oil adds a vivid, flavorful punch when drizzled on a plate with grilled vegetables or a seafood appetizer. Combined with a dish containing cilantro, it can reinforce the herb flavor as well as provide attractive color. It makes a beautiful salad dressing when 4 parts of this oil are whisked together with 1 part uncolored vinegar, such as champagne or white wine.

¼ cup fresh cilantro leaves

1 cup olive oil

Half-fill a small saucepan with water and bring to a boil. Place iced water in a small bowl. Place the cilantro in a strainer and, using a large spoon to keep the cilantro submerged, blanch in the boiling water for 30 seconds. Immediately place the cilantro in the ice bath. When the cilantro is cold, gently dry by blotting with paper towels. Coarsely chop the cilantro and transfer to a blender. Add the oil and puree for 4 minutes.

Place a coffee filter in a strainer and strain the oil into a bowl; the process will take about 1 hour. Pour into a sterilized jar or bottle and seal tightly (page 206). Store in a cool, dark, dry place for up to 1 month. Unsealed, the oil can be refrigerated for up to 2 weeks.

MAKES ABOUT 1 CUP

Raspberry Vinegar

Although this was the ubiquitous flavored vinegar of the 1980s, that should not stop you from making your own. The color is a beautiful shade of red and the flavor truly is unique. It makes a terrific vinaigrette or marinade. This vinegar is flavored in two separate steps, each requiring about 4 cups of raspberries. Plan to obtain the second half of the fresh berries when the time for the second steeping arrives, after about 2 weeks.

8 cups raspberries, rinsed and drained well

3 cups white wine vinegar (or rice wine vinegar or cider vinegar)

Crush 4 cups of the berries and place in a sterilized, dry, heatproof 2-quart jar (page 206). Add the vinegar. Set in a deep saucepan and fill the pan with enough water to come halfway up the sides of the jar. Bring the water to a boil over medium heat; reduce the heat and simmer for 20 minutes. Remove the jar, set it aside, uncovered, and let cool completely.

Cover the jar and place it on a counter or somewhere obvious in your kitchen where you will remember to give it a shake every day for 2 weeks.

After 2 weeks, crush 4 more cups of raspberries in a bowl and strain the vinegar from the jar onto them through a fine sieve, pressing the old berries lightly to extract the juice. Discard the pulp in the sieve. Return the vinegar with the new raspberries to the jar and repeat the heating process. Let the raspberry vinegar stand for 2 more weeks; do not shake the jar.

Strain the vinegar through a fine sieve, pressing the berries lightly to extract the juice. Discard the pulp. Line a funnel with a coffee filter, dampen the filter, and set out 2 sterilized dry quart jars or bottles (or use 3 pint-size jars). Filter the vinegar through the funnel into the jars and seal tightly. (The vinegar will develop sediment as it stands, which is harmless. If you prefer a sparkling-clear vinegar, filter it again before using.) Keeps sealed in a cool, dark, dry place for up to a year or unsealed in the refrigerator for 3 months.

MAKES ABOUT 5 CUPS

Rosemary-Garlic Vinegar

Rosemary and garlic are two pungent ingredients that always form the perfect marriage. Rosemary is a member of the mint family that has been cultivated in its native Mediterranean region for thousands of years, both for its medicinal and culinary qualities (like garlic—see Garlic-Onion Pickles, page 18). Combine 1 part of this vinegar with 3 parts olive oil for an aromatic marinade for spring vegetables such as asparagus or artichokes.

1 cup loosely packed fresh sprigs rosemary

6 to 8 garlic cloves, peeled and flattened with the side of a large knife

2 to 3 cups champagne vinegar (or white wine vinegar or cider vinegar)

Place the rosemary and garlic in a sterilized, dry, heatproof quart jar (page 206). In a saucepan, heat 2 cups of the vinegar until simmering and pour it over the rosemary and garlic; the rosemary and garlic should be completely immersed. If necessary, heat more vinegar and add it to the jar.

Let cool and seal the jar. Let the vinegar steep for at least 10 days, shaking the jar every 2 days or so.

Strain the vinegar into a sterilized jar or bottle. Fresh sprigs of rosemary and peeled garlic cloves may be added (both for flavor and presentation) before sealing, if desired. Keeps unopened in a cool, dark, dry place for up to a year or unsealed in the refrigerator for 3 months.

MAKES ABOUT 3 CUPS

Tarragon-Citrus Vinegar

At one time, tarragon was best known in the United States as the herb used in béarnaise sauce. It is widely used in French cuisine and it bears distinctive aniselike tones that are assertive, yet subtly aromatic. For these reasons, it pairs well with the citrus flavors in this vinegar. Use it with olive oil to dress delicate greens such as red oakleaf or baby Boston lettuce.

4 cups champagne vinegar

10 sprigs fresh tarragon

2 oranges, zested and juiced

2 limes, zested and juiced

2 lemons, zested and juiced

In a saucepan, combine the vinegar, 5 sprigs of tarragon, half of the citrus zests, and all of the citrus juices and bring to a boil. Remove from the heat and let sit for 1 hour.

Meanwhile, place the remaining 5 sprigs of tarragon and the remaining zests into a large sterilized decorative bottle. Set aside.

Strain out the tarragon and zests, pour the vinegar into a clean saucepan, and bring to a simmer. Using a funnel, carefully pour the hot vinegar into the bottle and let cool to room temperature. Seal tightly and let sit for 2 weeks before using. Keeps unopened in a cool, dark, dry place for up to a year or unsealed in the refrigerator for 3 months.

MAKES ABOUT 5 CUPS

CHAPTER TWO
SALSAS RELISHES SAUCES AND VINAIGRETTES

SALSAS, RELISHES, AND CHUTNEYS

Pico de Gallo

This is probably the most commonly used salsa in Texas and Southwestern cuisine, where it is often used in place of ketchup. Sometimes, this recipe goes by the name "salsa fresca." Either way, it is extremely versatile. In Spanish, the name of this salsa means "beak of the rooster," referring to the habit of roosters to peck and chop their food before eating it, just as the salsa is finely chopped. Another theory is that the name comes from the Mexican tradition of eating this salsa with the thumb and forefinger, mimicking the pecking action of the rooster.

5 ripe tomatoes, blanched, peeled, seeded, and finely diced (page 203)
1 tablespoon chopped fresh cilantro leaves
1 garlic clove, minced
1/2 cup minced onion
Juice of 1/2 lime
2 serrano chiles, seeded and minced
Salt and freshly ground black pepper to taste

In a mixing bowl, place the tomatoes, cilantro, garlic, onion, lime juice, chiles, and salt and pepper and combine thoroughly. Let stand for 30 minutes at room temperature before serving. Serve at room temperature or chilled. Keeps for 3 to 4 days, refrigerated.

MAKES ABOUT 3 CUPS

Mango-Basil Salsa

Ripe mango, aromatic basil, and the kick of the chile and ginger combine to create a refreshing salsa that I use with Coconut-Ginger Rice Tamales (page 113). Be sure to use a good ripe mango.

(photograph on page 34)

2 ripe mangos, peeled, pitted, and finely diced
2 tablespoons chopped fresh basil leaves
1 serrano chile, seeded and minced
1 tablespoon peeled minced fresh ginger
Juice of 1 lime
Salt to taste

In a mixing bowl, combine the mangos, basil, chile, ginger, lime juice, and salt and gently mix thoroughly. Keeps, refrigerated, 3 to 4 days. Serve chilled or at room temperature.

MAKES ABOUT 2 CUPS

Griddled Tomato-Chipotle Salsa

This is another wonderful all-purpose salsa. It goes particularly well with eggs and any dish containing black beans. The essential technique in this recipe is the blackening of the tomatoes. That and the chipotle chile give the salsa its deep, smoky flavor.

6 ripe tomatoes, cut in half
2 tablespoons olive oil
1 cup sliced onions
4 jalapeño chiles, seeded and sliced
4 garlic cloves, chopped
2 tablespoons chipotle chile puree (page 206)
½ cup chopped fresh cilantro leaves
½ cup freshly squeezed lime juice
2 teaspoons salt

Place a large cast-iron skillet over high heat for about 3 minutes, or until smoking. Add the tomatoes to the skillet and char on both sides until black and somewhat soft, about 8 to 10 minutes. Remove from the skillet and set aside. Reduce the heat to medium and, after 2 minutes, pour the olive oil into the skillet. Immediately add the onions, jalapeños, and garlic and sauté for about 3 minutes, stirring occasionally, until the vegetables are soft. Transfer the onion mixture to a food processor with the griddled tomatoes. Process until all the ingredients are well blended. Transfer to a mixing bowl, add the chile puree, cilantro, lime juice, and salt, and stir well to combine. Serve at room temperature. Keeps for up to 1 week, refrigerated.

MAKES ABOUT 4 CUPS

Avocado-Tomatillo Salsa

This colorful all-purpose salsa goes with almost any savory dish. Avocados and tomatillos make a natural partnership, which the cilantro and lime juice complement perfectly by providing a little "edge" to the flavors. *(photograph on page 34)*

2 avocados, peeled, pitted, diced
½ tablespoon diced red bell pepper
½ tablespoon diced green bell pepper
1 tablespoon sliced scallion
4 tomatillos, husked, rinsed, and diced
1 garlic clove, minced
2 tablespoons fresh cilantro leaves
2 serrano chiles, seeded and minced
2 teaspoons freshly squeezed lime juice
3 tablespoons olive oil
Salt to taste

In a large mixing bowl, combine the avocados, bell peppers, scallion, and half of the tomatillos. Place the remaining tomatillos in a blender and add the garlic, cilantro, chiles, and lime juice. Puree until smooth and then, with the motor running, drizzle in the oil. Pour the puree into the mixing bowl, combine thoroughly, and season with salt. Let sit for at least 30 minutes. Keeps, refrigerated, up to 2 days. Serve chilled.

MAKES ABOUT 1½ CUPS

Tomatillo-Serrano Salsa

This is simply a cooked *salsa verde,* so prevalent throughout Mexico and the Southwest. Enjoy it as a dip with a bowl of tortilla chips. The pleasant acidity of the tomatillos also makes it a great accompaniment with vegetable enchiladas, white fish, shellfish, and poultry.

8 tomatillos (about 10 ounces), husked, rinsed, and cut in half
2 garlic cloves, cut in half
1/2 onion, quartered
2 serrano chiles, stemmed
1 1/2 cups Vegetable Stock (page 211) or water
2 tablespoons freshly squeezed lime juice
1/2 cup fresh cilantro leaves
Salt to taste

In a saucepan, combine the tomatillos, garlic, onion, and serranos, cover with vegetable stock or water, and bring to a boil. Reduce the heat to a simmer and cook for 8 minutes. Remove from the heat and pour the mixture through a strainer, discarding the liquid. Place the strained solids in a food processor, add the lime juice and cilantro, and puree until smooth. Season with salt. Serve warm or let cool to room temperature. Keeps for up to 1 week, refrigerated.

MAKES ABOUT 1 1/2 CUPS

Golden Gazpacho Salsa

This salsa, which is inspired by the classic Spanish soup, has the perfect balance of fruit, acidity, and spice, making it a terrific match with any fish or shellfish, as well as with grilled or roasted vegetables. I use it with the Celery Root Pancakes (page 88). In addition to being delicious, this salsa is also appealing to the eye.

5 to 6 golden or yellow tomatoes, blanched, peeled, seeded, and diced (page 203), about 3 cups
1/4 cup diced yellow or green bell pepper
1/4 cup diced cantaloupe melon
1/4 cup diced papaya
1/4 cup diced mango
1 cucumber, peeled, cut in half, seeded, and diced
1/4 cup diced jicama
6 scallions, white parts only, sliced
3 serrano chiles, seeded
3/4 cup Vegetable Stock (page 211) or store-bought
1/4 teaspoon saffron threads
2 tablespoons freshly squeezed lime juice
1/2 teaspoon salt, or to taste

In a mixing bowl, combine the tomatoes, bell pepper, melon, papaya, mango, cucumber, jicama, and scallions. Set aside.

Place the serrano chiles and stock in a blender and puree. Transfer to a mixing bowl, stir in the saffron, and let infuse for 10 minutes.

Meanwhile, transfer three quarters of the reserved vegetable and fruit mixture to a blender or food processor and puree. Add back to the remaining fruit-vegetable mixture. Using a medium-mesh strainer, strain the pureed stock mixture into the bowl and stir in the lime juice and salt.

Place the salsa, uncovered, in the refrigerator and let chill for at least 1 hour. Keeps for 3 to 4 days, refrigerated. Serve chilled or at room temperature.

MAKES ABOUT 2 CUPS

Chayote–Black-Eyed Pea Relish

Chayote, also called mirliton and vegetable pear, is a pale green, pear-shaped member of the squash family that has crisp flesh and an earthy flavor similar to zucchini and cucumber. Chayotes grow on vines and were a much prized food staple of the Aztecs and Mayas. Although chayote is often used split, stuffed, and baked like an eggplant or acorn squash, I prefer its raw crunchiness in salads and relishes. Here, it is perfectly paired with one of the standbys of Southern cooking—black-eyed peas.

1 small chayote, peeled, cut in half, seeded, and finely diced
1 cup cooked black-eyed peas (page 214)
1 small garlic clove, minced
1 serrano chile, seeded and minced
2 teaspoons chopped fresh cilantro leaves
¼ cup diced mango or papaya
2 scallions, white parts only, thinly sliced
¼ cup roasted fresh corn kernels (page 204)
2 teaspoons freshly squeezed lime juice
2 teaspoons fruity white wine, such as Riesling or Gewürztraminer
Salt to taste

In a mixing bowl, place the chayote, black-eyed peas, garlic, chile, cilantro, mango, scallions, corn, lime juice, wine, and salt and mix gently. Let sit for at least 1 hour before serving. Adjust the seasonings before serving if necessary. Serve at room temperature. Keeps for 3 to 4 days, refrigerated.

MAKES ABOUT 2 CUPS

Mango-Basil Salsa; Avocado-Tomatillo Salsa;
Tomatillo-Jalapeño Chutney

Cherry Tomato–Mozzarella Relish

This recipe is my Southwestern adaptation of the classic Italian combination of tomatoes, mozzarella, and basil. The jalapeño chile gives this relish an added zip, making it a great garnish for grilled vegetables, fish, or chicken. Combine it with garden greens for a tasty salad. Use it up as soon as you can, as it does not keep well. My favorite mozzarella comes from the Dallas Mozzarella Company, but any good mozzarella will work well.

(photograph on page 38)

1 pint cherry tomatoes, rinsed and quartered
8 ounces fresh mozzarella cheese, diced
2 tablespoons chopped fresh basil
2 tablespoons balsamic vinegar
3 tablespoons extra-virgin olive oil
1 jalapeño chile, seeded and minced
Salt to taste

In a mixing bowl, combine the tomatoes, cheese, basil, vinegar, olive oil, chile, and salt. Let marinate in the refrigerator for 30 minutes before serving. Serve chilled. Best used the same day, but keeps for 2 to 3 days, refrigerated.

MAKES ABOUT 2 CUPS

White Bean–Oven-Dried Tomato Relish

Cooked dried beans are a great medium for carrying other flavors. In this recipe, the white beans combine with the intense tones of the tomatoes, the herbs, and the green chile for a highly satisfying relish. I use it with Butternut Squash Empanadas (page 127).

1 cup cooked white beans (page 213)
1/3 cup oven-dried cherry tomatoes (page 205)
1 New Mexico or Anaheim green chile, roasted, peeled, seeded, and diced (page 204)
1 tablespoon chopped fresh cilantro leaves
1 tablespoon chopped fresh basil
2 tablespoons fresh lime juice
1/4 cup extra-virgin olive oil
2 tablespoons roasted garlic puree (page 203)
Salt to taste

In a mixing bowl, combine the beans, tomatoes, chile, cilantro, and basil. In another mixing bowl, combine the lime juice, olive oil, and garlic and whisk together until combined. Pour the dressing over the bean mixture, toss to combine, and season with salt. Before serving, relish should marinate for 1 hour, refrigerated. Keeps, refrigerated, for up to 1 week.

MAKES ABOUT 2 1/2 CUPS

Jicama-Papaya Relish

Jicama is a root vegetable native to the Amazon basin that has long been cultivated in Mexico, and is often referred as to "the Mexican potato." Its crisp, white flesh is slightly sweet and refreshing, which makes it a great ingredient for salsas and relishes. Combined with the tropical fruity tones of papaya and melon, this relish conveys the essence of summer. You can substitute melon for the papaya, but in either case, make sure the fruit is perfectly ripe. I use this relish with the Avocado Soup (page 64). *(photograph on page 38)*

1 small ripe papaya, peeled and seeded
1 serrano chile, seeded
Juice of 1 lime
1½ tablespoons finely diced red bell pepper
½ cup finely diced cantaloupe melon
½ cup finely diced honeydew melon
2 tablespoons peeled, seeded, and finely diced cucumber
½ cup peeled and finely diced jicama
2 teaspoons chopped fresh cilantro leaves
¼ teaspoon salt
¼ teaspoon freshly ground black pepper
2 tablespoons sour cream

Place the papaya, serrano, and lime juice in a food processor or blender and puree. In a mixing bowl, place the bell pepper, both melons, cucumber, and jicama, add the puree, and combine thoroughly. Mix in the cilantro, salt, and pepper. Gently fold in the sour cream and serve. Use the same day.

MAKES ABOUT 2 CUPS

Apple-Almond Chutney

Almonds are believed to have originated in the eastern Mediterranean, but more almonds are now grown in California than anywhere else in the world. They make a complementary partnership with apples, as this sweet and tart chutney proves.

1½ cups cider vinegar
¾ cup loosely packed dark brown sugar
1 cup sliced blanched almonds, toasted and coarsely chopped (page 211)
2 tart green apples, cored and diced
Juice of 2 lemons
¼ cup diced onion
2 tablespoons diced red bell pepper
2 tablespoons diced green bell pepper
Salt to taste

In a large saucepan, combine the vinegar and sugar and cook over high heat for 15 minutes, whisking for the first 30 seconds to dissolve the sugar. Add the almonds, apples, lemon juice, onion, and bell peppers and cook for 10 minutes longer. Remove from the heat, let cool completely, and season with salt.

MAKES ABOUT 2 CUPS

Pineapple–Green Chile Chutney

I have long loved the sweet and spicy combination of fruit and chiles. Pineapples seem to have a natural affinity for chiles, fresh green ones in particular, as well as those with fruity tones. I like this chutney with grilled food, especially chicken and fish.

⅔ cup cider vinegar
¾ cup sugar
1 pineapple, peeled, cored, and diced
2 tablespoons peeled minced fresh ginger
2 poblano chiles, roasted, peeled, seeded, and diced (page 204)
2 tablespoons diced red onion
1 teaspoon minced lime zest
2 tablespoons freshly squeezed lime juice
1 garlic clove, minced
Pinch of cayenne
Pinch of ground allspice
Pinch of ground cloves
Salt to taste

Bring the vinegar and sugar to a boil in a saucepan. Add the pineapple, ginger, chiles, onion, lime zest and juice, garlic, cayenne, allspice, cloves, and salt and return to a boil. Reduce the heat to a simmer and cook for 15 minutes. Remove from the heat and let cool. Serve at room temperature. Keeps for up to 2 weeks, refrigerated.

MAKES 2 CUPS

Jicama-Papaya Relish and
Cherry Tomato–Mozzarella Relish

Tomatillo-Jalapeño Chutney

The firm-fleshed tomatillos look like green tomatoes, and they are distantly related. Tomatillos have a tart, slightly lemony flavor that has a natural affinity for the cilantro, garlic, and green chiles in this recipe. The tomatillos take on a sweet, pickled flavor and texture in this chutney, and that makes it an excellent accompaniment with roasted or grilled vegetables. I pair this chutney with Grilled Blue Corn Polenta Cakes (page 92), and it is especially delicious with poultry such as duck and quail. Try it also as a condiment with your favorite sandwich in Chapter 10. *(photograph on page 34)*

12 tomatillos (about 1 pound), husked, rinsed, and chopped

2 small red bell peppers, seeded and diced

1 small green bell pepper, seeded and diced

8 scallions, thinly sliced

4 jalapeño chiles, seeded and minced

2/3 cup red wine vinegar

1/2 cup fresh corn kernels

1/4 cup firmly packed light brown sugar

1 tablespoon chopped fresh cilantro leaves

1 teaspoon salt

1 garlic clove, minced

1/4 teaspoon cayenne

1/4 teaspoon ground cumin

In a large saucepan, place the tomatillos, bell peppers, scallions, chiles, vinegar, corn, brown sugar, cilantro, salt, garlic, cayenne, and cumin and bring to a boil, stirring frequently. Reduce the heat and boil gently for 20 to 30 minutes, until thick, stirring occasionally. Let cool completely. Cover and refrigerate until ready to serve. Keeps for up to 2 weeks, refrigerated.

MAKES ABOUT 2 CUPS

SAUCES AND VINAIGRETTES

Mole Verde

Mole (pronounced MOH-lay) sauces are among the most complex in Latin American cuisine, but they are well worth the effort involved. The state of Oaxaca in southern Mexico is known as "the land of seven moles," and this recipe is my adaptation of the classic Oaxacan green mole sauce. Grinding the toasted pumpkin seeds gives the sauce an interesting consistency, but for a smooth, rather than textured, mole sauce, pour the cooked sauce back into the blender or food processor, blend until smooth, and strain. This sauce goes really well with the Risotto and Corn Chile Rellenos (page 114).

1 cup (about 4 ounces) pumpkin seeds
3 cups (or more as needed) Vegetable Stock (page 211) or store-bought
8 tomatillos, husked and rinsed
3 serrano chiles, seeded
1/2 onion, chopped
3 garlic cloves, chopped
1 cup fresh basil leaves
1/2 cup fresh cilantro leaves
2 fresh hoja santa leaves, chopped (optional)
1 tablespoon chopped fresh epazote (optional)
1/8 teaspoon ground cumin
3/4 teaspoon ground cinnamon
Pinch of ground cloves
1 1/2 tablespoons vegetable oil
1/2 teaspoon salt

Heat a large skillet over medium heat for several minutes, then add the pumpkin seeds in a single layer. When the first one pops, stir them constantly for 5 to 6 minutes, until all have toasted and popped. Let cool completely. In batches, grind the seeds in a spice grinder. Sift them through a medium-mesh sieve into a bowl and stir in 1 cup of the stock.

Bring a saucepan of salted water to a boil, add the tomatillos and serranos, and simmer, covered, until tender, about 10 to 15 minutes. Drain the tomatillos and chiles, transfer to a blender or food processor, and puree. Add the onion, garlic, basil, cilantro, hoja santa, epazote, cumin, cinnamon, and cloves and blend until smooth.

In a large saucepan over medium heat, heat the oil until lightly smoking. Add the reserved pumpkin seed mixture and stir constantly as it thickens and darkens, about 4 to 5 minutes. Add the vegetable puree and stir for 2 to 3 minutes longer, until very thick. Stir in the remaining 2 cups of vegetable stock, reduce the heat to medium-low, and simmer, partially covered, for about 30 minutes. Season with salt and thin to a lighter consistency with additional stock, if desired. Keeps, refrigerated, 4 to 5 days. Serve warm.

MAKES ABOUT 3 CUPS

Pasilla Mole

The pasilla chile, also known as *chile negro,* is a dried version of the fresh chilaca chile. "Pasilla" means "little raisin," and it has a wrinkly appearance and dark brown coloring similar to raisins, which are also included in this sauce to reinforce the flavor tones. Most people believe that all mole sauces contain chocolate, like this one, but as the previous recipe proves, this is not always the case. Serve this sauce with the Cilantro Ravioli with Black Olive–Goat Cheese Stuffing (page 121), with sautéed or grilled vegetables, or with vegetable empanadas.

1 cup Vegetable Stock (page 211) or store-bought

1 large ripe tomato, blanched, peeled, seeded, and quartered (page 203)

2 tomatillos, husked, rinsed, peeled, and quartered

1/2 cup minced onion

2 garlic cloves, minced

1/2 cup sesame seeds

1/2 teaspoon coriander seeds

2 tablespoons pumpkin seeds

1/4 cup sliced blanched almonds

1/4 cup raisins

1/4 teaspoon ground cloves

1/2 teaspoon ground cinnamon

1/4 teaspoon freshly ground black pepper

1/4 cup pasilla chile puree (page 206)

2 tablespoons ancho chile puree (page 206)

1 ounce bitter chocolate, chopped (about 2 1/2 tablespoons)

1/4 cup vegetable oil

In a saucepan, bring the stock to a boil, reduce the heat, and add the tomato, tomatillos, onion, and garlic. Simmer for 10 minutes. Transfer to a blender, puree, and set aside.

In a skillet, toast the sesame seeds, coriander seeds, pumpkin seeds, and almonds over medium heat for 3 to 4 minutes while shaking the pan. In a large saucepan, combine the raisins, cloves, cinnamon, pepper, pasilla and ancho chile purees, and the chocolate. Add the toasted seeds and nuts and the pureed tomato mixture. Cook over low heat until the chocolate melts. Transfer to a blender and puree.

Heat the vegetable oil in a skillet until lightly smoking. Cook the puree for 3 to 5 minutes over medium-high heat until dark and thick. The mole will keep for 4 to 5 days in the refrigerator. Serve warm.

MAKES ABOUT 2 1/2 CUPS

Roasted Garlic Sauce

This is one of the few recipes in this book that calls for cream, reflecting the trend nowadays away from these kinds of sauces. Occasionally, however, only the satisfying rich nuttiness of a cream sauce will do. Another way of justifying this sauce is that roasted garlic has a real affinity for cream! Use it with Cumin, Black Bean, and Queso Fresco Quesadillas (page 128), with grilled vegetables, or with grilled chicken or fish.

4 heads of garlic, cut in half crosswise
2 tablespoons olive oil
1 tablespoon unsalted butter
½ small onion, diced
½ cup white wine
1 tablespoon Worcestershire sauce
2 cups heavy cream
Salt and freshly ground black pepper to taste

Preheat the oven to 350°F.

In a small baking dish, toss the garlic with 1 tablespoon of the oil and 1 teaspoon of water. Cover the dish with aluminum foil and seal the edges tightly. Place in the oven and roast for 30 to 40 minutes. Remove and let cool. Once cool, squeeze out the pulp from the skin.

In a saucepan, heat the remaining 1 tablespoon of olive oil and the butter until lightly smoking. Add the onion and cook, stirring occasionally, for 6 minutes over medium heat, or until it has just started to brown. Add the wine and Worcestershire sauce and reduce the liquid until the pan is almost dry, about 4 minutes. Reduce the heat to low, add the cream, and reduce by half, about 15 minutes. Season with salt and pepper, whisk in the reserved garlic, and strain. Keeps, refrigerated, for 2 days. Serve warm.

MAKES 1½ CUPS

Watercress Puree

Use this puree to add flavor and color to vinaigrettes. It's also a great complement to roasted or grilled vegetables such as asparagus and artichokes. Serve it also with grilled chicken or fish.

1 pound watercress, washed
½ cup (or more as needed) Vegetable Stock (page 211) or store-bought
1 teaspoon grated lemon zest
Salt to taste

Fill a stainless steel bowl with ice water and place next to the stove. Discard any discolored or bruised watercress leaves and cut off any thick stems. Fill a saucepan halfway with water and bring to a boil. Have a bowl of ice water ready. Submerge the watercress in the boiling water for 15 seconds and then immediately drain and plunge into the ice water.

Once the watercress has chilled, remove and gently squeeze out any excess water. Transfer to a blender, add the stock and lemon zest, and pulse briefly before blending for 4 minutes, thinning with additional stock if necessary. Season with salt and pass through a fine-mesh strainer. Serve chilled or at room temperature. Use the same day.

MAKES ABOUT 1 CUP

Tomato Salsa Coulis

The word *coulis* is a French term for a thick puree or sauce, and this Southwestern coulis is like a refined and delicately textured salsa that's full of flavor. It makes a tasty accent for just about any type of roasted or grilled vegetable, chicken, or fish. It's especially good drizzled on tomato salads.

1 tablespoon olive oil
½ small onion, diced
4 garlic cloves, chopped
1 jalapeño chile, seeded and chopped
4 tomatoes, blanched, peeled, seeded, and chopped (page 203)
2 tablespoons freshly squeezed lime juice
2 tablespoons chopped fresh cilantro leaves
Salt to taste

In a small saucepan, heat the olive oil until lightly smoking. Add the onion, garlic, and jalapeño and cook over medium heat for 3 minutes, or until the onion and garlic just start to turn golden. Add the tomatoes and lime juice and cook for 5 minutes longer. Transfer the mixture to a blender and puree for 2 to 3 minutes, until very smooth.

Pass the sauce through a fine-mesh strainer into a clean saucepan. Over medium heat, reduce the sauce until it thickens and reaches the consistency of heavy cream, 4 or 5 minutes. Remove from the heat and stir in the cilantro. Season with salt and serve chilled or at room temperature. Coulis will keep for 3 to 4 days in the refrigerator.

MAKES ABOUT 1½ CUPS

Cranberry-Chipotle Sauce

The fruit flavors of the cranberries and orange in this recipe are highlighted by the smoki-ness of the chipotle chile. While this is the perfect condiment for the Thanksgiving table, it also makes a great addition to the Red Cabbage, Blue Cheese, and Walnut Empanadas (page 123) and other vegetable empanadas or chilaquiles.

1 orange
⅔ cup sugar
1 canned chipotle chile in adobo sauce
2 cups fresh cranberries
2 tablespoons chopped fresh mint leaves
3 tablespoons chopped toasted pecans (page 211)

Zest the orange and place the zest in a food processor. Cut off the white pith of the orange and discard. Cut the fruit into 8 pieces, discard the seeds, and add the fruit to the food processor. Add the sugar and chipotle and blend until the orange mixture resembles coarse cornmeal. Add the cranberries, mint, and pecans and pulse until just chopped; the mixture should be a little chunky. Let stand for 30 minutes for the flavors to marry. Serve chilled or at room temperature. Keeps, refrigerated, for 4 to 5 days.

MAKES ABOUT 1½ CUPS

Black Bean—Cumin Sauce

Cumin, a spice native to the Mediterranean region, has been used in the kitchen for centuries and was also used by Egyptians as a preservative for mummies. Its aromatic, nutty quality makes it the perfect seasoning for black beans. Reducing the liquid in which the beans cooked keeps the vibrant black color of the sauce, which I match with the Potato—Goat Cheese Pie with Leeks (page 75). It also goes well with any of the enchiladas in Chapter 9. Reserve the extra black beans for a side dish or to make salsa.

8 ounces dried black beans, cleaned, soaked overnight, and drained
4 cups Vegetable Stock (page 211) or store-bought
½ tablespoon olive oil
2 garlic cloves, chopped
¼ onion, chopped
½ teaspoon cumin seeds
½ tablespoon chopped fresh cilantro leaves
Freshly squeezed lime juice to taste
Salt to taste

In a saucepan, place the beans and add the stock. Bring to a boil and reduce the heat to medium-low. Cook for 1½ hours, or until the beans are tender, adding more stock or water as necessary to keep the beans covered.

Remove the beans from the heat and strain, reserving the cooking liquid and the beans separately. Place the cooking liquid in a clean saucepan and reduce over medium-high heat until 1½ cups remain, about 10 to 12 minutes. Set aside.

In another saucepan, heat the olive oil and when lightly smoking, add the garlic, onion, and cumin. Cook, stirring, over high heat for 4 or 5 minutes, or until the onion just starts to turn golden. Add the reserved cooking liquid and transfer to a blender. Add ¼ cup of the cooked black beans and blend until smooth. Pass the pureed sauce through a fine-mesh strainer into a clean saucepan and stir in the cilantro, lime juice, and salt. Serve hot. Keeps, refrigerated, for 3 to 4 days.

MAKES ABOUT ½ CUP

Fiery Tropical Fruit Sauce

Try this zesty sauce drizzled on sliced fresh fruits such as melon, peaches, or tropical fruit. With the addition of a little more lime juice and ½ cup of olive oil, it becomes a deliciously fruity dressing for salad greens.

1 cup diced mango
1 cup diced papaya
½ banana, peeled and chopped
1 habanero chile, seeded, minced
¼ cup fresh orange juice
Juice of 1 lime
2 tablespoons apple juice
3 tablespoons light rum
Salt to taste

In a blender, place the mango, papaya, banana, habanero, orange juice, lime juice, apple juice, and rum and puree until smooth. Pass through a fine-mesh strainer and season with salt. Serve chilled or at room temperature. Keeps, refrigerated, up to 2 days.

MAKES ABOUT 2 CUPS

Wild Mushroom Sauce

Of the many thousand different types of mushroom, only a handful—twenty or so—are used culinarily; the rest are either poisonous, unpleasant, or otherwise inedible. But what magnificent flavors and textures those few mushrooms provide! This is a delicious sauce to serve with marinated, grilled portobello mushrooms for a meatless "steak dinner." It's also the perfect accessory for the Morel and Dried Cherry Empanadas (page 124).

2 tablespoons (¼ stick) unsalted butter
2 tablespoons all-purpose flour
2 tablespoons olive oil
½ onion, diced
2 garlic cloves, minced
1 pound assorted wild mushrooms, such as shiitake, cremini, and portobello, sliced
4 cups full-bodied red wine, such as Merlot or Cabernet
1 tablespoon chopped fresh thyme leaves
Salt to taste

In a small bowl, combine the butter and flour with your fingertips until the flour is fully incorporated. Set aside.

In a saucepan, heat the oil until lightly smoking and add the onion. Sauté over high heat for 4 minutes, or until the onion begins to turn brown. Add the garlic and cook for 1 minute longer. Add the mushrooms and sauté for 5 minutes, or until fully cooked. Add the red wine and cook until the liquid is reduced to 2 cups, about 8 minutes. While the mixture is lightly boiling, whisk in the butter mixture until completely combined. Add the thyme, reduce the heat to a simmer, and cook for 3 minutes longer. Season with salt and serve hot. This dish can be made ahead and stored, refrigerated, for 3 to 4 days.

MAKES ABOUT 2 CUPS

Preserved Lemon–Tarragon Vinaigrette

This dressing is wonderful with asparagus and artichokes and salads containing either vegetable. If you prefer, you can use the Preserved Lemons in Chapter 1 (page 16) if you have them on hand, rather than the simmered lemons in this recipe. If you do take the shortcut for the lemons offered in this recipe, save the syrup in which the lemons simmered for iced tea.

3 lemons, washed
1 cup sugar
1 shallot, minced
1 tablespoon chopped fresh tarragon leaves
¼ cup freshly squeezed lemon juice
1 cup extra-virgin olive oil
Salt to taste

Preserved Lemon–Tarragon Vinaigrette and Mango Habanero Vinaigrette

Cut the ends off the lemons and then slice into ⅛-inch rounds. Cut the rounds into quarters and reserve. In a saucepan, place the sugar and 1 cup water and stir over medium heat until the sugar is dissolved. Add the reserved lemon slices and bring to a gentle simmer. Let simmer for 2 hours, or until the lemon rind is translucent. Remove from the heat, drain the lemons from the syrup, and lay out the lemons flat on wax paper.

In a mixing bowl, combine the shallot, tarragon, and lemon juice. Gradually whisk in the olive oil and then stir in the lemon slices. Season with salt. Keeps, refrigerated, up to 1 week.

MAKES ABOUT 1½ CUPS

Annatto-Rosemary Vinaigrette

Annatto seeds are used commercially in the United States for coloring dairy products such as cheese and margarine. In Mexico, annatto is ground and used as a paste mainly for marinades (see also page 25). It adds a beautiful orange color to this vinaigrette while imparting a subtle earthy flavor—a good marriage with the aromatic rosemary. This assertive dressing is best used in salads with stronger-tasting greens and lettuces such as arugula, radicchio, and chicory.

2 garlic cloves, minced
4 sprigs fresh rosemary
1/4 cup freshly squeezed lemon juice
1 tablespoon champagne vinegar
2 tablespoons grated orange zest
1 teaspoon honey
1 cup Annatto Oil (page 25)
Salt to taste

In a mixing bowl, combine the garlic, rosemary, lemon juice, vinegar, orange zest, and honey. Using a whisk, gradually incorporate the annatto oil. Season with salt. Keeps, refrigerated, up to 1 week.

MAKES ABOUT 1 CUP

All-Purpose Herbed Vinaigrette

The name of this vinaigrette pretty much sums it up! Not only is it the perfect dressing for salads, but it also makes a delicious marinade for grilled vegetables.

1 shallot, minced
2 garlic cloves, minced
2 tablespoons minced fresh thyme leaves
2 tablespoons chopped fresh basil leaves
2 tablespoons minced fresh cilantro leaves
1 tablespoon Dijon mustard
1/4 cup sherry vinegar
1 tablespoon balsamic vinegar
1/4 cup corn oil
3/4 cup extra-virgin olive oil
Salt and freshly ground black pepper to taste

In a mixing bowl, combine the shallot, garlic, thyme, basil, cilantro, mustard, and both vinegars. While whisking slowly, gradually pour both oils into the bowl. Whisk until the vinaigrette is slightly emulsified. Season with salt and pepper. Keeps, refrigerated, up to 1 week.

MAKES ABOUT 1 1/2 CUPS

Mango-Habanero Vinaigrette

One of the great combinations of tropical ingredients is mango and habanero chile, and it's one that is seen more and more in today's cooking. Here, the tropical fruitiness of the ripe mango is balanced by the acidity of the lime and the spiciness of the habanero. Use this vinaigrette with a black bean and avocado salad for a dish of complex and pleasing flavors.

(photograph on page 46)

1 garlic clove, peeled and minced

1/2 shallot, peeled and minced

1 ripe mango, peeled, pitted, and diced

1 habanero chile, seeded and minced

2 tablespoons freshly squeezed lemon juice

6 tablespoons olive oil

2 tablespoons corn oil

1 tablespoon chopped fresh cilantro leaves

1 tablespoon chopped fresh mint leaves

Salt to taste

In a blender, place the garlic, shallot, mango, habanero, and lemon juice and puree until smooth. Gradually add the olive oil and corn oil while the motor is running. Stir in the cilantro and mint and season with salt. Keeps, refrigerated, up to 1 week.

MAKES ABOUT 1 CUP

CHAPTER THREE

SLAWS AND SALADS

Cactus-Watercress Slaw with Red Chile–Citrus Zest Pesto

Long popular in Mexico, nopales—the leaves or pads of the prickly pear cactus—are finally entering the culinary mainstream, at least in the Southwest and in major cities in the United States, where they are available at Hispanic markets. Nopales are usually sold dethorned, but if not, wear thick gloves and use a vegetable peeler to remove the fine thorns. Nopales are delicious grilled, and it is best to slice them into a fan after they are cooked, leaving one end intact; this helps ensure that the mucilaginous or "slimy" quality that cactus can sometimes take on is minimized or eliminated. In this recipe, cooking the cactus with the scallion tops has the same effect.

2 nopales (cactus pads), cut into ¼-inch strips

1 bunch of scallions, green tops only, chopped

Salt to taste

2 bunches of watercress, washed and stemmed

1 red bell pepper, roasted, peeled, seeded, and cut into ¼-inch strips (page 204)

1 yellow bell pepper, roasted, peeled, seeded, and cut into ¼-inch strips (page 204)

½ cup toasted pumpkin seeds (page 211)

1 cup Red Chile–Citrus Zest Pesto (page 21)

In a saucepan, place the cactus and scallions and cover with water. Lightly salt the water and bring to a boil over high heat. Boil the cactus for 5 minutes, or until the cactus is tender but al dente. Remove from the heat, strain, and rinse the cactus twice in cold water. Remove the scallion tops and discard. Transfer the cactus to a mixing bowl and add the watercress, bell peppers, pumpkin seeds, and pesto. Toss together and season with salt. Transfer to the refrigerator and serve chilled. Keeps, refrigerated, for 2 days.

SERVES 4 TO 6

Spicy Pickled Cucumber Slaw with Yogurt-Cumin Dressing

This slaw is ideal for a summer picnic or as an accompaniment for barbecued foods. The combination of yogurt, cucumber, and cumin is inspired by the Indian side dish called raita (pronounced RIGHT-ah), a cooling yogurt-based dish served with curries to counter their heat. The habanero used in this recipe is the hottest chile of all, so you might consider adding it to taste, or using a milder chile, such as rehydrated dried ancho.

(photograph on page 58)

½ cup plain yogurt (nonfat, low-fat, or whole milk)

2 tablespoons sour cream

1 tablespoon toasted ground cumin seeds (page 211)

2 tablespoons freshly squeezed lime juice

1 tablespoon chopped fresh cilantro leaves

1 tablespoon chopped fresh parsley leaves

1 small onion, thinly sliced

2 English cucumbers, peeled, seeded, and julienned

1 small head of Napa cabbage (or half a large head), cut in half, stemmed, and shredded

1 habanero chile, seeded and minced

Salt to taste

In a large bowl, combine the yogurt, sour cream, cumin, lime juice, cilantro, and parsley and whisk together. Add the onion, cucumbers, cabbage, and chile, toss together well, and season with salt. Cover and let stand for 1 hour in the refrigerator. Serve chilled. Keeps, refrigerated, for 2 days.

SERVES 4

Carrot-Jicama Slaw with Ancho Chiles

Jicama, the root vegetable native to Mexico, derives its name from the Aztec word *xícamatl*. It is best served in its raw, crunchy state, when the flavors of apple and water chestnut prevail. The combination of jicama, carrot, and mild but flavorful ancho chile in a creamy slaw is particularly appealing. *(photograph on page 58)*

2 small ancho chiles, seeded
1 tablespoon chopped fresh cilantro leaves
1/2 cup Mayonnaise (page 212) or store-bought
1/2 cup sour cream
2 tablespoons freshly squeezed lime juice
2 carrots, peeled and julienned
1 large jicama, peeled and julienned
1 small red onion, very thinly sliced
Salt to taste

Preheat the oven to 400°F.

Place the anchos on a cookie sheet and toast in the oven for 2 minutes. Transfer to a mixing bowl, cover with warm water, and weight down with a plate or pan so the anchos stay submerged. Let soak for 10 to 15 minutes, or until just pliable.

Meanwhile, in a mixing bowl, combine the cilantro, mayonnaise, sour cream, and lime juice and whisk to combine. Set aside. Combine the carrots, jicama, and red onion in another bowl.

Drain the anchos; stem and seed under running water. Cut into very thin strips and add to the carrot mixture. Add the mayonnaise mixture to the slaw and toss well to coat. Season with salt and refrigerate. Serve cold. Keeps, refrigerated, for up to 2 days.

SERVES 4 TO 6

Asparagus-Artichoke Salad with Roasted Portobello Dressing

What is more representative of the arrival of spring than asparagus and artichokes? This combination is made even more interesting with the added flavor of the portobello mushrooms and takes a decidedly Italian turn with the addition of balsamic vinegar, capers, and Asiago cheese.

(photograph opposite)

FOR THE MUSHROOM MARINADE

¼ cup balsamic vinegar

½ cup extra-virgin olive oil

2 garlic cloves, minced

1 teaspoon dried red pepper flakes

1 teaspoon salt

2 portobello mushrooms, stems removed

FOR THE DRESSING

3 tablespoons balsamic vinegar

2 tablespoons roasted garlic puree (page 203)

½ cup extra-virgin olive oil

3 tablespoons chopped fresh basil leaves

2 tablespoons chopped fresh oregano leaves

Salt and freshly ground black pepper to taste

FOR THE SALAD

1 pound asparagus, bottoms trimmed by 1 inch

8 artichoke bottoms, sliced (page 205) and blanched

2 Roma tomatoes, blanched, peeled, seeded, and diced (page 203)

2 tablespoons capers, drained

¼ cup grated Asiago cheese

Preheat the oven to 400°F.

To prepare the marinade, whisk together the vinegar, olive oil, garlic, red pepper flakes, and salt in a small mixing bowl. Place the mushrooms in the bowl and toss to coat. Transfer the mushrooms and marinade into an 8-inch square baking dish, cover with foil, and bake for 20 minutes, or until the mushrooms are tender. Remove from the oven and let cool. When cool, slice the mushrooms.

To prepare the dressing, combine the vinegar and garlic puree in a mixing bowl. While whisking, slowly drizzle in the olive oil. Add the diced mushrooms, basil, and oregano and season with salt and pepper.

To prepare the salad, blanch the asparagus in a saucepan of boiling salted water for 3 to 4 minutes. Transfer to an ice bath and, when cool, drain well and place in a mixing bowl. Add the artichokes, tomatoes, and capers and combine thoroughly. Add the dressing and toss to mix well. Divide evenly among serving plates and garnish with the cheese.

SERVES 4 TO 6

Egg-Free Southwestern Caesar Salad with Herbed Ricotta

This dressing has all the flavor and punch of a great Southwestern Caesar salad but without the egg. Caesar salads have come a long way since they were created in Tijuana, Mexico, in the 1920s by restaurateur Caesar Cardini. They have gone in and out of fashion, but over the last few years they have taken restaurant menus by storm. Ricotta cheese is a by-product from making other types of cheese such as mozzarella and provolone, and infusing it with herbs and roasted garlic creates a delicious highlight for this salad.

FOR THE DRESSING

- 1 small shallot, minced
- 4 teaspoons Dijon mustard
- 2 garlic cloves, minced
- 1 teaspoon tamarind paste
- 2 tablespoons chipotle chile puree (page 206)
- 1 tablespoon balsamic vinegar
- 2 tablespoons freshly squeezed lemon juice
- 1 teaspoon pure red chile powder
- 1 teaspoon ground cumin
- 2 tablespoons grated Asiago cheese
- 2/3 cup extra-virgin olive oil
- 1/3 cup vegetable oil
- Salt to taste
- Cayenne to taste

FOR THE HERBED RICOTTA

- 1 cup ricotta cheese
- 1 tablespoon chopped fresh chives
- 1 tablespoon chopped fresh basil leaves
- 1 tablespoon chopped fresh oregano leaves
- 1 tablespoon roasted garlic puree (page 203)
- 2 tablespoons extra-virgin olive oil
- Salt and freshly ground black pepper to taste

FOR THE SALAD

- 4 heads of romaine lettuce

To prepare the dressing, place the shallot, mustard, garlic, tamarind paste, chipotle puree, balsamic vinegar, lemon juice, chile powder, cumin, and cheese in the bowl of a food processor and process until smooth. Slowly drizzle in the olive oil and vegetable oil while the motor is running and blend until all the ingredients are fully incorporated. Season with salt and cayenne and set aside.

To prepare the herbed ricotta, combine the ricotta, chives, basil, oregano, garlic, oil, and salt and pepper in a small mixing bowl and stir until thoroughly incorporated.

To prepare the salad, discard the tough outer leaves from each head of romaine and then tear the remaining leaves into bite-size pieces. Transfer to a large salad bowl and toss the romaine with the dressing. Divide the tossed greens evenly among serving plates and serve with 3 teaspoon-size scoops of the herbed ricotta. Season the salad with salt and pepper.

SERVES 6

Black Bean–Saffron Rice Salad with Mango-Habanero Vinaigrette

This salad derives its complex flavors from a number of complementary ingredients. Saffron, basmati rice, mango, black beans, and habanero chiles all work surprisingly well together, the sum being even more interesting than any of the parts.

2 tablespoons olive oil
1/2 onion, finely diced
2 garlic cloves, minced
1 cup raw basmati rice
1 1/2 cups Vegetable Stock (page 211) or store-bought
Salt to taste
1/4 teaspoon saffron threads
1 cup cooked black beans, cooled (page 213)
1/2 red onion, diced and blanched for 1 minute
1 small red bell pepper, seeded and diced
2 jalapeño chiles, seeded and minced
1 tablespoon chopped fresh cilantro leaves
1 tablespoon chopped fresh oregano leaves
1/2 cup Mango-Habanero Vinaigrette (page 49)

In a saucepan with a lid, heat the olive oil, uncovered, until lightly smoking. Add the diced onion and sauté for 1 minute over medium-high heat. Add the garlic and sauté for 1 minute longer. Add the rice and stir until coated. Add the stock, salt, and saffron and bring to a boil. Reduce the heat to a simmer, cover the pan, and cook until the rice has absorbed the liquid, about 15 minutes. Remove from the pan and spread out evenly on a cookie sheet. Refrigerate until cool.

Transfer the cooled rice to a mixing bowl and add the beans, red onion, bell pepper, chiles, cilantro, and oregano. Mix together well, add the vinaigrette, and combine thoroughly. Season with salt and serve at room temperature. This salad can be made 1 day ahead.

SERVES 4 TO 6

Three-Grain Salad with Dried Fruit, Almonds, and Grapefruit-Chipotle Vinaigrette

Here's a salad that features some ingredients with a history. Barley is one of the oldest cultivated grains, dating back at least ten thousand years to southwestern Asia or northeastern Africa. Quinoa, which is native to South America, has been cultivated for at least five thousand years and was a staple sacred food of the Inca civilization. Wild rice, which is not a grain at all but a seed of a type of aquatic grass, has been harvested by Native Americans of the Great Lakes region of North America for centuries. All are highly nutritious, and the addition of dried fruits and almonds makes this salad even more healthful.

FOR THE GRAPEFRUIT-CHIPOTLE VINAIGRETTE

- 1 shallot, minced
- Juice of 2 ruby red grapefruit
- Juice of 1 orange
- 1 tablespoon chipotle chile puree (page 206)
- 1 tablespoon roasted garlic puree (page 203)
- 1/4 cup champagne vinegar
- 1 teaspoon honey
- 1 cup olive oil
- Salt to taste

FOR THE SALAD

- 1/2 cup barley
- 1/2 cup quinoa
- 1/2 cup wild rice
- 1/4 cup sliced almonds, toasted (page 211)
- 2 tablespoons diced dried apricot
- 2 tablespoons golden raisins
- 2 tablespoons diced dried pineapple
- 1 grapefruit, peeled and sectioned (page 211)
- 1 tablespoon chopped fresh cilantro leaves
- 1/2 tablespoon chopped fresh mint leaves
- Salt to taste

To prepare the vinaigrette, place the shallot, grapefruit juice, and orange juice in a saucepan set over medium heat. Reduce the juices to 3 tablespoons and transfer to a mixing bowl. Add the chipotle puree, garlic, vinegar, and honey and whisk to combine. While whisking, drizzle in the oil and season with salt.

Heat 3 saucepans of boiling water and separately cook the barley, quinoa, and wild rice according to the directions on the packages (see Note). Drain and let each cool.

To make the salad, place the cooked grains, almonds, apricot, raisins, pineapple, grapefruit, cilantro, mint, and salt in a bowl and mix well. Add the vinaigrette and toss to combine thoroughly. Serve chilled or at room temperature. This dish can be made 1 day ahead, adding the almonds just before serving.

SERVES 4 TO 6

Note: If not using packaged grains, add the barley to 4 cups of salted water and boil for 25 to 30 minutes over medium-high heat, until tender. Add more water if necessary. Drain.

Add the quinoa to 3 cups salted water and boil for 18 to 20 minutes over medium heat, until tender. Add more water if necessary. Drain.

For the wild rice, see page 213.

Three-Grain Salad with Dried Fruit, Almonds, and Grapefruit-Chipotle Vinaigrette; Spicy Pickled Cucumber Slaw with Yogurt-Cumin Dressing; Carrot-Jicama Slaw with Ancho Chiles

Jicama-Mango Tortilla Salad with Citrus Vinaigrette

This salad, which is wonderful either on its own or served with grilled fish, has a great diversity of flavors and textures. The sweet lushness of the mango, the acidity of the lime, the crunch of the tortillas, and the refreshing crispness of the jicama and bell pepper presented in an assortment of colors make this a treat for all the senses.

3 cups vegetable oil
2 yellow corn tortillas, julienned
1 red corn tortilla, julienned
1 blue corn tortilla, julienned
¼ cup freshly squeezed lime juice
½ cup olive oil
Salt to taste
1 jicama, peeled and julienned
½ ripe mango, peeled, pitted, and julienned
½ red bell pepper, julienned
¼ cup fresh cilantro leaves

In a sauté pan, heat the vegetable oil until lightly smoking. Add the julienned tortillas and fry over high heat until crisp, about 2 minutes. Remove from the oil with a slotted spoon and drain on paper towels.

Pour the lime juice into a mixing bowl and gradually drizzle in the olive oil while whisking until an emulsion forms. Season the vinaigrette with salt. In a large mixing bowl, combine the jicama, mango, bell pepper, and cilantro leaves. Pour the vinaigrette over the salad and toss to combine. Add the fried tortillas and toss gently, being careful not to break up the tortillas too much.

SERVES 4 TO 6

Wilted Mustard Greens with Apples and Pecans

This salad is inspired by Southern flavors such as mustard greens, pecans, and apples, which are given starring roles here. The crunch of the tart apples and the texture of the pecans balance the sweet macerated apple puree and the pungent greens. This unusual salad is the quintessence of heartwarming, autumnal fare.

3 green apples, such as Granny
   Smith or Pippin, peeled,
   cored, and chopped
1/4 cup sugar
1/4 cup olive oil
2 shallots, minced
2 garlic cloves, minced
1/4 cup corn oil
2 tablespoons balsamic vinegar
2 tablespoons red wine vinegar
2 sprigs fresh rosemary, leaves
   removed and chopped
1/2 cup chopped toasted pecans
   (page 211)
8 ounces mustard greens, rinsed
   and dried
Salt and freshly ground black
   pepper to taste

Place one third of the apples and all of the sugar in a blender and process for 30 seconds. Set aside.

In a sauté pan, heat 1 tablespoon of the olive oil. Add the shallots and garlic and sauté over medium-high heat for 2 or 3 minutes, or until soft. Add the remaining 3 tablespoons of olive oil, the corn oil, balsamic vinegar, and red wine vinegar and whisk together. Add the rosemary, pecans, the macerated apple puree, and the remaining 2 chopped apples and cook for 1 minute. Add the greens, toss just until wilted, about 20 to 30 seconds, and season with salt and pepper. Divide evenly among serving plates.

SERVES 4

CHAPTER FOUR

SOUPS STEWS AND CHOWDERS

Charred Tomato-Eggplant Soup with Garlic

Eggplant (a berry) and tomato (a fruit) belong to the same botanical family—solanum—and while combining them in recipes is quite common, the charring technique for the tomatoes adds an exciting and unusual smoky quality to the pairing. The thin and elongated Japanese eggplant is now much more common than it used to be in the United States, and it has a slightly sweeter flavor than the large, oval Italian variety.

8 Roma tomatoes (about 1 pound), cut in half

5 tablespoons extra-virgin olive oil

1/2 cup chopped onion, plus 1 cup diced onion

10 garlic cloves, peeled and chopped

2 tablespoons (1/4 stick) unsalted butter

1 Japanese eggplant, cut in half lengthwise and sliced into half-moons

1 carrot, peeled and diced

1 celery stalk, peeled and diced

1/2 cup red wine

3 cups Vegetable Stock (page 211) or store-bought

3 tablespoons ancho chile puree (page 206)

2 tablespoons chopped fresh basil leaves

1 tablespoon chopped fresh oregano leaves

Salt to taste

6 tablespoons sour cream

Place a cast-iron skillet over high heat and heat for 5 minutes. Place the tomatoes, cut-side down, in the skillet and blacken completely, about 10 minutes, turning occasionally. Set aside. Carefully add 2 tablespoons of the olive oil to the skillet and sauté the chopped onion and garlic for 3 to 4 minutes, until the onion becomes translucent. Set aside.

In a large saucepan set over medium-high heat, add the remaining 3 tablespoons of olive oil and the butter. When the butter has fully melted and has started to brown, add the eggplant. Sauté for 10 minutes, or until the eggplant has caramelized fully. Add the diced onion, carrot, and celery and cook for 2 minutes longer. Deglaze the skillet with the red wine and reduce to a syrupy glaze, about 4 or 5 minutes.

Add the stock, the reserved tomato-onion-garlic mixture, and the ancho puree. Bring to a boil and then reduce the heat to a simmer. Add the basil and oregano and continue to simmer for 2 minutes longer. Transfer the mixture to a blender in batches and puree until smooth, about 3 minutes per batch. Season with salt. Ladle the soup into serving bowls and garnish each serving with 1 tablespoon of sour cream. The soup can be made 1 day ahead. The soup may be reheated or served chilled.

SERVES 4 TO 6

Avocado Soup with Jicama-Papaya Relish

This delightfully refreshing soup is a must on a hot summer's day. Like the word *jicama,* the word *avocado* is derived from a word in the Aztec language, *ahuacatl,* meaning "testicle." I'll let you take it from there! The rich buttery quality of avocado makes it ideal for chilled soups, and it goes especially well with the ripe melon and the crunchy jicama in the relish. You can find avocado leaves at Mexican specialty food stores.

1   tablespoon olive oil
½ onion, chopped
1   avocado leaf (optional)
1   garlic clove
1   serrano chile, stemmed and
      chopped (with seeds)
½ cup loosely packed fresh
      cilantro leaves
½ cup loosely packed spinach
      leaves
3   avocados, peeled, pitted, and
      chopped
2   cups Vegetable Stock (page
      211) or store-bought
¼ cup heavy cream
Salt to taste
4   to 6 tablespoons Jicama-
      Papaya Relish (page 37)

In a saucepan, heat the olive oil until lightly smoking. Add the onion and avocado leaf and cook for 1 minute over medium heat. Add the garlic and serrano and cook for 2 minutes longer. Discard the avocado leaf. Place the onion mixture in a blender, add the cilantro, spinach, avocados, stock, and 2 cups water, and puree until smooth. Strain the mixture through a medium-mesh sieve and chill thoroughly in the refrigerator. Stir in the cream, season with salt, and place 1 tablespoon of the relish in the center of each portion of the chilled soup. If making the soup 1 day ahead, the avocados will thicken. Thin by adding vegetable stock.

SERVES 4 TO 6

Winter Root Vegetable Stew

This satisfying stew brings all the rich heartiness of a winter stew without the fat and protein usually associated with meat and cream. If any of the vegetables called for here are unavailable, you can increase the others, or substitute potatoes and turnips, for example. I have always been fascinated by the word *rutabaga* and, on doing a little research, I discovered that it comes from the Swedish word *rotabagge*. The vegetable dates from medieval times in that country, which also explains why it is called a "swede" in England.

2 tablespoons olive oil

8 garlic cloves, chopped

½ onion, thinly sliced

1 carrot, peeled and finely diced

1 cup celery root, peeled and finely diced

1 cup parsnips, peeled and finely diced

1 cup rutabaga, peeled and finely diced

1 small beet, peeled and finely diced

1 turnip, peeled and finely diced

½ cup red wine

4 cups (or more as needed) Vegetable Stock (page 211) or store-bought

1 teaspoon chopped fresh sage leaves

1 teaspoon chopped fresh thyme leaves

1 teaspoon chopped fresh oregano leaves

1 tablespoon chopped fresh parsley leaves

Salt and freshly ground black pepper to taste

In a large saucepan, heat the olive oil until lightly smoking and add the garlic, onions, carrots, celery root, parsnips, rutabaga, beet, and turnips. Cook the vegetables over high heat until they are slightly golden, about 4 minutes, stirring occasionally. Deglaze the pan with the red wine and reduce by half. Add the stock, bring to a simmer, and cover the pan. Cook at a simmer, covered, for about 8 minutes, or until all the vegetables are tender; add more stock as necessary to keep the vegetables covered. Add the sage, thyme, oregano, and parsley, season with salt and pepper, and serve. The soup can be made 1 day ahead and reheated.

SERVES 6

Asparagus–Pine Nut Soup with Pecorino-Lime Crisps

If you've never tried the combination of asparagus and pine nuts, you're in for a real treat. The pecorino-lime crisps are easy to make and they add a pleasantly salty, acidic flavor. Parmesan or Romano cheese can be substituted for the pecorino, which is an Italian sheep's milk cheese. The crisps are also delicious in salads; for example, try them with the Egg-Free Southwestern Caesar Salad (page 56) instead of the herbed ricotta. *(photograph opposite)*

FOR THE CRISPS

- 1 cup coarsely grated pecorino cheese
- 2 tablespoons grated lime zest

FOR THE SOUP

- 1 bunch of large asparagus (about 15 spears), trimmed to 4 or 5 inches in length
- 2 teaspoons salt
- 2 tablespoons olive oil
- 1 onion, diced
- 1/4 cup peeled and diced carrot
- 1/2 cup diced celery
- 4 garlic cloves, minced
- 1 cup white wine
- 1/2 cup heavy cream
- 3 cups Vegetable Stock (page 211) or store-bought
- 1 cup firmly packed spinach leaves, thoroughly cleaned
- Juice of 2 limes
- 1/4 cup toasted pine nuts (page 211)

Preheat the oven to 350°F.

To prepare the crisps, combine the cheese and zest in a mixing bowl. Place four 3-inch circles of the mixture (about 3/8 inch thick) on a nonstick baking sheet. Place in the oven and bake for 25 to 30 minutes, or until golden brown. Remove and let cool before serving.

To prepare the soup, cut the tips from the asparagus spears and set aside. Chop the asparagus stems into 1-inch lengths and set aside separately from the tips.

In a medium saucepan, pour enough water to come about 3 inches up the sides. Add the salt and bring the water to a boil. Add the asparagus tips and blanch until just tender, about 3 minutes. Drain and refresh under cold running water to stop the cooking process. Drain and set aside.

In a large saucepan, heat the olive oil until lightly smoking. Add the asparagus stems, onion, carrot, and celery and cook until the onion is translucent, about 4 minutes. Add the garlic and cook for 1 minute longer. Deglaze the pan with the white wine and reduce until syrupy, about 8 minutes. Add the cream and stock and bring to a boil. Reduce the heat to a simmer and cook for 10 minutes. Remove from the heat and add the spinach. Transfer the soup in batches to a blender and puree until smooth, 3 to 5 minutes (alternatively, use a hand-held blender to process the soup in the saucepan). Strain the soup through a medium-mesh strainer into a clean saucepan and bring to a simmer. Add the lime juice and asparagus tips and continue to simmer for 2 minutes, or until the asparagus tips are warm. Season to taste with salt and ladle into serving bowls. Garnish each serving with 1 tablespoon of pine nuts and a pecorino-lime crisp.

SERVES 4

Curried Lima Bean Soup with Apple-Almond Chutney

The plump, glossy, cream or pale green lima beans—also called butter beans because of their pallor and richness—have been cultivated for at least seven thousand years in their native South America. The name is derived from the anglicized version of Lima, the capital of Peru, which is where the oldest archaeological examples of the bean have been found. I have always enjoyed the blended spice flavors of curry matched with lima beans, and this well-balanced soup is rounded out perfectly with the addition of the apple-almond chutney, which makes another bow (like the curry) to the cuisine of India.

2 tablespoons olive oil
1/2 onion, diced
1 small carrot, peeled and chopped
1 celery stalk, chopped
1 jalapeño chile, seeded and chopped
2 garlic cloves, minced
2 tablespoons curry powder
1 green apple, such as Granny Smith or Pippin, peeled, cored, and chopped
1/2 cup white wine
1 cup dry lima beans, soaked overnight and drained
5 cups Vegetable Stock (page 211) or store-bought
Salt to taste
1/4 cup Apple-Almond Chutney (page 39)

In a large saucepan, heat the oil over medium heat until lightly smoking. Add the onion, carrot, celery, jalapeño, and garlic and sauté for 4 minutes, stirring occasionally. Add the curry powder and apple and sauté for 2 minutes longer.

Deglaze the pan with the white wine and reduce the liquid for 3 minutes, or until the pan is almost dry. Add the lima beans and stock and bring to a boil. Reduce the heat to a simmer and cook for 40 minutes, or until the lima beans are soft. In a blender, blend the soup in batches and pass through a medium-mesh strainer into a clean saucepan. Warm through, season with salt, and ladle into soup bowls. Place 1 tablespoon of the chutney in the center of each serving. The soup can be made ahead and reheated.

SERVES 4

Black and White Bean Soup

Using two different color beans, and then blending them at the last moment, creates a colorful soup—a delicious version of traditional bean soup.

2 tablespoons olive oil
1 small onion, chopped
1 small carrot, peeled and chopped
2 celery stalks, chopped
1 poblano chile, seeded and chopped
4 garlic cloves, chopped
2 teaspoons chopped thyme leaves
1 tablespoon chopped epazote
6–8 cups Vegetable Stock (page 211) or store-bought
2 teaspoons pure chile powder
1 tablespoon ground cumin
1½ cups (½ pound) great Northern white beans, soaked overnight and drained
1½ cups (½ pound) black turtle beans, soaked overnight and drained
1 tablespoon chopped fresh cilantro leaves
Salt to taste
½ cup sour cream, for garnish
Pickled Japapeños (page 17), for garnish

In a large pot, heat the olive oil until lightly smoking. Add the onion, carrot, celery, poblano, garlic, thyme, and epazote, and cook for 3 minutes, or until the onions are translucent. Add 6 cups of the vegetable stock and bring to a boil; skim the surface to remove any residue. Whisk in the chile powder and cumin, then equally divide the liquid and sautéed vegetables between two smaller pots. Add the white beans to one pot and the black beans to the other. Bring both back to a boil; lower heat and simmer for 1½ to 2 hours. Add more stock if the level of liquid falls below the surface of the beans.

Puree each soup for 3 to 4 minutes in the blender at high speed with ½ tablespoon of the cilantro, then season with salt.

To serve, reheat both soups in separate pans. Simultaneously ladle some of each into warmed bowls. Garnish with sour cream and Pickled Jalapeños.

SERVES 4 TO 6

Wild Mushroom–Chipotle Consommé

This dish brings together the subtle and delicate nature of classic wild mushroom consommé and the earthy smokiness of chipotle chiles. Consommés are clarified broths that are usually made with meat or fish, but as this recipe proves, they can be made with equally delicious results using vegetables. *(photograph opposite)*

4 pounds fresh wild mushrooms, such as morels, cèpes, or shiitakes, cleaned

8 cups Vegetable Stock (page 211) or store-bought

8 large leeks, thoroughly cleaned and chopped

6 garlic cloves

2 cups dried mushrooms, such as porcini

2 canned chipotle chiles in adobo sauce, cut in half and seeded

12 sprigs fresh thyme

2 cups loosely packed fresh basil leaves and stems

4 sprigs fresh rosemary

6 large egg whites

2 large ripe tomatoes, blanched, peeled, seeded, and diced (page 203)

¼ cup sliced fresh chives

Salt to taste

Remove the stems from the fresh mushrooms and reserve. Slice the caps thinly and set aside. In a large saucepan set over high heat, bring the vegetable stock to a boil. Add the reserved mushroom stems, the leeks, garlic, dried mushrooms, chiles, thyme, basil, and rosemary and reduce the heat to a simmer. Cook this mushroom broth for 30 minutes. Strain through a medium-mesh sieve and return to the saucepan. Let cool completely.

In a mixing bowl, lightly beat the egg whites until just frothy. Whisk into the mushroom broth and return the pan to the stove over low heat. Bring to a low simmer and let simmer gently without stirring until the egg whites coagulate, forming a "raft," about 5 minutes. Gently ladle the clarified broth through a strainer lined with cheesecloth or a coffee filter, being careful not to disturb the "raft."

Return the strained consommé to a clean saucepan and add the sliced mushroom caps, the diced tomatoes, and the chives. The soup can be made 4 to 5 days ahead. Reheat gently, season with salt, and serve.

SERVES 6

Butternut Squash Chowder with Pears and Ginger

This autumnal dish is especially appropriate and welcome as the first course on a cool fall evening. The subtle sweetness of the squash is enhanced by the flavors of the pears, orange, and ginger, making it a great addition also to the Thanksgiving table.

2 Anjou or Bosc pears, peeled, cored, and diced

Juice of 2 lemons

2 tablespoons olive oil

1 cup peeled and diced Vidalia or Spanish onion

1 stalk celery, diced

1 small carrot, peeled and diced

1 tablespoon minced garlic

1 teaspoon peeled minced fresh ginger

1/2 cup dry white wine

2 small butternut squash, peeled, seeded, and diced (about 3 cups)

1 baking potato (about 12 ounces), peeled and diced

5 cups Vegetable Stock (page 211) or store-bought

1/4 cup freshly squeezed orange juice

1 tablespoon freshly squeezed lemon juice

1/2 cup heavy cream

Salt to taste

Place the pears in a bowl with the lemon juice, cover with water, and set aside.

In a large saucepan, heat the olive oil over high heat until lightly smoking. Add the onion, celery, and carrot and sauté for 2 to 3 minutes, or until the onion is translucent. Add the garlic and ginger and sauté for 1 minute longer, stirring constantly. Add the white wine and reduce the liquid until the pan is almost dry, about 3 minutes.

Drain half of the pears, reserving the other half in the lemon water for garnish. Add the drained pears to the pan with the squash, potato, and stock and bring to a boil. Reduce the heat to a simmer and cook for 30 minutes, or until the squash is tender. Transfer half of the soup in batches to a blender and puree until smooth. Strain through a fine-mesh sieve back into the saucepan with the unpureed mixture. Add the orange juice, lemon juice, cream, salt, and the reserved pears and gently warm the chowder through (do not boil). The chowder can be made 1 day ahead.

SERVES 6

Roasted Corn and Sweet Potato Chowder with Fried Scallions

If I was stranded on a desert island with a range and only two main ingredients, I would probably choose corn and sweet potatoes. That is one of the reasons why this is one of my all-time favorite chowders. Sweet potatoes, which have been cultivated for over ten thousand years in their native South America, are not related to potatoes. Neither should they be confused with yams, which are a different species of tuber native to Africa and later introduced to South America and the Caribbean.

FOR THE CHOWDER

- 2 ears of corn, in their husks
- 2 large sweet potatoes (2½ to 3 pounds)
- 2 teaspoons corn oil
- ½ onion, diced
- 1 celery stalk, diced
- 1 small carrot, peeled and diced
- ½ red bell pepper, seeded and diced
- ½ yellow bell pepper, seeded and diced
- 1 garlic clove, finely minced
- 1 tablespoon chopped fresh thyme leaves
- ¼ cup white wine
- 1½ quarts Vegetable Stock (page 211) or store-bought

FOR THE FRIED SCALLIONS

- ⅓ cup all-purpose flour
- ⅓ cup cornstarch
- ¾ cup very cold water
- 1 teaspoon salt

Vegetable oil, for frying
- 1 cup scallions cut on the bias into 1-inch lengths

Salt to taste

Preheat the oven to 350°F.

To prepare the chowder, place the corn on a baking sheet and bake in the oven for 20 minutes. When cool enough to handle, remove the husks and silks from the corn and then cut the kernels from the cob.

Place the sweet potatoes on a baking sheet and place in the oven. Remove one of the potatoes from the oven after 30 minutes. When cool enough to handle, peel, cut into ¼-inch dice, and set aside. Continue baking the remaining potato for 30 minutes longer, or until fork-tender. Remove from the oven and let cool.

In a large saucepan over medium heat, heat the corn oil. Add the onion, celery, carrot, bell peppers, garlic, and thyme. Cook for 3 to 5 minutes, or until the onion becomes translucent. Add the white wine and reduce to a syrupy glaze, 4 or 5 minutes.

Meanwhile, peel the roasted sweet potato, roughly chop, and add to the vegetables in the saucepan. Add the vegetable stock, bring to a simmer, and cook for 45 minutes.

Prepare the fried scallions: Using a whisk, combine the flour, cornstarch, water, and salt in a small mixing bowl. Refrigerate for 20 minutes. Meanwhile, heat 2 to 3 inches of the vegetable oil in a large saucepan to 350°F. Dunk the scallions in the batter with a slotted spoon and allow the excess liquid to drip off. Carefully place the dipped scallions in the oil and cook for 2 minutes, or until golden brown. Remove the scallions from the hot oil with a slotted spoon or skimmer and drain on paper towels.

Ladle the soup into a blender in batches and puree. Pass through a strainer and return to a clean saucepan. Stir in the reserved diced sweet potato and the roasted corn. Warm through and season with salt. Ladle the soup into warm bowls and sprinkle the fried scallions over the top.

SERVES 4 TO 6

CHAPTER FIVE
POTATOES
CORN AND
BEANS

Potato–Goat Cheese Pie with Leeks

Potatoes and leeks are a time-honored combination beloved by soup lovers, especially connoisseurs of vichyssoise. The leek is the national symbol of Wales, although it is native to the eastern Mediterranean and was probably taken to the British Isles by the Romans. Its delicate flavor—milder and sweeter than onions or garlic—combines perfectly with the potatoes and goat cheese in this recipe.

FOR THE CRUST

1½ cups all-purpose flour
¼ teaspoon salt
½ cup vegetable shortening
4 to 5 tablespoons cold water

FOR THE FILLING

2 tablespoons Vegetable Stock (page 211) or store-bought
½ cup heavy cream
6 ounces fresh goat cheese
⅔ cup diced leeks, white parts only, washed and drained
¼ cup roasted garlic puree (page 203)
1½ pounds russet or new potatoes, peeled and diced
Salt to taste

To prepare the crust, combine the flour and salt in a mixing bowl. Add the shortening and incorporate with your fingertips until the mixture resembles very coarse cornmeal. Sprinkle 3 to 4 tablespoons of the water over the flour mixture in 1-tablespoon increments while stirring with a fork. Add more water if needed. Form the dough into a ball, wrap in wax paper or plastic, and let rest for 1 hour in the refrigerator.

Preheat the oven to 425°F.

On a lightly floured work surface, roll out the dough into an 11-inch circle with a ⅛-inch thickness. Place the dough into an 8-inch pie pan, trimming and crimping the edges. Place the pie shell in the freezer for 20 minutes.

To prepare the filling, combine the stock and cream in a saucepan and bring to a simmer. Remove from the heat and whisk in the goat cheese until the mixture is smooth. In a mixing bowl, combine the leeks, garlic puree, and potatoes. Add the goat cheese mixture and salt and toss until thoroughly combined. Remove the pie shell from the freezer, fill with the mixture, and bake in the oven for 45 minutes, or until the potatoes are tender and the top is golden brown. Serve hot.

SERVES 6

Red Potatoes in Ancho-Saffron-Orange Broth

Ancho chiles and orange have become a pretty common combination in Southwestern cooking. Saffron and orange is another common pairing in certain cultures—Spain and other parts of the Mediterranean, for example. The three ingredients together, however, make a surprisingly harmonious team, individually and collectively enhancing the red potatoes.

1 tablespoon olive oil
1/2 onion, diced
3 garlic cloves, minced
Zest and juice of 2 oranges
5 cups Vegetable Stock (page 211) or store-bought
1/4 cup julienned ancho chile
1/4 teaspoon saffron threads
1 pound small red potatoes, unpeeled, cut into wedges
2 tablespoons chopped fresh cilantro leaves
Salt to taste

In a saucepan, heat the oil until lightly smoking. Add the onion and sauté over high heat for 3 minutes. Add the garlic and orange zest and cook for 2 minutes longer. Deglaze the pan with the orange juice and reduce until 2 tablespoons of liquid remain. Add the stock, ancho, saffron, and potatoes and bring to a boil. Reduce the heat to a simmer and cook for 20 minutes, or until the potatoes are tender. Stir in the cilantro and season with salt.

SERVES 6

Twice-Baked Sweet Potatoes with Candied Ginger and Orange

Here is a dish just begging to be taken to the Thanksgiving table. It is composed of some of my favorite ingredients that define the South: sweet potatoes, orange, ginger, and pecans. Southern cooking is one of the many antecedents of Texas cooking, and its influence remains strong, especially in the eastern part of the state.

6 small sweet potatoes (about 1 pound each), cut in half lengthwise
Juice of 4 oranges (about 4 cups)
2 tablespoons grated orange zest
Pinch of cayenne
1/4 cup candied ginger, minced
2/3 cup toasted chopped pecans (page 211)
Salt to taste

Preheat the oven to 350°F.

Place the sweet potatoes on a lightly oiled cookie sheet, cut-side down. Place in the oven and bake for 30 minutes, or until they yield a little when pressed. Remove and let cool; keep the oven on. Meanwhile, place the orange juice in a small saucepan and reduce by one quarter over medium-high heat. Remove from the heat and reserve.

Once the potatoes have cooled enough to handle, carefully scoop the flesh into the work bowl of a food processor, leaving the skins intact; reserve 8 of the skin halves. Add the orange zest, reduced orange juice, and cayenne to the food processor and process until smooth, about 1 minute. Transfer to a mixing bowl and fold in half of the candied ginger and half of the pecans. Season to taste with salt.

Place the reserved potato skins on a lightly oiled cookie sheet and scoop equal amounts of the potato mixture into each skin. Place the potatoes in the oven and bake for 25 minutes, or until the tops of the potatoes start to caramelize. Remove from the oven and garnish with the remaining ginger and pecans.

SERVES 6

Saffron-Corn Mashed Potatoes

Saffron is the most expensive spice in the world. Why? Because it is highly labor-intensive. Saffron is derived from the dried stigmas of a small purple crocus native to Greece and the eastern Mediterranean, and the stigmas must be collected individually by hand. The good news is that a very little saffron packs a wallop of flavor and color, as these potatoes prove.

2½ pounds russet or new
    potatoes, peeled and roughly
    chopped
2 tablespoons olive oil
½ onion, diced
1 cup fresh corn kernels
4 garlic cloves, minced
1 cup heavy cream
2 teaspoons saffron threads
2 tablespoons (¼ stick)
    unsalted butter
Salt to taste

In a large saucepan, place the potatoes and cover with cold water. Cover the pan and bring to a boil over high heat. Reduce the heat to a simmer and cook for 25 to 30 minutes, or until a paring knife penetrates the potatoes easily; drain the potatoes in a colander. Mash the potatoes by working them through a food mill or by beating with a mixer.

While the potatoes are cooking, heat the olive oil over medium heat in a small sauté pan until lightly smoking. Add the onion to the pan and sauté for 2 minutes. Add the corn and garlic and continue cooking until the onion is lightly caramelized and the corn is soft, about 4 minutes. Add the cream, saffron, and butter and bring just to a boil. Cover the pan, remove from the heat, and let the saffron infuse for 15 minutes.

When the potatoes are mashed, fold in the cream and corn mixture and season with salt.

SERVES 4 TO 6

Smoked Salmon–Horseradish Mashed Potatoes

There's something about the combination of smoked salmon, horseradish, and potatoes that seems both down-home and exotic. As well as a side dish, these potatoes make a great hors d'oeuvre simply spooned onto croutons or, better yet, onto the Corn Griddle Cakes (page 90).

2½ pounds Yukon gold, fingerling, or yellow fingerling potatoes, peeled and roughly chopped
⅓ cup unsalted butter
3 tablespoons prepared horseradish
1 cup sour cream
3 tablespoons sliced fresh chives
8 ounces smoked salmon, thinly sliced
Salt to taste

In a large saucepan, place the potatoes and cover with cold water. Cover the pan and bring to a boil over high heat. Reduce the heat to a simmer and cook for 25 to 30 minutes, or until a paring knife penetrates the potatoes easily; drain the potatoes in a colander. Mash the potatoes by working them through a food mill or by beating with a mixer. Transfer to a mixing bowl.

In a saucepan, melt the butter and, off the heat, whisk in the horseradish and sour cream. Fold into the potatoes with the chives and salmon; season with salt.

SERVES 4

Roast Garlic Mashers

To me, these potatoes are the very essence of comfort food. I enjoy them with grilled vegetables, such as eggplant and squash, and grilled corn on the cob with Red Chile Butter (page 85). They are also the perfect accompaniment to simply grilled or roasted meat, poultry, or fish.

2½ pounds russet or yellow fingerling potatoes, peeled and roughly chopped
½ cup heavy cream
2 tablespoons (¼ stick) unsalted butter
¼ cup roasted garlic puree (page 203)
Salt to taste

In a large saucepan, place the potatoes and cover with cold water. Cover the pan and bring to a boil over high heat. Reduce the heat to a simmer and cook for 25 to 30 minutes, or until a paring knife penetrates the potatoes easily; drain the potatoes in a colander. Mash the potatoes by working them through a food mill or by beating with a mixer.

Place the cream and butter in a saucepan and bring to a boil. Whisk in the roasted garlic, then add to the potatoes while whisking. Season with salt.

SERVES 4

An assortment of Mashed Potatoes

Refried Black Bean Casserole with Queso Fresco

Black beans are native to Central America, where they are a staple, and they have an appealing meaty quality. They have become very popular over recent years in the United States, especially on Southwestern menus. Serve one of the salsas in Chapter 2—for example, the Griddled Tomato-Chipotle Salsa (page 32)—with this hearty dish. It's also a delicious accompaniment to poultry and beef dishes, or as part of a vegetarian platter, especially if it contains roasted corn and sweet potatoes.

2 cups dried black beans, soaked overnight and drained
6 cups Vegetable Stock (page 211) or store-bought
½ cup red wine
½ cup chopped onion
2 garlic cloves, minced
Vegetable oil, for frying
9 corn tortillas
3 Pickled Jalapeños (page 17), seeded and diced
Salt to taste
2 tablespoons chopped fresh cilantro leaves
½ cup Garlic-Onion Pickles (page 18)
½ cup grated *queso fresco* or Muenster cheese
½ cup Pico de Gallo (page 31)

Rinse the beans under cold running water. In a large saucepan, bring the stock and wine to a boil. Add the beans, onion, and garlic. Bring the liquid back to a boil, reduce the heat, and simmer for 1½ hours, or until tender. Drain the beans and transfer the cooking liquid to a clean saucepan. Over high heat, reduce the liquid to ½ cup and set aside.

While the beans are cooking, pour enough vegetable oil into a large skillet to come 1 inch up the sides and heat to 350°F. Add 2 or 3 tortillas and deep-fry for about 3 minutes, or until crispy. Remove with tongs and drain on paper towels. Repeat for the remaining tortillas. Set aside.

Preheat oven to 350°F.

In a clean skillet over medium-high heat, heat 3 tablespoons more of the vegetable oil until lightly smoking. Add the cooked beans and pickled jalapeños and mash with a large fork or a potato masher until the beans have a roughly pureed texture. Add the reserved ½ cup of cooking liquid and bring to a boil. Reduce the heat to low and let the beans simmer for a few minutes, stirring constantly, until they are a little thinner than the desired consistency. Stir in the salt and cilantro. Spread one third of the beans in an 8-inch square casserole. Spread one third of the pickled onions on top of the beans and then roughly crumble 3 of the deep-fried tortillas on top of the onions. Sprinkle one third of the *queso fresco* on top of the tortillas, then repeat the process, ending with the remaining cheese. (The casserole may be refrigerated at this point, 1 day ahead, until ready to cook and serve.)

Place the casserole in the oven and bake for 15 to 20 minutes; the cheese will be completely melted and golden brown. (Allow an additional 10 minutes of baking if the casserole has been refrigerated.) Garnish with the Pico de Gallo.

SERVES 4

Posole with Southern Greens, Chayote, Dried Cherries, and Pecans

Posole is a thick, hearty stew typically containing corn and pork that originated in Jalisco, Mexico. Since I wanted to make this recipe vegetarian anyway, I decided to take it in an entirely new direction. The dried cherries may seem a little odd at first, but they lend a pleasant sweet-tartness to the dish while the pecans take it a bit deeper into the South. In the United States, we call the dried posole "hominy."

½ cup dry posole, soaked
    overnight
6 cups Vegetable Stock (page
    211) or store-bought
2 tablespoons olive oil
½ cup diced onion
2 garlic cloves, peeled and
    minced
1 pound greens (such as mustard
    greens, collards, and/or
    Swiss chard), washed and
    roughly chopped
2 chayotes, cut in half, pitted, and
    julienned
½ cup dried cherries
½ cup toasted chopped pecans
    (page 211)
¼ cup cider vinegar
3 tablespoons unsalted butter
Salt to taste

Drain the posole and place in a saucepan. Cover with the stock and bring to a boil. Reduce the heat to a simmer and cook for 1 hour, or until the posole is tender. Drain and reserve the posole and cooking liquid separately.

In a stockpot, heat the olive oil until lightly smoking. Add the onion and sauté for 1 minute over high heat. Add the garlic and cook for 1 minute longer. Add the greens, chayotes, and 1 cup of the posole cooking liquid. Cover the pan, reduce the heat to a simmer, and cook for 20 minutes, or until the greens are tender. Remove the lid and add the dried cherries, pecans, vinegar, and reserved posole. Cook over low heat, uncovered, for 10 minutes. Stir in the butter and season with salt. Serve immediately.

SERVES 4 TO 6

Tri-Color Potato Chips

These colorful chips are a terrific accompaniment to any of the sandwiches in Chapter 10. Try them also as a snack sprinkled with a crumbly cheese and placed under the broiler just long enough to melt the cheese. A mandoline slicer is really the best way to go for making these chips, and you'll find it's a great investment. If you are using a sharp knife, you'll need to add more time for the chips to cook, as they will be slightly thicker. *(photograph opposite)*

2 Peruvian purple potatoes, peeled
2 small sweet potatoes, peeled
2 small baking potatoes, peeled
Peanut or canola oil, for deep-frying
Salt to taste
Cayenne to taste (optional)

Using a mandoline slicer, slice all the potatoes wafer thin. As you cut them, place in separate bowls of hot water so they are covered and do not oxidize.

In a deep-fryer or large saucepan, place the oil and heat to 325°F. Thoroughly drain and pat dry the purple potatoes and carefully add to the oil (take care, as the hot oil may spatter). Deep-fry for 8 to 10 minutes, or until crispy. Remove the potatoes with a slotted spoon and drain on paper towels. The potatoes will crisp further as they cool. Repeat for each of the remaining potatoes. Sprinkle with salt and cayenne if desired.

SERVES 4 TO 6

Texas Red Beans and Rice

While this dish gets its inspiration from Louisiana, it is a preparation quite commonly seen in Texas, especially on the Gulf Coast, which shares more than a little culture with our neighbor state to the east. Serve this recipe with some good corn bread or warm tortillas, or as a side dish with great burgers, vegetarian or otherwise. If you have the time, smoke the onion (see page 209).

2 tablespoons olive oil
1/2 cup finely diced onion
1/4 cup finely diced celery
1 green bell pepper, seeded, diced
2 Pickled Jalapeños (page 17), chopped
6 garlic cloves, minced
6 cups Vegetable Stock (page 211) or store-bought
1 cup red beans, soaked overnight and drained
3/4 cup rice
Salt and black pepper to taste
4 scallions, chopped
3 tablespoons chopped fresh cilantro leaves

In a large saucepan set over high heat, heat the oil until lightly smoking. Add the onion, celery, bell pepper, jalapeños, and garlic and cook for 2 minutes, or until the onion is translucent. Add the stock and beans and bring to a boil, reduce the heat to a simmer, and cook for 1 hour, or until the beans are almost tender.

Add the rice, cover the pan, and simmer for 20 minutes longer, or until the rice and beans are tender (add a little water if necessary). Season with salt and pepper and stir in the scallions and cilantro. This dish can be made ahead and reheated.

SERVES 4

Canyon Cowboy Beans with Mexican Corn Bread

This is my version of the classic Mexican *borracho* ("drunken") beans. It's a dish I was served with great regularity at my grandmother's house when I was growing up. Whenever I serve this with Mexican Skillet Corn Bread (page 175), I am practically transported back to my childhood. The only thing missing here is a "mess of greens," in which case you may want to serve this with the Wilted Mustard Greens with Apples and Pecans (page 61) or the Posole with Southern Greens, Chayote, Dried Cherries, and Pecans (page 81).

FOR THE BEANS

- 2 tablespoons olive oil
- 1 onion, sliced and smoked (page 209) (optional)
- 2 garlic cloves, minced
- 2 cups pinto beans, soaked overnight and drained
- 4 cups Vegetable Stock (page 211) or store-bought
- 2 cups dark beer, such as Shiner Bock or Negra Modelo
- 2 tablespoons Worcestershire sauce
- 4 jalapeño chiles, thinly sliced, with seeds

Salt and freshly ground black pepper to taste
- 2 tablespoons chopped fresh cilantro leaves

FOR THE CORN BREAD

- 1 cup yellow cornmeal
- 1 teaspoon salt
- 1/2 teaspoon baking soda
- 2 large eggs
- 2/3 cup buttermilk
- 1/3 cup vegetable shortening, melted and cooled
- 3/4 cup fresh corn kernels
- 1/2 cup heavy cream
- 2 jalapeño chiles, seeded and minced
- 1 small poblano or Anaheim chile, roasted, peeled, seeded, and diced (page 204)
- 1 cup grated sharp Cheddar cheese

To prepare the beans, heat the olive oil until lightly smoking, add the onion, and sauté over high heat for 3 minutes, or until just translucent. Add the garlic and cook for 1 minute longer. Add the beans, stock, beer, and Worcestershire sauce and bring to a boil. Reduce the heat to a simmer and cook for about 1 hour, checking after 30 minutes every 10 minutes or so for doneness, adding more stock as needed to keep the beans covered. Add the jalapeños after the first 30 minutes of cooking. When the beans are tender, season with salt and pepper and stir in the cilantro.

While the beans are cooking, preheat the oven to 375°F.

To prepare the corn bread, combine the cornmeal, salt, and baking soda in a mixing bowl and set aside. In another bowl, lightly whisk the eggs, add the buttermilk and melted shortening, and combine thoroughly. Add the liquid ingredients to the dry ingredients and fold in the corn, cream, and chiles.

Place a large cast-iron skillet in the oven for 5 minutes to heat through. Remove the skillet and pour in half of the mixture. Sprinkle in the cheese and then pour in the remaining mixture. Return the skillet to the oven and bake for 30 to 35 minutes, until golden brown. Serve the corn bread with the beans.

SERVES 4

Corn Grilled in Its Husk with Red Chile Butter

This is great side for barbecued food and makes a striking visual presentation, not only because the corn husks are kept intact, but also because the red-flecked butter spread on the corn contrasts with the bright yellow kernels. The smoky flavor of the corn gives a further interesting twist to an old standby.

8 ears of corn, in the husk

FOR THE RED CHILE BUTTER

3 tablespoons freshly squeezed lime juice
1 tablespoon plus 1 teaspoon salt
1 cup (2 sticks) unsalted butter, at room temperature
2 tablespoons pure red chile powder
1 tablespoon paprika
1/4 teaspoon cayenne
2 tablespoons roasted garlic puree (page 203)
2 tablespoons chopped fresh cilantro leaves

Prepare the grill.

Soak the ears of corn in warm water for 15 minutes. Meanwhile, to prepare the red chile butter, combine the lime juice and 1 tablespoon of salt in a small bowl and stir to dissolve the salt. Place the butter, chile powder, paprika, cayenne, garlic puree, and the remaining 1 teaspoon of salt in a food processor and blend until combined thoroughly, scraping down the sides as needed. Add the reserved lime juice mixture and the cilantro and blend until incorporated. Set aside.

Remove the corn from the water and carefully peel the husk back, leaving the leaves attached and intact. Remove the corn silks and spread the butter mixture on the kernels; fold the leaves back over the corn. Wrap the corn with foil, place on the grill over medium-high heat, and grill for 35 minutes, turning the ears every 10 minutes. Remove from the grill, unwrap and discard the foil, and serve. This dish can also be made by roasting the corn for 25 to 30 minutes at 350°F.

SERVES 8

CHAPTER SIX

PANCAKES
FRITTERS
AND HASHES

Poblano–Dried Fruit Risotto Cakes with Green Mango–Habanero Jam

The flavors and textures of this dish are about as complex as any in this book. The chewy and slightly acidic dried fruit is the perfect foil for the creamy but firmly textured risotto and the spicy sweet-tartness of the jam. If there is anything that might make this dish even better, it would be roast duck. The shiny green poblanos are the fresh form of dried ancho chiles.

FOR THE RISOTTO CAKES

- 5 cups Vegetable Stock (page 211) or store-bought
- 4 tablespoons (½ stick) unsalted butter
- ¼ cup minced onion
- 1½ cups Arborio rice
- ½ cup dry white wine
- ⅓ cup grated *queso fresco,* or Parmesan or pecorino cheese
- 2 poblano chiles, roasted, peeled, seeded, and diced (page 204)
- 2 tablespoons diced dried papaya
- 2 tablespoons diced dried pineapple
- 2 tablespoons diced dried mango

Pinch of cayenne
Salt to taste
- 3 tablespoons olive oil
- 1 cup coarse cornmeal, for dredging

Green Mango–Habanero Jam (page 12)

In a saucepan, bring the stock to a simmer. Meanwhile, in a large heavy saucepan over medium heat, heat 3 tablespoons of the butter. Add the onion and sauté over high heat for about 2 minutes, until translucent. Add the rice to the pan and stir for 1 minute, making sure that the rice is well coated. Add ¼ cup of the wine and stir until it is completely absorbed. Begin adding the stock, ½ cup at a time, stirring until almost completely absorbed before adding the next ½ cup; this process will take about 20 to 25 minutes until the stock is all absorbed. Stir frequently to prevent sticking.

When the rice is tender but still firm, add the remaining ¼ cup of wine. Turn off the heat and immediately add the remaining 1 tablespoon of butter, the *queso fresco*, poblanos, papaya, pineapple, mango, and cayenne. Stir well to combine the ingredients, season with salt, and let cool in an even layer on a baking sheet.

Form the rice by hand into large, round cakes about 3 inches across and ½ inch thick. In a cast-iron skillet, heat the olive oil until lightly smoking. Dredge the rice cakes in the cornmeal and sauté over low heat for 2 minutes on each side. Drain on paper towels and serve with the Green Mango–Habanero Jam.

SERVES 4 TO 6
MAKES 12 RISOTTO CAKES

Carrot Pancakes with Dill Yogurt

These pancakes make a great appetizer for a vegetarian dinner. Smaller pancakes also make terrific passed hors d'oeuvres at cocktail parties. The flavors of carrot and ginger are particularly complementary (it's a good combination for soup), while the aromatic dill yogurt provides a pleasing counterpoint. Dill is best used fresh, as here.

FOR THE DILL YOGURT
- 1 cup plain yogurt (nonfat, low-fat, or whole milk)
- 2 tablespoons chopped fresh dill
- 1 tablespoon freshly squeezed lemon juice
- Salt and cayenne to taste

FOR THE PANCAKES
- 2 cups grated carrots
- 1 tablespoon peeled grated fresh ginger
- 1 scallion, finely chopped
- 1 jalapeño chile, stemmed and minced
- 1/4 cup bread crumbs
- 2 eggs, lightly beaten
- 2 tablespoons (1/4 stick) unsalted butter, melted
- 1/2 tablespoon salt
- Olive oil, for frying

In a small mixing bowl, combine the yogurt, dill, and lemon juice. Add the salt and cayenne and mix thoroughly. Keep refrigerated.

To prepare the pancakes, combine the carrots, ginger, scallion, jalapeño, bread crumbs, eggs, melted butter, and salt in a mixing bowl and toss until thoroughly combined.

Pour enough olive oil into a large cast-iron skillet to come 1/8 inch up the sides. Heat the oil to 350°F., or until lightly smoking. Pour 1/4 cup of the batter into the oil, flatten evenly with a spatula to form a 3-inch pancake, and repeat for as many pancakes as will fit comfortably into the skillet. Cook for 2 minutes on each side, or until the pancakes are golden brown. Remove and let drain on a cookie sheet lined with paper towels. To keep warm, place the pancakes in a 250°F. oven. Repeat for the remaining pancakes. Serve with the dill yogurt.

SERVES 4 TO 8
MAKES 8 PANCAKES

Celery Root Pancakes and Golden Gazpacho Salsa

Celery root, also called celeriac, is a roundish, brown-skinned vegetable root of a type of celery. It's grown specifically for the coconut-size root—the leaves and stem of the plant are inedible. It has white, crisp flesh and a strong flavor, with tones of celery and parsley, and it can be eaten raw or cooked. It is usually available from early fall through late spring. In this recipe, the celery root is complemented nicely by the acidic sweetness of the salsa.

- 1 pound celery root, peeled and grated
- 2 scallions, sliced
- 1 small garlic clove, minced

Combine the celery root, scallions, garlic, jalapeño, bell pepper, thyme, oregano, flour, bread crumbs, half-and-half, egg, baking powder, and salt in a large bowl. Stir together until well incorporated and the mixture forms a thick batter.

1 jalapeño chile, seeded and
    minced
¼ cup diced red bell pepper
1 teaspoon chopped fresh thyme
    leaves
1 teaspoon chopped fresh
    oregano leaves
½ cup all-purpose flour
¼ cup fresh bread crumbs
½ cup half-and-half
1 large egg, lightly beaten
1 teaspoon baking powder
½ tablespoon salt
Olive oil, for frying
¾ cup Golden Gazpacho Salsa
    (page 33)

In a large cast-iron skillet, pour enough olive oil to come ¼ inch up the sides. Heat the oil to 350°F., or until lightly smoking. Using a large spoon, drop about ¼ cup of the batter into the pan and flatten evenly with a spatula to form a 3-inch pancake. Cook for 3 minutes on each side, or until the pancake is golden brown. Remove and let drain on a cookie sheet lined with paper towels. Repeat for the remaining pancakes. To keep warm, place the pancakes in a 250°F. oven. Serve with Golden Gazpacho Salsa.

SERVES 4 TO 6
MAKES 12 PANCAKES

Black Bean–Chayote Cakes

Chayote has a unique, earthy flavor that pairs well with black beans, and it is an excellent source of potassium (see also the headnote on page 35). These cakes are great served with just a little sour cream or Pico de Gallo (page 31); the flavors of the cakes will be further developed by serving them with grilled or sautéed sea scallops.

2½ cups black beans, cooked,
    drained, and cooled
    (page 213)
2 tablespoons duck fat, bacon
    fat, or lard
1 tablespoon ancho chile puree
    (page 206)
2 tablespoons pure red chile
    powder
1 tablespoon ground cumin
2 tablespoons chopped fresh
    cilantro leaves
½ teaspoon salt
1 chayote, pitted and diced

Preheat the oven to 350°F.

In a food processor, place the beans and duck fat and puree until smooth. Add the ancho puree, chile powder, cumin, cilantro, and salt and process for 1 minute longer. Transfer to a mixing bowl and fold in the chayote.

Cut twelve 6-inch squares of parchment or wax paper and oil lightly. Form the bean mixture into 6 balls and flatten slightly between your hands. Place the patties on 6 of the oiled squares and place the remaining squares on top, oil side down. Press down evenly with a metal spatula to make the cakes ¼ inch tall and about 4½ inches across. Transfer to a lightly greased cookie sheet and bake in the oven for 7 to 8 minutes, or until the cakes are warmed through. Remove the top layer of paper from each cake and invert onto serving plates; remove the remaining paper. The cakes can be made up to 1 day ahead.

SERVES 3 TO 6
MAKES 6 CAKES

Corn Griddle Cakes

These simply but richly flavored pancakes are excellent with a dollop of caviar topped with a little crème fraîche or sour cream. Their versatility also makes them an appropriate partner for the Black Bean–Saffron Rice Salad with Mango-Habanero Vinaigrette (page 57). I also enjoy them with the Black Bean–Cumin Sauce (page 45) and Tomatillo-Serrano Salsa (page 33). The cakes can be made ahead and reheated for later use; place them on a lightly oiled cookie sheet and heat in the oven at 325°F for 3 or 4 minutes. *(photograph opposite)*

1/2 cup fine cornmeal
1/2 cup all-purpose flour
1/2 teaspoon baking powder
2 cups fresh corn kernels
1/2 cup whole milk
2 tablespoons diced red bell pepper
2 tablespoons diced yellow bell pepper
2 teaspoons minced serrano chile
6 tablespoons (3/4 stick) unsalted butter, melted
2 large eggs plus 4 large egg yolks
1 teaspoon salt
1 cup clarified butter or vegetable oil, for frying

Combine the cornmeal, flour, and baking powder in a mixing bowl and set aside.

In a blender, puree 1 cup of the corn kernels until smooth and transfer to a large mixing bowl. Add the remaining corn kernels, milk, diced bell peppers, serrano, and butter and whisk together. Add the cornmeal mixture and stir to combine. In a separate bowl, whisk together the eggs, egg yolks, and salt. Add the egg mixture to the batter and stir to combine thoroughly.

On a griddle or in a large cast-iron skillet, heat half of the clarified butter. When lightly smoking, pour in half of the batter to make 6 round pancakes. Cook for 2 minutes on each side, or until the pancakes are golden brown. Remove and let drain on a cookie sheet lined with paper towels. Repeat for the remaining batter.

SERVES 4 TO 6
MAKES 12 CORN CAKES

Grilled Blue Corn Polenta Cakes with Tomatillo-Jalapeño Chutney

Blue corn was cultivated by Native Americans of the Southwest for ceremonial as well as culinary purposes. It has a slightly sweeter flavor than most types of yellow corn and it makes great polenta. These cakes can also be sautéed, broiled, or baked instead of grilled, and they can be served with shellfish or chicken.

4½ cups Vegetable Stock (page 211) or store-bought
2 jalapeño chiles, seeded and minced
2 tablespoons roasted garlic puree (page 203)
2 cups blue cornmeal
½ cup diced red bell pepper
½ cup diced yellow bell pepper
½ cup grated Parmesan cheese
Salt to taste
Tomatillo-Jalapeño Chutney (page 40)

In a saucepan, bring the stock, jalapeños, and garlic puree to a boil. Slowly stir in the cornmeal. Reduce the heat to low and continue stirring. Cook over low heat, stirring often, for 15 minutes; the polenta should be the consistency of mashed potatoes. Remove from the heat, stir in the bell peppers and cheese, and season with salt. Turn out the polenta into a lightly greased 9 by 12-inch baking dish (or onto a cookie sheet) and refrigerate until firm, 35 to 45 minutes.

Prepare the grill.

Cut the polenta into 3-inch squares and cut the squares in half to form triangles. Place the triangles on the grill and cook over medium-high heat for 3 to 4 minutes per side, or until fully cooked through. Serve with Tomatillo-Jalapeño Chutney.

SERVES 4 TO 6
MAKES 12 POLENTA CAKES

Apple-Pecan Fritters with Canela

Canela, the Mexican cinnamon (see page 217), was brought to the New World from Sri Lanka and has about half the seasoning power as regular cinnamon (*cinnamonum cassia*). However, its flavor is more mellow and subtle, which suits many Southwestern and Mexican recipes better. These fritters make a great brunch item either as an appetizer before an egg course or as part of the brunch buffet. The syrup can also accompany a not-too-sweet dessert, such as apple spice cake or pound cake.

3 cups all-purpose flour

3 large eggs, lightly beaten

3 tablespoons unsalted butter, melted

1¼ cups champagne or sparkling wine, at room temperature

¾ cup sparkling water

3 tablespoons apple brandy

1½ cups white wine, such as Chardonnay

1½ cups sugar

1 vanilla bean, split in half lengthwise and seeds scraped

10 whole cloves

8 black peppercorns

6 green apples, such as Granny Smith or Pippin, peeled, cored, and quartered

Vegetable oil, for frying

3 cups gingersnap or macaroon cookie crumbs

3 tablespoons ground canela or 1½ tablespoons ground cinnamon

3 tablespoons powdered sugar

Candied Pecans (page 192)

Sift the flour into a mixing bowl. In a separate bowl, beat the eggs with the melted butter, champagne, sparkling water, and brandy until smooth. Gradually drizzle the mixture into the flour while whisking and continue whisking until the batter is smooth. Let the batter stand for 1 hour at room temperature before using (if the batter is too thick, thin with a little more sparkling water).

In a large saucepan, combine the wine, sugar, vanilla pod and seeds, cloves, and peppercorns. Bring to a boil, reduce the heat to medium-low, and boil slowly for about 8 minutes until syrupy. Reduce the heat to low, add the apples, and cook until just tender when pierced with a fork, 6 to 8 minutes.

In a large skillet, pour enough vegetable oil to come 2 inches up the sides and heat to 375°F., or until smoking. Test the oil by drizzling a drop of batter; it should rise to the top and brown within a few seconds. Roll the cooked apple quarters in the cookie crumbs, then dip into the batter and lower gently into the oil using tongs. Fry the apples until golden brown, about 4 minutes. Remove and drain on paper towels.

In a small mixing bowl, combine the canela and powdered sugar. Transfer to a sifter and sprinkle over the fritters. Garnish with the Candied Pecans and serve.

SERVES 4 TO 6
MAKES ABOUT 24 FRITTERS

Wild Rice—Grilled Corn Fritters

Wild rice (see also page 59) has a wonderful, nutty flavor that is perfectly complemented by the smoky grilled corn in this recipe. If you prefer, the corn can be roasted in its husk rather than grilled. Place the ears on a cookie sheet and roast in a 375°F. oven for 20 to 25 minutes, or until the kernels are dark yellow. Serve these fritters with fish or poultry, especially duck.

(photograph opposite)

2 ears of corn, husks and silks removed
Vegetable oil, for frying
1 cup all-purpose flour
½ cup fine cornmeal
1 tablespoon baking powder
2 teaspoons salt
1 cup whole milk
2 large eggs
1 cup wild rice, cooked and cooled (page 213)
½ cup diced red bell pepper
1 serrano chile, seeded and minced

Prepare the grill. Grill the corn over medium-high heat until tender, about 12 to 15 minutes, turning often. Remove from the grill, let cool, and cut the corn kernels from the cobs.

In a deep saucepan, pour enough vegetable oil to come 2 inches up the sides and heat to 350°F., or until smoking.

Meanwhile, sift the flour, cornmeal, baking powder, and salt into a mixing bowl and stir to combine. In a separate bowl, whisk the milk and eggs together. Pour the milk-egg mixture into the flour mixture and stir until smooth. Fold in the grilled corn, wild rice, bell pepper, and serrano.

To test the oil, drop a drizzle of batter; it should bubble up and brown within a few seconds. Using two tablespoons, scoop the batter with one spoon and carefully scrape it into the oil with the other (each fritter should be made with about 1½ tablespoons of batter). Cook the fritters for 4 minutes, turning after 2 to 3 minutes when the first side darkens. Remove the fritters with a slotted spoon or tongs and drain on paper towels.

SERVES 6
MAKES ABOUT 30 FRITTERS

Tomatillo Fritters

Also known as jamberries, tomatillos are members of the nightshade or solanum family, along with tomatoes, eggplants, chiles, and potatoes. Buy tomatillos that are unblemished and that completely fill their papery, parchmentlike husks. I use tomatillos most for salsa, which makes a fine accompaniment for these fritters served as a snack. Alternatively, serve the fritters as a side dish for fish, poultry, and even game meat. The champagne adds both fruitiness and carbonation.

Vegetable oil, for frying
  1 cup all-purpose flour
  1 tablespoon baking powder
  1 teaspoon baking soda
  1 tablespoon paprika
Pinch of cayenne
  1 teaspoon ground cumin
Salt to taste
  1 large egg
  1 cup champagne or sparkling
    water
  6 large tomatillos, husked, rinsed,
    and each end sliced off

In a deep saucepan, pour enough vegetable oil to come 1 inch up the sides and heat to 325°F., or until lightly smoking.

Meanwhile, sift the flour, baking powder, baking soda, paprika, cayenne, cumin, and salt into a mixing bowl and stir to combine. In a separate bowl, beat the egg and champagne together. Gradually sprinkle in the flour mixture while whisking.

Slice the tomatillos into ¼-inch-thick slices and cut each slice into ¼-inch strips. Test the oil by drizzling a drop of batter; it should bubble up and brown within a few seconds. Dip the strips into the batter and let all but a thin film run off the strips, lifting them with a slotted spoon. Fry the tomatillo strips in the hot oil until golden brown, about 1 minute. Drain on paper towels.

SERVES 4 TO 6
MAKES ABOUT 36 FRITTERS

Wild Mushroom and Green Pea Fritters with Ginger-Honey Mustard

Any number of types of wild mushrooms can be used for this recipe, either in combination or alone. I love the flavor combination of wild mushrooms and green peas, and they work well in this tempura-like batter. In this recipe, the Ginger-Honey Mustard is used as a dip to accompany the fritters; you can also serve them alone as "croutons" with your favorite green salad.

FOR THE FRITTERS
Vegetable oil, for frying
¼ cup all-purpose flour
¼ cup masa harina
Pinch of cayenne
½ teaspoon ground cumin
  1 teaspoon salt
  2 large eggs

To prepare the fritters, pour enough vegetable oil into a deep saucepan to come 1½ inches up the sides and heat to 350°F., or until smoking.

Meanwhile, sift the flour, masa harina, cayenne, cumin, and salt into a mixing bowl and stir to combine. Whisk in the eggs and gradually add the sparkling water, whisking to make a smooth batter. Fold in the mushrooms and peas.

⅓ cup sparkling water
1 cup finely diced wild
   mushrooms such as
   portobellos, shiitakes, or
   pleurottes
1 cup fresh green peas

Ginger-Honey Mustard (page 22)

To test the oil, drop a drizzle of batter into the oil; it should bubble up and brown within a few seconds. Using a slotted spoon (so the excess batter runs off), place about 1½ tablespoons of the vegetables coated with batter in the hot oil and fry for 4 minutes, flipping them over after 2 minutes to evenly cook both sides. Remove with a slotted spoon and drain on paper towels. Serve with the Ginger-Honey Mustard.

SERVES 4 TO 6
MAKES ABOUT 30 FRITTERS

Grilled Fennel and Onion Hash

The white fennel bulb has a pleasant aniseed flavor and it can be eaten cooked or raw. In Italy, in the past, it was served as a dessert! In this recipe, as an alternative to grilling, the fennel can be roasted in a lightly oiled pan in a 350°F. oven for 20 minutes; it should be turned once. One of my favorite combinations with fennel is hazelnuts, and when the two are partnered with the sweet onions in this recipe, it produces an irresistible dish. I like to serve this hash with a grilled or sautéed white fish such as halibut or sea bass, preferably garnished with a relish made with orange segments and diced hazelnuts.

2 fennel bulbs, about 14 ounces
   each, split, cored, and each
   cut into 8 wedges
1 red onion, cut into ¼-inch
   slices
1 sweet onion, such as Vidalia or
   Texas Sweet, cut into ¼-inch
   slices
Salt to taste
¼ cup heavy cream
2 tablespoons olive oil plus more
   for coating
½ cup hazelnuts, toasted and
   chopped (page 211)
2 tablespoons roasted garlic
   puree (page 203)
2 tablespoons chopped fresh
   parsley leaves
2 tablespoons chopped fresh
   oregano leaves
2 oranges, sectioned (page 211),
   about ½ cup

Prepare the grill.

Lightly oil the fennel and onion slices, season with salt, and grill over medium-high heat until tender, about 10 minutes, turning often to prevent the vegetables from coloring too much. Allow the fennel and onions to cool, and then chop into small pieces and reserve.

Meanwhile, pour the cream into a saucepan and bring to a boil. Lower the heat to a simmer and reduce the cream until 2 tablespoons remain. Set aside.

In a large cast-iron skillet, heat the 2 tablespoons of olive oil to 350°F., or until lightly smoking. Add the reserved onions and fennel and sauté for 2 minutes over high heat. Add the hazelnuts, garlic, parsley, and oregano and sauté for 2 minutes longer. Add the reduced cream and toss to combine. Add the orange segments and season with salt. Serve immediately.

SERVES 4 TO 6

CHAPTER SEVEN

GRATINS
CASSEROLES AND
STUFFED
VEGETABLES

Maple-Baked Squash with Candied Pecans

This quintessentially Southern dish comes straight from my childhood. I was probably in my teens before I realized that squash didn't have to be mushy and overcooked. The maple and pecans give this recipe a festive holiday flavor, but it can be enjoyed year-round.

2 tablespoons vegetable oil

2½ pounds butternut squash, peeled, seeded, and diced

½ cup (1 stick) unsalted butter, melted

¼ cup maple syrup

2 tablespoons whole milk

1 tablespoon bourbon

1 tablespoon peeled minced fresh ginger

½ teaspoon ground canela or ¼ teaspoon ground cinnamon

Pinch of ground cloves

1 teaspoon grated lemon zest

Juice of 1 lemon

1 tablespoon salt

1 cup Candied Spiced Pecans (page 214), for garnish

Preheat the oven to 350°F.

In a large sauté pan or skillet, heat the vegetable oil and sauté the squash over medium-high heat for 5 minutes. Drain on paper towels and transfer to a mixing bowl. Add the melted butter, maple syrup, milk, bourbon, ginger, canela, cloves, lemon zest, lemon juice, and salt and toss together until the squash is completely coated.

Transfer the mixture into an 8-inch square glass or metal baking dish and bake in the oven for 45 minutes, or until the squash is tender but not mushy. Top with the pecans and serve.

SERVES 4 TO 6

Potato–Goat Cheese Gratin with Artichokes

The artichoke plant is a type of thistle, and you will see thousands of acres of them growing in the central coast region of California. If you are a carnivore who happens to love vegetarian cooking, this dish makes a great accompaniment to roast spring lamb. It is also delicious served with a mixed green salad or blanched asparagus dressed with a simple vinaigrette.

Salt
- 2 baking potatoes (about 10 ounces each), peeled and cut into 1/2-inch slices
- 6 artichoke bottoms, blanched (page 205) and sliced in half crosswise
- 2 tablespoons Rosemary-Garlic Vinegar (page 29)
- 3 tablespoons olive oil
- 3 tablespoons sliced fresh chives
- 1 1/4 pounds fresh goat cheese, at room temperature
- 2 tablespoons heavy cream
- 3 large eggs

Preheat the oven to 400°F.

In a saucepan of boiling salted water, place the potatoes and cook for 4 or 5 minutes, or until just tender. Drain the potatoes and set aside. Grease an 8-inch square glass baking dish and layer the potatoes and artichoke bottoms alternately, overlapping them slightly. Sprinkle with salt, vinegar, olive oil, and 1 tablespoon of the chives.

In a food processor, combine the goat cheese, cream, and eggs and pulse until just combined; do not overmix. Spread this mixture evenly over the potatoes and artichokes. Transfer the baking dish to the oven and bake for 15 minutes, or until light brown and firm in the center. Remove from the oven and garnish with the remaining 2 tablespoons of chives. This dish is best served warm.

SERVES 4 TO 6

Crab-Stuffed Avocados with Tortilla Gratin

The combination of crabmeat and avocados is tried-and-true, and the addition of the toasty, crunchy tortillas brings the flavors right back to the Southwest. Like some other fruits, avocados (also called "alligator pears" because of the texture of the skin) ripen best once picked. For more on avocados, see page 64.

FOR THE CRAB STUFFING

- 1 pound jumbo lump crabmeat, cleaned of shell and cartilage
- 2 Roma tomatoes, blanched, peeled, seeded, and diced (page 203)
- 2 tablespoons diced roasted red bell pepper (page 204)
- 2 tablespoons diced roasted yellow bell pepper (page 204)
- 2 stalks celery, diced
- 2 serrano chiles, seeded, minced
- 2 large hard-boiled eggs, diced
- 1 tablespoon chopped fresh basil
- 1 tablespoon chopped fresh cilantro leaves
- 1 tablespoon chopped fresh marjoram leaves
- ¼ cup Smoked Tomato Aioli (page 25)

Salt to taste

FOR THE TORTILLA GRATIN

Vegetable oil, for frying
- 6 corn tortillas
- 2 garlic cloves
- ¼ cup grated Asiago or Parmesan cheese
- 1 tablespoon pure red chile powder
- ¼ teaspoon ground cumin

Pinch of cayenne
Pinch of salt
- ¼ cup (½ stick) unsalted butter, chilled and diced

FOR THE AVOCADOS

- 4 ripe avocados

Salt to taste

To prepare the stuffing, place the crabmeat, tomatoes, red and yellow bell peppers, celery, chiles, eggs, basil, cilantro, marjoram, and aioli in a mixing bowl. Toss to combine, season with salt, and refrigerate.

To prepare the gratin, pour enough oil to come 2 inches up the sides of a sauté pan or skillet and heat to 350°F., or until lightly smoking. Place 2 tortillas at a time in the hot oil and fry over medium-high heat for 3 or 4 minutes, until crisp. Remove with tongs and drain on paper towels. When cool enough to handle, crumble the fried tortillas into the work bowl of a food processor and add the garlic, cheese, chile powder, cumin, cayenne, and salt. Process for about 2 minutes, until the mixture resembles coarse cornmeal. Add the butter and process until just combined. Set aside.

Preheat the broiler.

Using a very sharp knife, slice ⅛ inch off the long sides of each avocado. Then split each avocado lengthwise down the middle and remove the pit by planting the blade of the knife into the pit and twisting. Scoop out the avocado flesh with a spoon and place the avocado halves, cavity-side up, on a cookie sheet. Sprinkle with salt and fill each cavity with the reserved crab stuffing, mounding evenly to accommodate all of the crab mixture. Sprinkle the gratin mixture over the stuffed avocados and broil on a middle rack for 5 minutes, or until the gratin begins to brown. Remove from the oven and serve immediately.

SERVES 4 (OR 8 AS APPETIZERS)

Polenta Gratin with Wild Mushrooms and Three Cheeses

Like risotto, polenta is a staple of Northern Italy, so much so that many Europeans associate corn with that region. In fact, corn was introduced there from the New World only in the seventeenth century. This dish is wonderful winter fare that is both elegant and comfortably homey. The Gorgonzola lends a salty, pungent flavor while the mascarpone enriches it. Avoid using "instant" polenta or cornmeal. This dish can be refrigerated a day in advance before the final step of baking.

(photograph opposite)

2 tablespoons olive oil

1/2 onion, diced

8 ounces assorted wild mushrooms such as shiitakes or portobellos, trimmed and sliced

Salt to taste

3 tablespoons roasted garlic puree (page 203)

1 tablespoon chopped fresh oregano leaves

1/2 tablespoon chopped fresh rosemary leaves

6 cups Vegetable Stock (page 211) or store-bought

2 cups polenta or yellow cornmeal

1/2 cup (1 stick) unsalted butter

1/2 cup mascarpone cheese

1/2 cup grated Parmesan cheese

2/3 cup crumbled Gorgonzola cheese

2 red bell peppers, roasted, peeled, seeded, and cut into 2 by 1/2-inch strips (page 204)

2 yellow bell peppers, roasted, peeled, seeded, and cut into 2 by 1/2-inch strips (page 204)

1/3 cup pine nuts

1/2 cup seasoned bread crumbs

In a sauté pan set over high heat, heat the olive oil to 350°F., or until lightly smoking. Add the onion and sauté for 1 minute. Add the mushrooms and sauté for 5 minutes longer, or until the mushrooms are fully cooked. Season with salt and stir in the roasted garlic puree, oregano, and rosemary. Remove from the heat and set aside.

Place the stock in a large saucepan and bring to a strong boil. Reduce the heat to a gentle boil. Add 2 teaspoons of salt and slowly drizzle in the polenta. Continuously and slowly, stir the polenta for 15 to 20 minutes, until the polenta thickens and pulls away from the sides of the pan with each stir.

Remove the pan from the heat, add the butter, mascarpone, and Parmesan, and stir until completely absorbed by the polenta. Transfer half of the polenta into an 8-inch square ovenproof glass or metal baking dish and smooth with a spatula; keep the remaining polenta over very low heat. Spread the reserved mushroom mixture over the polenta and sprinkle half of the Gorgonzola over the mushrooms. Lay the bell pepper strips evenly over the cheese. Gently add the remaining polenta and spread into an even layer. Top with the remaining Gorgonzola, the pine nuts, and the seasoned bread crumbs. Let cool for at least 1 hour, or until it becomes firm. The polenta can be made up to 2 days ahead.

Preheat the oven to 350°F.

Place the casserole in the oven for 30 minutes. Remove from the oven and let cool for 10 minutes. Serve with a spoon.

SERVES 8

Tortilla and Three Onion Casserole with Tomato-Ginger Jam

Here is another recipe inspired by childhood meals when I was growing up in West Texas. The ubiquitous "tortilla casserole" was served at every religious or social function; sometimes ten different versions would be on the table! What sets this recipe apart is the tomato-ginger jam, which may seem an odd combination at first glance but lends a pleasant acidic sweetness to the dish. Don't worry if you can't find red or blue tortillas—yellow will do fine.

FOR THE CASSEROLE

- 2 tablespoons olive oil
- 1 yellow onion, julienned
- 1 red onion, julienned
- 4 scallions, sliced
- 2 jalapeño chiles, seeded and julienned
- 4 Roma tomatoes, blanched, peeled, seeded, and julienned (page 203)
- 10 yellow corn tortillas, julienned
- 10 red corn tortillas, julienned
- 10 blue corn tortillas, julienned
- 1/4 cup chopped fresh cilantro leaves
- 2 tablespoons roasted garlic puree (page 203)
- 3 cups Vegetable Stock (page 211) or store-bought
- 1/2 cup heavy cream
- Salt to taste
- 3/4 cup grated Monterey Jack cheese
- 1 cup Tomato-Ginger Jam (page 13)

FOR THE GARNISH

- Vegetable oil, for frying
- 2 yellow corn tortillas, julienned
- 2 red corn tortillas, julienned
- 2 blue corn tortillas, julienned

Preheat the oven to 350°F.

In a large sauté pan, heat the olive oil until lightly smoking. Add the yellow onion, red onion, scallions, and chiles and sauté over high heat for 2 minutes. Add the tomatoes, julienned tortillas, cilantro, and garlic and toss to coat. Transfer to a large mixing bowl and set aside.

Pour the stock and cream into a saucepan and bring to a boil. Pour over the tortilla mixture and let sit for 5 minutes, tossing occasionally. Season with salt. Transfer the mixture to a lightly greased 9 by 12-inch baking dish, pressing all of the mixture below the rim of the dish. Sprinkle the cheese over the top, cover with foil, and bake in the oven for 20 minutes.

Meanwhile, to prepare the garnish, heat enough vegetable oil to come 2 inches up the side of a saucepan and heat to 375°F., or until lightly smoking. Add one third to one half of the julienned tortillas and fry for 1 minute. Remove with a slotted spoon and drain on paper towels. Repeat with the remaining julienned tortillas in 1 or 2 batches.

Remove the baking dish from the oven and set the oven to broil. Remove the foil and when the broiler is hot, return the dish to cook for 3 minutes, or until the top of the casserole is golden brown. Garnish with the tortilla strips. Serve with the Tomato-Ginger Jam. The casserole can be baked up to 2 days ahead and broiled before serving.

SERVES 4 TO 6

Grilled Eggplant "Lasagna"

Instead of the sheets of pasta normally used to make lasagna, this recipe is layered with "planks" of eggplant, zucchini, and yellow squash and structured in the classic way. The chile powder and fresh poblano mark this as a distinctively Southwestern dish. Another element that makes it stand out from the traditional lasagna is the use of red chile and green chile salsas.

2 eggplants, 8 to 10 ounces each, trimmed and cut lengthwise into 1/2-inch "planks"

2 small zucchini, trimmed and cut lengthwise into 1/2-inch "planks"

2 small yellow squash, trimmed and cut lengthwise into 1/2-inch "planks"

Salt to taste

1/4 cup olive oil

1 pound ricotta cheese

1/2 cup grated pecorino cheese

2 large eggs

2 tablespoons chopped fresh cilantro leaves

2 tablespoons chopped fresh chives

2 tablespoons pure red chile powder

1/4 teaspoon cayenne

2 cups fresh bread crumbs

1 cup Griddled Tomato-Chipotle Salsa (page 32)

2 red bell peppers, roasted, peeled, seeded, and cut into 3 by 1/2-inch strips (page 204)

2 yellow bell peppers, roasted, peeled, seeded, and cut into 3 by 1/2-inch strips (page 204)

2 poblano chiles, roasted, peeled, seeded, and cut into 3 by 1/2-inch strips (page 204)

1 1/2 cups Tomatillo-Serrano Salsa (page 33)

1 cup grated Monterey Jack cheese

Prepare the grill.

Lay the slices of eggplant, zucchini, and squash on a work surface and season with salt. With a pastry brush, brush both sides of the slices with olive oil. Grill or broil the eggplant, zucchini, and squash until tender, about 2 to 3 minutes on each side. Remove from the grill and set aside on a platter to cool.

In a food processor, combine the ricotta, pecorino, eggs, cilantro, chives, chile powder, and cayenne and pulse until just combined. Set aside.

Preheat the oven to 350°F. Lightly grease a square 12-inch baking dish.

Line the bottom of the baking dish with one third of the eggplant, zucchini, and squash, alternating and overlapping. Sprinkle one third of the bread crumbs over the vegetables and cover with one third of the tomato-chipotle salsa. Then evenly spread one third of the ricotta mixture over the salsa and cover with one third of the pepper and chile strips. Repeat with 2 more alternating layers of the grilled vegetables, bread crumbs, salsa, ricotta mixture, and strips of pepper and chile. Spread 3/4 cup of the Tomatillo-Serrano Salsa over the top and sprinkle with the cheese.

Bake in the oven for 35 minutes, or until the cheese is bubbly and golden brown. Remove the baking dish and let cool for 10 minutes. Cut into 3-inch squares and serve on the remaining 3/4 cup of Tomatillo-Serrano Salsa.

SERVES 8

Caramelized Onions Stuffed with Sweet Potato–White Bean Ragout

I like to use the crisp, sweet, and mild Texas 10/15 onions for this recipe, which derive their name from the fact that they are traditionally planted on (or around) October 15 for best results—they prefer growing in the shorter daylight of the winter months. Other Texas sweet onions that work equally well are Noonday and Spring Sweet. All these onions are the fore-bears of the more famous Vidalia variety from Georgia, and they contain unusually high amounts of sugar. This makes them delicious when eaten raw, as they lack the hot bitter-ness associated with uncooked yellow onions.   *(photograph opposite)*

6   large sweet onions, about
      3 inches in diameter,
      unpeeled
1   sweet potato (about 12 ounces),
      peeled and finely diced
2   tablespoons olive oil
1/2   yellow onion, diced
4   garlic cloves, minced
1   jalapeño chile, seeded and
      minced
1/2   cup white wine
1/2   cup cooked white beans
      (page 213)
1   red bell pepper, roasted, peeled,
      seeded, and diced (page 204)
1   yellow bell pepper, roasted,
      peeled, seeded, and diced
      (page 204)
1/4   cup toasted pumpkin seeds
      (page 211)
1   tablespoon chopped fresh
      marjoram leaves
1   tablespoon chopped fresh
      parsley leaves
1   teaspoon chopped fresh thyme
      leaves
1/4   cup fresh bread crumbs
1/4   cup grated Romano cheese
Salt to taste

Preheat the oven to 375°F.

Place the sweet onions in a roasting pan and roast in the oven for 1½ hours. Remove from the oven and let sit until the onions are cool enough to handle. Peel the onions and cut about 1 inch off the tops and enough from the bottoms that the onions will sit upright. Using a paring knife, extract the flesh from the center of the onion, leaving the edges about 3/8 inch thick. (Save the flesh to make stock or soup later.)

Bring a saucepan of salted water to a boil and blanch the sweet potato for 1 minute. Drain and set aside.

Preheat the broiler. In a large sauté pan, heat the olive oil until lightly smoking. Add the diced yellow onion and sauté over high heat for 3 minutes, or until golden brown, stirring occasionally. Add the garlic and chile and sauté for 1 minute longer. Add the wine and deglaze the pan. Reduce the liquid for 2 minutes, or until the mixture is almost dry. Add the blanched sweet potato, beans, peppers, pumpkin seeds, marjoram, parsley, and thyme, and heat through. Add the bread crumbs and cheese, stir to combine, and season with salt.

Stuff the onions with this mixture, place under the broiler, and cook for 5 minutes, or until the top of the stuffing turns brown. The onions can be prepared 1 day ahead, but should be warmed for 10 minutes in a 350°F. oven before broiling.

SERVES 6

Cabbage Stuffed with Wild Mushrooms and Golden Raisins

Cabbage, a native of Asia Minor or northern Europe, depending on which sources of information you believe, was beloved by the ancient Greeks and Romans. The Emperor Claudius even persuaded the senate to vote that cabbage and corned beef constituted the consummate meal! Of the many medicinal properties claimed for cabbage in antiquity, perhaps the most unusual was as a protection against drunkenness. The crinkly-leaved Savoy variety works best here. I usually associate stuffed cabbage with winter fare, so the addition of the wild mushrooms and raisins is particularly appropriate.

Vegetable oil, for frying
2 corn tortillas
1 head of Savoy cabbage, outer leaves removed
2 tablespoons olive oil
½ cup diced onion
1 shallot, minced
1 pound assorted wild mushrooms, such as shiitake, portobello, and oyster, finely diced
¼ cup sherry vinegar
¼ cup pasilla chile puree (page 206)
2 tablespoons roasted garlic puree (page 203)
½ cup golden raisins
½ cup grated *queso fresco* or Chihuahua or Monterey Jack cheese
3 tablespoons chopped fresh cilantro leaves
Salt to taste

In a sauté pan or skillet, heat enough vegetable oil to come 1 inch up the sides and heat to 350°F., or until lightly smoking. Add the tortillas, and fry over medium-high heat for 3 to 4 minutes, until crisp. Remove with tongs and drain on paper towels. When cool enough to handle, finely crush the tortillas with your hands. Set aside.

Fill a large saucepan halfway with water and bring to a boil. Meanwhile, remove 8 of the outer cabbage leaves and set aside. Cut the remaining head of cabbage in half lengthwise, remove the hard core and thick stem, and julienne the cabbage. Prepare an ice bath in a large bowl and set aside. Cook the 8 cabbage leaves in the boiling water for 3 minutes, or until just tender. Remove with tongs and plunge into the ice water to stop the cooking process. When cold, transfer the cabbage leaves to a colander and let drain.

In a large sauté pan, heat the olive oil until lightly smoking. Add the onion and cook over high heat for 30 seconds. Add the shallot and cook for 30 seconds longer. Add the reserved julienned cabbage and cook for 3 minutes more. Add the mushrooms and cook for 6 or 7 minutes, or until they are tender. Add the vinegar and deglaze the pan by scraping to loosen any particles stuck to the bottom. Reduce the heat to medium and cook for 2 or 3 minutes longer, or until the liquid has almost evaporated.

Transfer the mixture to a mixing bowl and add the pasilla puree, garlic puree, raisins, crushed tortillas, cheese, and cilantro. Combine thoroughly and season with salt. Let cool until the mixture can be handled comfortably.

Prepare a steamer or set a vegetable basket over a saucepan of boiling water. Lay the blanched cabbage leaves out on a work surface and, with a paring knife, cut out the thickest part of the large center veins. Divide the cooled mixture evenly among the leaves, placing it on the uncut side of each leaf. With the cut side of the leaves away from you, fold in the sides and roll up the leaves like burritos, making sure the filling is fully enclosed. Place the rolls in the steamer, seam-side down, and steam for 6 minutes, or until heated through. Serve immediately. The stuffed cabbage rolls can be made 1 day ahead.

SERVES 4

CHAPTER EIGHT

GRAINS AND PASTA

Green Chile–Pineapple Risotto

Risotto is the classic dish from northern Italy made with high-starch, short-grain Arborio rice. Risottos are labor-intensive—this one is no exception—but it is worth every second spent in preparing it. Pineapples and green chiles (especially poblanos) make a wonderfully well-balanced, sweet-acidic-spicy combination, giving this dish a distinctly south-of-the-border tweak.

5 cups Vegetable Stock (page 211) or store-bought
3 tablespoons olive oil
1/2 onion, diced
2 garlic cloves, minced
1 cup Arborio rice
1/2 cup dry sherry
2 tablespoons chopped fresh cilantro leaves
2 tablespoons chopped fresh basil leaves
2 poblano chiles, roasted, peeled, seeded, and diced (page 204)
3/4 cup diced fresh pineapple
1/2 cup freshly grated Romano or Parmesan cheese
Salt to taste

In a stockpot, bring the stock to a boil. Reduce the heat to low so the stock is just simmering. Meanwhile, in a saucepan, heat the olive oil until lightly smoking. Add the onion and sauté for 3 minutes over medium-high heat. Add the garlic and sauté for 1 minute longer. Add the rice and cook, while stirring with a wooden spoon, for 3 more minutes, or until the rice has a nutty aroma. Add the sherry and cook until it is absorbed by the rice, about 2 minutes. Stir 1/2 cup of the stock into the rice mixture and stir until the stock is almost completely absorbed. Continue adding the stock in 1/2 cup increments, stirring until each addition is absorbed. When the last 1/2 cup is added, remove the risotto from the heat and stir in the cilantro, basil, poblanos, pineapple, and cheese. Season with salt and serve. Total cooking time is approximately 25 minutes.

SERVES 4

Black Barley "Risotto"

Barley is one of the oldest grains ever cultivated, and we know it was used in prehistoric times. Black-hulled barley, available at most natural foods stores, is high in starch content, making it a good substitute for Arborio rice in this "mock risotto" recipe.

1 cup black barley
2 tablespoons olive oil
1/2 onion, diced
2 garlic cloves, minced
1 cup white wine, such as Chardonnay
1 cup heavy cream
Pinch of cayenne
1/2 cup freshly grated Asiago or Parmesan cheese
Salt to taste

Place the barley in a saucepan, add 2 cups of water, and bring to a boil. Reduce the heat to a strong simmer and cook for 30 to 40 minutes, or until tender. Drain and set aside.

In a saucepan, heat the oil until lightly smoking. Add the onion and sauté over high heat for 3 minutes. Add the garlic and cook for 2 minutes longer. Add the white wine and deglaze the pan by scraping to loosen any particles stuck to the bottom. Reduce over medium heat until syrupy, about 7 minutes. Add the cream and bring to a boil, being careful not to let the mixture boil over. Reduce the cream by half and then add the cooked barley and cayenne. When the barley is warmed through, remove from the heat and stir in the cheese. Season with salt and serve.

SERVES 4

Wild Mushroom Risotto

This dish is a wild mushroom lover's dream come true! You can use as many different types of mushroom as you like in the risotto, and the porcinis (also called cèpes) in the broth give the dish a delightfully rich, woodsy flavor. Porcinis are rarely available fresh—the best times for finding them are late spring and early fall—but the dried porcinis used in this recipe provide plenty of "oomph" to flavor the risotto.

2 pounds assorted fresh wild mushrooms, such as shiitake, cremini, or portobello, wiped clean, stems removed and reserved

FOR THE MUSHROOM BROTH

1 cup dried porcini mushrooms
6 scallions, chopped
3 garlic cloves, chopped
1 onion, chopped
1 leek, cleaned and chopped
2 sprigs of fresh thyme
4 black peppercorns
1 cup white wine, such as Chardonnay

FOR THE RISOTTO

3 tablespoons olive oil
1 onion, chopped
2 garlic cloves, minced
1 cup Arborio rice
1/2 cup white wine, such as Chardonnay
2 tablespoons mixed fresh herbs, such as chives, thyme, rosemary, and parsley
2 tablespoons (1/4 stick) unsalted butter
Salt and freshly ground black pepper to taste
1/4 cup grated Parmesan or pecorino cheese

Dice the mushroom caps and reserve in the refrigerator, covered with a damp towel.

To prepare the mushroom broth, place the mushroom stems, dried mushrooms, scallions, garlic, onion, leek, thyme, peppercorns, wine, and 4 cups of water in a stockpot and bring to a boil. Reduce the heat to a simmer and let the broth simmer for 1 hour. Strain through a fine-mesh sieve or cheesecloth into a large clean saucepan and return to a simmer. Add more water if necessary to yield 5 cups.

Meanwhile, to prepare the risotto, place the olive oil in a heavy saucepan set over high heat. When lightly smoking, add the onion and sauté for 1 minute. Add the garlic and continue to cook for 1 minute. Reduce the heat to medium and add the rice, stirring for 1 minute, making sure each grain is coated with oil. Add the white wine and cook until it is completely absorbed, about 3 minutes. Add 1/2 cup of the simmering broth and stir with a wooden spoon until it is completely absorbed. Continue adding the broth in 1/2-cup increments until 1 cup of broth remains, stirring until each addition is absorbed. The rice should be almost tender but still a bit al dente, about 25 minutes in all.

Add the reserved mushrooms and 3/4 cup of the remaining broth. Cook until the mushrooms are cooked through and the liquid is absorbed, while continuing to stir. Add the herbs, butter, and the remaining 1/4 cup of broth. Season with salt and pepper and remove from the heat. Stir in the cheese and serve.

SERVES 4 TO 6

Coconut-Ginger Rice Tamales with Mango-Basil Salsa

This recipe involves a little Mexican-Asian fusion, which is usually a pretty wonderful pairing. Sticky, or glutinous, rice is the short-grained variety that is widely used in Japan and other Asian countries, partly because it's easier to eat with chopsticks. Banana leaves are sold, fresh or frozen, in Latin or Southeast Asian grocery stores. These tamales are the perfect accompaniment with grilled white fish that has been marinated in a little soy sauce and brown sugar.

2 cups short-grain sticky rice, soaked in water overnight

2 cans unsweetened coconut milk (14 ounces each)

2 tablespoons minced peeled fresh ginger

1 teaspoon salt

1 tablespoon chopped fresh cilantro leaves

2 large banana leaves, 12 by 24 inches

2 cups Mango-Basil Salsa (page 31)

Drain the soaked rice in a fine-mesh sieve and rinse under cold running water. In a saucepan, place the rice, coconut milk, ginger, and salt and bring to a gentle boil. Reduce the heat to a simmer, cover with a lid, and cook over low heat for 1¼ hours, stirring frequently to prevent the rice from sticking to the bottom of the pan.

When the rice has finished cooking, stir in the cilantro and transfer the mixture to a baking sheet or cookie tray. Spread out the mixture evenly, about 1 inch thick. Cool to room temperature and then chill in the refrigerator for 1 hour.

When chilled, form the rice into 8 equal squares, about 4 inches on each side.

Soften the banana leaves over an open flame for 10 seconds on each side, being careful not to burn them; cut each leaf into 4 equal pieces, about 6 by 12 inches. Place one portion of the rice mixture in the center of each piece of banana leaf. Fold the tamales into "packets," picking up the two long sides of each leaf and bringing them together. Tuck one side under the other and fold the flaps on each end underneath the tamales.

Steam the tamales in a conventional steamer or in a strainer or vegetable basket set in a saucepan over boiling water and covered with a tight-fitting lid. It is important that little or no steam escapes while cooking. Steam the tamales for 15 to 20 minutes; the water should always be lightly boiling. The tamales can be made 2 days ahead.

Unwrap the tamales and place on serving plates. Spoon the Mango-Basil Salsa over the tamales and serve.

SERVES 8

Risotto and Corn Chile Rellenos

I love making chile rellenos—stuffed chiles—especially when they vary from the norm. These rellenos definitely do that. The risotto should be slightly undercooked, as it will be cooked again in the poblano chiles. These rellenos can be served with the Fiery Tropical Fruit Sauce, as called for in this recipe, or the Black Bean–Cumin Sauce (page 45). After cutting the corn from the cobs, save the cobs for stock. *(photograph opposite)*

FOR THE RISOTTO FILLING

- 2 ears of corn
- 1 tablespoon olive oil
- ¼ cup diced red bell pepper
- 2 jalapeño chiles, seeded and minced
- 1 small onion, minced
- 2 garlic cloves, minced
- 4 cups Vegetable Stock (page 211) or store-bought
- 2 tablespoons (¼ stick) unsalted butter
- 1 cup Arborio rice
- ½ cup white wine, such as Chardonnay
- ¾ cup grated Asiago or Parmesan cheese

Salt to taste

- 12 poblano chiles, roasted and peeled (stems intact) (page 204)

Fiery Tropical Fruit Sauce (page 45)

Preheat the oven to 350°F.

Cut the corn kernels from the cobs and set aside. In a sauté pan set over medium heat, heat the olive oil until lightly smoking. Add the bell pepper, jalapeños, and half of the onion to the pan and sauté for 2 to 3 minutes. Add the garlic and reserved corn kernels and sauté for 3 to 4 minutes longer, or until the corn is just tender. Remove from the heat and reserve.

In a saucepan, bring the stock to a simmer. Meanwhile, heat the butter in a heavy saucepan set over high heat. Add the remaining onion and sauté for 1 minute. Reduce the heat to medium and add the rice. Stir for 1 minute, making sure each grain is coated with butter. Add the white wine and cook until it is completely absorbed, while stirring, about 3 minutes. Add ½ cup of the simmering stock and stir with a wooden spoon until it is completely absorbed. Continue adding stock in ½-cup increments until ½ cup of stock remains, stirring until each addition is absorbed. After approximately 25 minutes, the rice should be almost tender but still a bit al dente.

Add the reserved corn mixture and the remaining ½ cup stock and stir until completely incorporated. Remove the pan from the heat. Finish the risotto by stirring in ½ cup of the cheese and season with salt. Set aside to cool to room temperature.

Carefully split the poblanos down one side, leaving the stems intact. Remove all the seeds and veins with a sharp knife and carefully stuff the poblanos with the rice mixture. Place the rellenos on a baking sheet and cover with the remaining ½ cup of cheese. Bake in the oven for 12 minutes, or until the cheese is slightly golden brown. Transfer the rellenos to a serving platter and serve with the fruit sauce. The rellenos can be stuffed and made 1 day ahead.

SERVES 6

Grilled Vegetable Couscous

This is a variation on the classic "couscous au sept légumes" that I experienced frequently on my travels in Morocco. Grilling the vegetables gives a smoky dimension to the dish, which contrasts with the traditional steaming process that tends to make the vegetables bland in flavor. Couscous is not only the name of the dish but also the main ingredient, which is actually granular semolina. In North Africa, couscous is nothing if not versatile: it is cooked in milk and served as a porridge, and mixed with fruit and sweetened for a dessert.

FOR THE VEGETABLES

- 1 small zucchini, cut lengthwise into 1/2-inch-thick "planks"
- 1 small yellow squash, cut lengthwise into 1/2-inch-thick "planks"
- 1 red bell pepper, seeded and quartered
- 1 yellow bell pepper, seeded and quartered
- 1 red onion, cut into 1/2-inch rounds
- 1 portobello mushroom, stem removed

Salt and freshly ground black pepper to taste

- 1 tablespoon chopped fresh oregano leaves
- 1 tablespoon chopped fresh parsley leaves
- 1 tablespoon sliced fresh chives
- 2 tablespoons balsamic vinegar
- 6 tablespoons olive oil

FOR THE COUSCOUS

- 2 cups couscous
- 4 cups Vegetable Stock (page 211) or store-bought

Salt to taste

- 2 teaspoons unsalted butter
- 2 tomatoes, blanched, peeled, seeded, and diced (page 203)
- 1 tablespoon chopped fresh basil leaves
- 1 tablespoon chopped fresh cilantro leaves
- 2 limes, zested and juiced
- 6 tablespoons toasted pine nuts (page 211)
- 1/4 cup crumbled *queso fresco* or feta cheese

Prepare the grill.

In a large mixing bowl, place the zucchini, squash, bell peppers, onion, and portobello and sprinkle with salt and pepper. In another mixing bowl, combine the oregano, parsley, chives, vinegar, and olive oil. Whisk to combine, pour over the vegetables, and toss to coat well. Place the vegetables on the grill or under a broiler and cook until tender, turning every couple of minutes, 5 to 8 minutes. Remove the cooked vegetables from the grill, let cool, and reserve. When cool, chop the vegetables.

Meanwhile, place the couscous in a 2-quart mixing bowl. Place the stock in a saucepan, season with salt, and bring to a boil. Pour over the couscous, stir in the butter, and cover with plastic wrap. Let the couscous stand for 10 minutes.

When the couscous is ready, fluff it with a fork, making sure there are no lumps. Add the tomatoes, basil, cilantro, lime juice and zest, pine nuts, and cheese and season with salt. Mound the couscous on a platter. Pour the chopped vegetables on top and serve.

SERVES 6 TO 8

Quinoa Salad with Smoked Salmon and Capers

The Incas of South America held quinoa (pronounced KEEN-wah) as a sacred food and called it the "mother seed." It is considered a complete protein because it contains all eight essential amino acids. In conquering the Inca civilization in the sixteenth century, the Spanish went to great lengths to destroy this important crop. Ultimately, it survived, and you'll often find quinoa on menus when visiting Ecuador and Peru today. It has certainly become popular in the United States over the last few years. Smoked salmon and capers give the quinoa a new look in this recipe.

1 tablespoon olive oil
1 tablespoon unsalted butter
2 garlic cloves, minced
1 cup quinoa
2 teaspoons salt
2½ cups Vegetable Stock (page 211) or store-bought (or water)
6 ounces sliced smoked salmon, julienned
½ cup capers, drained and rinsed
2 tablespoons prepared horseradish
2 tablespoons sliced fresh chives

In a saucepan over medium-high heat, heat the oil and butter until the butter melts and begins to foam. Add the garlic and quinoa to the pan and toast until the quinoa begins to pop, about 2 to 3 minutes. Add the salt and stock and bring to a boil. Reduce the heat to a simmer, cover the pan, and cook for 15 minutes, or until the liquid is absorbed. Remove from the heat, pour the mixture evenly onto a cookie sheet, and refrigerate for up to 1 day. Once the quinoa has cooled, add the salmon, capers, horseradish, and chives and toss to combine well. Serve chilled or at room temperature.

SERVES 4

Red Chile Linguine with Pumpkin Seed Pesto

Red chile pasta makes a nice base for a simple pasta dish, but any store-bought tomato-based pasta would work. This is the same pesto we use in our bread at Star Canyon. Use it to enliven vinaigrettes or to brush on fish or vegetables before grilling. *(photograph opposite)*

FOR THE PESTO
- ¼ cup toasted pumpkin seeds (page 211)
- 1 cup fresh cilantro leaves
- ¼ cup freshly grated Parmesan cheese
- 2 garlic cloves
- Juice of ½ lemon
- ½ cup extra-virgin olive oil

FOR THE LINGUINE
- 1 cup all-purpose flour
- ½ cup semolina flour
- 2 tablespoons Hungarian sweet paprika
- 1 tablespoon cayenne
- ¾ teaspoon salt
- 2 large eggs
- 1 tablespoon tomato paste
- ½ tablespoon olive oil

In a food processor, place the pumpkin seeds, cilantro, Parmesan, garlic, and lemon juice. Blend for 4 to 5 minutes, until perfectly smooth. With the machine running, slowly add the olive oil to form a thick paste. Set aside in the refrigerator, or freeze.

To prepare the linguine, combine both flours, the paprika, cayenne, and salt in a food processor or blender. In a small bowl, beat the eggs, tomato paste, and olive oil until thoroughly combined. With the machine running, add the egg mixture to the dry ingredients and blend until the dough is evenly moistened; do not allow the dough to form into a ball. Turn the dough out onto a lightly floured work surface, gather into a ball, and then, using the heel of your hand, flatten into a ½-inch-thick disk. Cover with plastic wrap and let stand at room temperature for 1 hour.

Cut the dough into 2 pieces; cover 1 piece with plastic wrap and set aside. Using the heel of your hand, flatten the remaining dough into disks that will fit the widest setting of the pasta machine. Roll out through the pasta machine on the #5 or widest setting. Fold the dough into thirds and roll through the same setting. Repeat this procedure four times, or until the dough is smooth and velvety. Dust with a little flour if the dough becomes sticky. Reduce the thickness on the machine by one setting and roll the dough through the machine. Continue to reduce the thickness each time the dough goes through the machine until the dough goes through at the third thinnest setting, dusting with flour as necessary.

Hang the dough sheet on a drying rack or lay flat on a cookie sheet lined with wax paper. Repeat with the remaining dough, using a towel or more wax paper to prevent the dough from touching. Set aside until the sheets look leathery and the edges begin to curl, 10 to 30 minutes, depending on their dampness.

Run the sheets through the linguine blade of the pasta machine. Arrange the pasta on a towel, overlapping as little as possible. Bring a large saucepan of salted water to a boil. Cook the linguine for 2 to 3 minutes, or until it rises to the top. Drain, transfer to a large bowl, and toss with the pesto. Serve immediately.

SERVES 4 TO 6

Basil and Epazote Fettuccine in Spicy Tomato Sauce

Epazote is a pungent herb (also called "stinkweed") that is popular in Mexico, where it is used with most bean dishes because it reduces their gaseousness. For many people, epazote is an acquired taste because the fragrance is a little like kerosene, but once that taste is acquired, its flavor is irreplaceable. Epazote is available in Latin markets, and if you can find it, add another teaspoon to the tomato sauce along with the basil.

FOR THE FETTUCCINE

1 1/2 cups all-purpose flour
2 large eggs
1/2 cup chopped fresh basil leaves
1 tablespoon chopped fresh epazote, 1 teaspoon dried epazote, or 2 tablespoons chopped fresh cilantro leaves

FOR THE SPICY TOMATO SAUCE

2 tablespoons olive oil
1 large onion, minced
6 garlic cloves, minced
2 serrano chiles, minced, with seeds
2 pounds ripe tomatoes, cut in half
1/2 cup red wine, such as Pinot Noir
1/2 cup Vegetable Stock (page 211) or store-bought
1 tablespoon chopped fresh basil leaves
Salt to taste

To prepare the fettuccine, in the bowl of an electric mixer fitted with a paddle attachment, place the flour. In a mixing bowl, combine the eggs, basil, and epazote and whisk well to combine. Slowly pour this mixture into the flour and mix on the lowest speed until the dough forms a ball. Let the machine run for 6 minutes on low speed, until the dough is smooth and silky. Transfer the dough to a lightly floured work surface, cover with a damp towel, and let rest for 15 minutes.

Cut the dough into 2 pieces and, using the heel of your hand, flatten each piece of dough into a disk that will fit through the widest setting of the pasta machine. Roll out each piece of dough through the pasta machine on the widest or #5 setting. Cut the rolled pasta to the desired length (about 10 inches, for example) and run it through the wide cutter on the machine (you will need to do this by hand if your machine does not have a cutting attachment). Place the pasta on a cookie sheet, swirl into "nests," and cover with a damp cloth until ready to cook. (Just before you are ready to serve, bring a large saucepan with 2 quarts of salted water to a boil. Place the fettuccine in the boiling water and cook, stirring gently, for 20 to 30 seconds, or until al dente. Drain in a colander and transfer to a large serving bowl.)

To prepare the sauce, heat the olive oil in a large saucepan until lightly smoking. Add the onion and sauté over high heat until translucent, about 1 minute. Add the garlic and chiles and sauté for 1 minute longer. Add the tomatoes, reduce the heat to medium, and cook until the tomatoes are softened, about 3 minutes. Add the wine, stock, and basil and cook for 5 minutes more. Season with salt and toss with the pasta. Divide evenly among warm plates and serve immediately.

SERVES 4 TO 6

Cilantro Ravioli with Black Olive–Goat Cheese Stuffing

Typically, green pasta is colored with spinach, but here I use cilantro, which also gives the pasta an aromatic quality. These raviolis can be served with several sauces from Chapter 2.

FOR THE CILANTRO RAVIOLI

- 3 large eggs
- 1 cup chopped fresh cilantro leaves
- 2 cups all-purpose flour
- 1/4 teaspoon salt
- 1 teaspoon olive oil

FOR THE BLACK OLIVE– GOAT CHEESE STUFFING

- 6 ounces goat cheese
- 1 tablespoon roasted garlic puree (page 203)
- 2 tablespoons fresh bread crumbs
- 2 tablespoons grated Parmesan cheese
- 1 tablespoon sliced fresh chives
- 1/4 cup pitted and chopped kalamata olives
- 1 large egg, lightly beaten
- Pinch of cayenne
- Salt and freshly ground black pepper to taste

FOR THE EGG WASH

- 1 large egg
- 1/4 cup water

SAUCE SUGGESTIONS

Roasted Garlic Sauce (page 43)

or

Black Bean–Cumin Sauce (page 45)

or

Tomato Salsa Coulis (page 44), gently heated

Place the eggs and cilantro in a bowl and whisk together. Place the flour in a food processor and, with the machine running, add the egg mixture a little at a time. After all the eggs have been added, add the salt and olive oil and process for 15 or 20 seconds. Turn out the dough onto a lightly floured work surface and knead for 5 minutes, or until the dough has formed a smooth, firm ball. Cover with a damp towel and let rest for 30 minutes.

Cut the dough into five pieces and, using the heel of your hand, flatten each piece of dough into a disk that will fit through the widest setting of the pasta machine. Roll out each piece of dough through the pasta machine on the widest setting. Fold the dough into thirds and roll through the widest setting again. Repeat this procedure four times, or until the dough is smooth and velvety. Dust with a little flour if the dough becomes sticky. Reduce the thickness on the machine by one setting and roll the dough through the machine. Continue to reduce the thickness each time the dough goes through the machine until the dough goes through at the third thinnest setting, dusting with flour as necessary. Place a rolled-out piece of dough on a cookie sheet lined with wax paper, cover with another piece of wax paper, and alternate the dough with wax paper so that none of the dough touches another piece. Cover with a towel and refrigerate.

In a mixing bowl, place the stuffing ingredients and stir until thoroughly combined. Lay out a sheet of pasta dough on a lightly floured work surface and, using a 3-inch cookie or biscuit cutter, cut out as many circles as possible. Place 1 1/2 tablespoons of the stuffing in the center of each circle. Repeat for the remaining circles, consolidating the remaining dough and running it through the pasta machine again to roll out for additional circles.

Whisk the egg and water together in a bowl. Brush the edges of each round of pasta. Carefully fold the circles in half, pressing the edges together, squeezing out as much air as possible. Place the ravioli on a clean cookie sheet lined with wax paper.

Bring a large saucepan of salted water to a boil. Cook the ravioli for 2 to 3 minutes, or until they rise to the top. Drain the ravioli in a colander and serve 3 or 4 in each bowl.

SERVES 6

CHAPTER NINE

EMPANADAS
QUESADILLAS
AND ENCHILADAS

Red Cabbage, Blue Cheese, and Walnut Empanadas

This may be an unusual combination of ingredients and flavors for empanadas, but the pairing of cabbage, blue cheese, and walnuts is a classic that makes a wonderful cold-weather dish. While these empanadas would serve as a delicious and hearty vegetarian main course with the addition of rice and beans, I love these flavors with pork.

FOR THE EMPANADA DOUGH

1 1/3 cups all-purpose flour
1 tablespoon dried oregano
6 tablespoons vegetable shortening
1/4 cup cold water
1/4 teaspoon salt

FOR THE FILLING

1/2 head of red cabbage, cored and julienned
1/2 onion, minced
1 jalapeño chile, seeded and minced
1 tablespoon whole-grain mustard
1 teaspoon prepared horseradish
Pinch of ground canela or cinnamon
Pinch of ground allspice
1 cup cider vinegar
1/2 cup sugar
1/2 tablespoon salt
1/3 cup crumbled Gorgonzola cheese
1/4 cup toasted chopped walnuts (page 211)

FOR THE EGG WASH

1 large egg
1/4 cup water

To prepare the dough, combine the flour and oregano in the bowl of an electric mixer fitted with a paddle attachment. Add the shortening and mix on low speed until the mixture resembles oatmeal. In a bowl, combine the water and salt and slowly drizzle into the mixer while on low speed. Mix until the water is fully absorbed; do not overwork the dough or it will form a ball. Wrap the dough in plastic and refrigerate for 30 minutes.

To prepare the filling, combine the cabbage, onion, jalapeño, mustard, horseradish, canela, allspice, vinegar, sugar, salt, and 1/2 cup water in a saucepan. Bring to a boil, reduce the heat to a simmer, and cook, covered, for 1 hour, or until the cabbage is tender. Remove the pan from the heat, let cool, and drain. In a mixing bowl, combine the cooled cabbage with the Gorgonzola and walnuts and set aside.

Preheat the oven to 400°F.

Remove the chilled dough from the refrigerator and cut into 16 equal pieces. Using a lightly floured rolling pin, roll out each piece into a circle about 1/8 inch thick. In a bowl, whisk together the egg and water. Divide the cabbage filling evenly among the circles, placing it in the center of each. With a pastry brush, brush the exposed edges of the dough with the egg wash. Carefully fold each circle in half, making sure the filling is completely sealed inside, and crimp the edges with a fork. Make a small slit in the top of each empanada to allow the steam to escape.

Place the empanadas on a lightly greased cookie sheet and brush with the remaining egg wash. Transfer to the oven and bake for 25 minutes, or until the pastry is shiny and golden brown.

SERVES 4 TO 8
MAKES 16 EMPANADAS

Morel and Dried Cherry Empanadas with Cilantro-Walnut Pesto

Morel mushrooms are closely related to truffles, and are almost equally prized—they deliver the same earthy, almost nutty aroma and flavor. Morels are usually available only in the spring, and they need cleaning, but like other mushrooms, do not let them soak in water or they will become soggy. I prefer the darkest morels I can find, as I think they have a more "foresty" flavor. The acidic flavor and chewy texture of the dried cherries make a delightful combination together with the morels, goat cheese, and black olives.

FOR THE EMPANADA DOUGH

1⅓ cups all-purpose flour
1 tablespoon chopped fresh cilantro leaves
6 tablespoons vegetable shortening
¼ cup cold water
¼ teaspoon salt

FOR THE FILLING

½ pound morel mushrooms or shiitakes, cleaned
5 tablespoons olive oil
½ tablespoon soy sauce
½ tablespoon balsamic vinegar
1 tablespoon dried cherries
½ cup Marsala wine
1 tablespoon diced onion
1 garlic clove, minced
1 tablespoon diced yellow bell pepper
1 tablespoon diced red bell pepper
1 tablespoon pitted and diced kalamata olives
1 teaspoon minced orange zest
1 teaspoon chopped fresh marjoram leaves
1 teaspoon sliced fresh chives
¼ teaspoon chopped fresh rosemary leaves
1 tablespoon crumbled goat cheese
Salt to taste

To prepare the dough, combine the flour and cilantro in the bowl of an electric mixer fitted with a paddle attachment. Add the shortening and mix on low speed until the mixture resembles oatmeal. In a bowl, combine the water and salt and slowly drizzle into the mixer while on low speed. Mix until the water is fully absorbed; do not overwork the dough or it will form a ball. Wrap the dough in plastic and refrigerate for 30 minutes.

Preheat the oven to 400°F.

To prepare the filling, place the mushrooms in a small roasting pan and drizzle with 4 tablespoons of the olive oil, the soy sauce, and the balsamic vinegar. Cover the pan with foil and roast in the oven for 25 to 30 minutes. Remove from the oven and, when cool enough to handle, cut the mushrooms into ¼-inch slices.

Soak the dried cherries in the Marsala for 20 minutes. In a skillet or sauté pan, heat the remaining 1 tablespoon of olive oil until lightly smoking. Add the onion, garlic, and bell peppers and sauté for 1 minute. Add the rehydrated cherries and soaking liquid to the pan with the olives. Cook until the Marsala has evaporated, about 3 or 4 minutes. Add the orange zest, marjoram, chives, rosemary, sliced morels, and goat cheese. Stir to combine thoroughly and then remove from the heat. Season with salt and let the mixture cool while rolling out the empanadas.

FOR THE EGG WASH

1 large egg

¼ cup water

Cilantro-Walnut Pesto (page 20)

Remove the chilled dough from the refrigerator and cut into 16 equal pieces. Using a lightly floured rolling pin, roll out each piece into a circle about ⅛ inch thick. In a bowl, whisk together the egg and water. Divide the filling evenly among the circles, placing it in the center of each. With a pastry brush, brush the exposed edges of the dough with the egg wash. Carefully fold each circle in half, making sure the filling is completely sealed inside, and crimp the edges with a fork. Make a small slit in the top of each empanada to allow the steam to escape.

Place the empanadas on a lightly greased cookie sheet and brush with the remaining egg wash. Transfer to the oven and bake for 25 minutes, or until the pastry is shiny and golden brown. Serve with Cilantro-Walnut Pesto.

SERVES 4 TO 8

MAKES 16 EMPANADAS

Butternut Squash Empanadas with White Bean–Oven-Dried Tomato Relish

Butternut squash is shaped like an elongated pear, measuring 9 to 12 inches in length. It has a cream- to light-brown-colored skin when ripe and mild, sweet-flavored, deep orange flesh. It is an excellent all-purpose winter squash that is a good substitute for pumpkin. White beans and butternut squash truly exemplify autumnal cooking at its best.

(photograph opposite)

FOR THE DOUGH

- 1 cup all-purpose flour
- 1/4 cup fine cornmeal
- 1/4 cup masa harina
- 3 tablespoons vegetable shortening
- 1/2 cup hot water
- 1 teaspoon salt

FOR THE FILLING

- 1/4 cup (1/2 stick) unsalted butter
- 1/4 cup light brown sugar, loosely packed
- 1 teaspoon dried red pepper flakes
- 1 small butternut squash (about 2 pounds), peeled, split in half, seeds removed, and cut into 1-inch chunks
- 1 tablespoon olive oil
- 1/2 onion, julienned
- 2 garlic cloves, minced
- 1 poblano chile, seeded and julienned
- 1 teaspoon ground cumin
- 1 tablespoon pure red chile powder
- 1/4 cup grated *queso fresco* or feta cheese
- 1 tablespoon freshly squeezed lemon juice
- 1 tablespoon chopped fresh mint marigold or tarragon leaves

FOR THE EGG WASH

- 1 large egg
- 1/4 cup water

White Bean–Oven-Dried Tomato Relish (page 36)

To prepare the dough, combine the flour, cornmeal, and masa harina in the bowl of an electric mixer fitted with a paddle attachment. Add the shortening and mix on low speed until the mixture resembles oatmeal. In a bowl, combine the water and salt and slowly drizzle into the mixer while on low speed. Mix until the water is fully absorbed; do not overwork the dough or it will form a ball. Wrap the dough in plastic and refrigerate for at least 30 minutes.

Preheat the oven to 350°F.

To prepare the filling, in a small saucepan, combine the butter, sugar, pepper flakes, and 1/4 cup of water and heat gently until the butter melts. Place the chunks of squash into an 8-inch square baking dish and pour the melted butter mixture over. Cover with foil and bake in the oven for 30 minutes, or until the squash yields easily when pressed with a fork. Remove from the oven and set aside.

In a sauté pan over high heat, heat the olive oil until lightly smoking. Add the onion, garlic, and poblano and sauté for 3 minutes, or until the onion is translucent. Add the cumin and chile powder and toss or stir gently to combine. Remove from the heat and transfer to a mixing bowl. Add the cooked squash, *queso fresco*, lemon juice, and mint marigold, fold to combine, and season with salt to taste. Set aside.

Increase the oven temperature to 400°F. Remove the chilled dough from the refrigerator and cut into 16 equal pieces. Using a lightly floured rolling pin, roll out each piece into a circle about 1/8 inch thick. In a bowl, whisk together the egg and water. Divide the filling evenly among the circles, placing it in the center of each. With a pastry brush, brush the exposed edges of the

(continued on next page)

dough with the egg wash. Carefully fold each circle in half, making sure the filling is completely sealed inside, and crimp the edges with a fork. Make a small slit in the top of each empanada to allow the steam to escape.

Place the empanadas on a lightly greased cookie sheet and brush with the remaining egg wash. Transfer to the oven and bake for 25 minutes, or until the pastry is shiny and golden brown. Serve with the relish.

SERVES 4 TO 6

MAKES 16 EMPANADAS

Cumin, Black Bean, and Queso Fresco Quesadillas

Cumin is a natural partner with beans, a combination that has found its way into the cuisine of more than one culture, Mexico included. Black beans are popular throughout Central America, and over the past few years they have taken North American menus by storm. Try these quesadillas with a puree of sweet potatoes flavored with a little brown sugar and butter, as these ingredients are particularly complementary to the bean mixture.

½ cup dried black beans, cleaned and soaked overnight
3 cups Vegetable Stock (page 211) or store-bought
1 ripe tomato, seeded and outer flesh diced
1 serrano chile, seeded and minced
2 tablespoons chopped fresh cilantro leaves
½ cup grated *queso fresco* or Monterey Jack cheese
½ teaspoon cumin seeds, toasted and ground (page 211)
Salt to taste
8 small Flour Tortillas (6 inches across) (page 184)
2 tablespoons (¼ stick) unsalted butter, melted

Combine the beans and stock in a saucepan and bring to a boil. Reduce the heat to low and simmer the beans for 1 hour, or until tender but not mushy. Remove from the heat and drain the beans in a colander. Transfer the beans to a cookie sheet, spread out, and let cool in the refrigerator. When cool, place the beans in a mixing bowl and add the tomato, serrano, cilantro, *queso fresco*, and cumin. Toss to combine and season with salt.

Lay the tortillas on a work surface and divide the filling evenly among the tortillas. Fold each tortilla over to make a semicircle. Brush each quesadilla lightly on both sides with the melted butter.

Preheat the oven to 200°F.

Set a dry, heavy cast-iron skillet or sauté pan over medium-low heat for 3 minutes. Place a quesadilla in the skillet and cook until golden brown, about 2 minutes. Carefully flip over using a large spatula and cook the other side until golden brown and the filling is heated through, about 2 minutes longer. Transfer to the oven to keep warm and repeat for the remaining quesadillas. Cut each quesadilla into 3 or 4 slices and serve.

SERVES 4

Oven-Roasted Vegetable Quesadillas

I love oven roasting vegetables because it caramelizes them and intensifies their flavors by developing the natural sugars. This simple recipe makes delicious quesadillas, which are a light, Southwestern form of sandwich in which the usual bread is replaced by tortillas. Quesadillas are wonderfully versatile, and I particularly enjoy their melt-in-the-mouth quality. Quesadillas make a great medium for flavors and ingredients, including all types of meat, fish, and vegetables.

1 small zucchini, finely diced

1 small yellow squash, finely diced

1 red bell pepper, seeded and finely diced

1 poblano chile, seeded and finely diced

2 tablespoons extra-virgin olive oil

1 tablespoon roasted garlic puree (page 203)

1 tablespoon pure red chile powder

1 teaspoon salt

1 teaspoon freshly ground black pepper

1 tablespoon chopped fresh oregano leaves

1 tablespoon chopped fresh rosemary leaves

8 small Flour Tortillas (6 inches across) (page 184)

3 tablespoons unsalted butter, melted

1 cup grated Monterey Jack cheese

Preheat the oven to 400°F.

In a mixing bowl, combine the zucchini, yellow squash, bell pepper, and chile and set aside. In another mixing bowl, whisk together the olive oil, garlic, chile powder, salt, pepper, oregano, and rosemary. Drizzle the oil mixture over the vegetables and toss to coat. Transfer the vegetables to a cookie sheet and roast in the oven for 10 to 12 minutes, or until tender. Remove from the oven and let cool. Reduce the oven temperature to 200°F.

Lay 4 of the tortillas on a work surface. Brush with 1 tablespoon of the melted butter and turn over. Sprinkle half of the cheese evenly over the buttered tortillas and top evenly with the cooled vegetable mixture. Sprinkle the remaining cheese over the vegetables and cover with the remaining 4 tortillas. Brush the top of the tortillas with the remaining butter.

Set a dry, heavy cast-iron skillet over medium heat for 3 minutes and place 1 or 2 quesadillas in the skillet. Cook the quesadillas until golden brown, about 2 minutes, and then carefully flip over using a large spatula. Cook the other side until golden brown and the filling is heated through, about 2 minutes longer. Transfer to the oven to keep warm and repeat for the remaining quesadillas. Cut each quesadilla into 6 pieces and serve.

SERVES 4

Market Vegetable Enchiladas with Avocado-Tomatillo Salsa

This is the perfect recipe for using whatever seasonal vegetables are available at your local market. In fact, the inspiration behind it came while I was filming a local television show where the focus was summer produce at the farmer's market. It then became the idea behind "enchiladas del dia" on the daily lunch menu at Star Canyon, where we use the best produce available that day.

(photograph opposite)

1/2 cup sweet potatoes, peeled and diced

2 tablespoons olive oil

2 onions, diced

2 tablespoons minced garlic

1 yellow squash, diced

1 small zucchini, diced

2 tablespoons chopped fresh cilantro leaves

1 tablespoon chopped fresh basil leaves

3 tablespoons ancho chile puree (page 206)

1 papaya, peeled, seeded, and diced

4 poblano chiles, roasted, peeled, seeded, and diced (page 204)

2 red bell peppers, roasted, peeled, seeded, and diced (page 204)

2 yellow bell peppers, roasted, peeled, seeded, and diced (page 204)

2 1/2 cups grated Chihuahua or Monterey Jack cheese

Salt and freshly ground black pepper to taste

Vegetable oil, for softening the tortillas

18 Corn Tortillas (6 inches across) (page 182)

Avocado-Tomatillo Salsa (page 32)

Preheat the oven to 350°F.

Heat a saucepan of boiling water and add the sweet potatoes. Blanch for 5 minutes, drain, and set aside. In a sauté pan, heat the olive oil until lightly smoking and sauté the onions and garlic for 2 minutes, until lightly browned. Add the squash and zucchini and continue to cook for 30 seconds longer. Add the cilantro, basil, ancho puree, papaya, poblanos, red and yellow bell peppers, and the reserved sweet potatoes. Cook for 30 seconds and then remove from the heat. Add 1 cup of the cheese, season with salt and pepper, and mix the ingredients thoroughly. Set aside.

Pour enough vegetable oil in a skillet to come 1/4 inch up the sides. Over medium heat, bring the oil to 350°F., or just smoking. Using tongs, dip each tortilla into the hot oil for 5 seconds and then drain on paper towels. Transfer the tortillas to a work surface, being careful not to overlap them, as they will stick together. Divide the reserved vegetable mixture evenly among the tortillas and roll up to form enchiladas. Place the enchiladas in a baking dish, seam-side down, placing them snugly together. Sprinkle the remaining cheese on top and cover the dish with foil. Bake in the oven for 8 minutes, or until the cheese has melted. Serve 3 enchiladas per plate and top with Avocado-Tomatillo Salsa.

SERVES 6

Stacked Cheese and Green Chile Enchiladas

This is my improvisation on the old Tex-Mex standby, green chile—sour cream enchiladas. To me, this recipe is the ultimate in comfort food, bringing back memories from childhood, when they were on the menu at my family's truck stop cafe. If you like, try these enchiladas with the Griddled Tomato-Chipotle Salsa (page 32) and of course with a side of rice and refried black beans.

4 poblano chiles, roasted, peeled, seeded, and cut into ¹/₂-inch strips (page 204)
1¹/₂ cups grated Monterey Jack cheese
1¹/₂ cups grated Cheddar cheese
2 tablespoons chopped dried Mexican oregano
¹/₂ teaspoon ground cumin
Salt to taste
12 to 14 tomatillos (about 1 pound), husked, rinsed, and quartered
2 serrano chiles, chopped
¹/₂ onion, chopped
4 garlic cloves
¹/₄ cup chopped fresh cilantro leaves
Vegetable oil, for softening the tortillas
12 blue or yellow corn tortillas (6 inches across) (page 182)

¹/₂ cup grated *queso fresco* or Monterey Jack cheese

Preheat the oven to 400°F.

Combine the poblanos, Monterey Jack and Cheddar cheeses, oregano, and cumin in a mixing bowl and mix thoroughly. Season with salt and set aside.

Place the tomatillos, serranos, onion, and garlic in a baking dish and bake in the oven for 12 minutes, or until the vegetables begin to brown. Remove from the oven and transfer to a food processor. Add the cilantro, process until smooth, and set aside. Reduce the oven temperature to 350°F.

Pour enough vegetable oil in a skillet to come ¹/₄ inch up the sides. Over medium heat, bring the oil to 300°F., or almost smoking. Using tongs, dip each tortilla into the hot oil for 5 seconds and then drain on paper towels. Transfer the tortillas to a work surface, being careful not to overlap them as they will stick together.

Place 4 of the tortillas in the bottom of an 8-inch square baking dish, overlapping them to cover the bottom of the pan. Sprinkle one third of the cheese mixture over the tortillas and top with one third of the pureed tomatillo sauce. Place 4 more tortillas over the sauce and repeat these layers, ending with a final layer of sauce on top. Cover the dish with foil and transfer to the oven. Bake for 10 to 12 minutes, until heated through.

Remove the baking dish from the oven, sprinkle with the *queso fresco,* and serve.

SERVES 4 TO 6

Huitlacoche Enchiladas with Pico and Garlic Crema

Huitlacoche is a gray-black corn fungus much prized as a cooking ingredient in Mexico (the name is derived from the ancient Nahuatl language). It is exotic looking—it makes the corn kernels swell to many times their normal size—and it tastes like sweet, smoky wild mushrooms. It is available in canned or frozen form, and it is just now beginning to be grown in the United States commercially. I predict that it will soon become available in fresh form. Ironically, it has long been considered a blight by American corn farmers, who destroyed infected ears.

1 cup heavy cream
5 tablespoons guajillo chile puree (page 206)
2 garlic cloves, minced
2 tablespoons freshly squeezed lime juice
Salt to taste
1 tablespoon olive oil
1/2 onion, diced
1 portobello mushroom, diced
1 7-ounce can huitlacoche
1/2 avocado, peeled, pitted, and finely diced
1/2 cup grated Chihuahua or Monterey Jack cheese
1 Roma tomato, seeded and diced
2 tablespoons chopped fresh cilantro leaves
8 Corn Tortillas (6 inches across) (page 182)

FOR THE GARLIC CREMA
2 cups heavy cream
2 tablespoons roasted garlic puree (page 203)

8 tablespoons Pico de Gallo (page 31)

Preheat the oven to 350°F.

In a saucepan, combine the 1 cup heavy cream, guajillo puree, and garlic and bring to a boil. Reduce the heat to low and simmer for 2 minutes. Remove from the heat, add the lime juice, and season with salt. Set aside.

In a sauté pan over medium-high heat, heat the olive oil until lightly smoking. Add the onion and portobello mushroom and sauté for 5 minutes, or until the onion is translucent and the mushroom is fully cooked. Add the huitlacoche and 2 tablespoons of the reserved cream mixture and simmer over medium heat for 4 minutes. Remove from the heat and transfer to a mixing bowl. Fold in the avocado, cheese, tomato, and cilantro and season with salt. Set aside.

In a sauté pan over medium heat, heat the remaining reserved cream mixture until it begins to simmer. Using tongs, dip each tortilla into the cream mixture for 30 seconds to soften and then transfer to a cooking sheet or platter, being careful not to tear them. Divide the reserved vegetable mixture evenly among the tortillas and roll up to form enchiladas. Place the enchiladas in a baking dish, seam-side down, placing them snugly together. Spoon the remaining cream mixture over the top and cover the dish with foil. Bake in the oven for 10 minutes.

Meanwhile, make the Garlic Crema. Place the 2 cups heavy cream in a large sauté pan and bring to a boil, stirring often. Turn the heat down to a simmer and reduce until 1 cup remains, 5 to 7 minutes. Transfer the reduced cream to a bowl and stir in the roasted garlic. Set aside.

Remove the enchiladas from the oven and, with a spatula, carefully place them on a serving platter. Garnish each enchilada with a dollop of Garlic Crema and a tablespoon of Pico de Gallo.

SERVES 4

CHAPTER TEN

TORTAS
SANDWICHES
AND PIZZAS

Grilled Pepper and Onion Torta with Arugula Pesto

The vegetables for this simple torta can be roasted instead of grilled, if you prefer, and the results will be just as good. If you can find orange bell peppers, use them too, or use one yellow and one orange bell pepper. The pesto is easy to make and versatile in its uses. Try it brushed on fish before roasting or grilling, or flavor a pasta or salad dressing with it, just as you would use basil pesto.

FOR THE ARUGULA PESTO
- 1 garlic clove, chopped
- 1/2 cup arugula
- 1/4 cup grated Parmesan cheese
- 2 tablespoons toasted pine nuts (page 211)
- 1/2 cup extra-virgin olive oil

FOR THE TORTA
- 2 red bell peppers, seeded and cut lengthwise into quarters
- 2 yellow bell peppers, seeded and cut lengthwise into quarters
- 2 poblano chiles, seeded and cut lengthwise into quarters
- 2 red onions, cut into 1/4-inch slices
- 2 tablespoons olive oil

Salt to taste
- 1/4 cup balsamic vinegar
- 2 tablespoons chopped fresh cilantro leaves
- 8 pieces (4 inches square) Ancho Focaccia (page 176) or store-bought

Prepare the grill.

To prepare the pesto, combine the garlic, arugula, Parmesan, and pine nuts in a food processor and puree until smooth. While the machine is running, slowly drizzle in the olive oil. Transfer to a bowl and refrigerate.

Place the red and yellow bell peppers, poblanos, and onions on a large platter and brush with 2 tablespoons of olive oil. Sprinkle the vegetables on both sides with salt. Grill the vegetables on both sides over medium heat for 5 to 7 minutes, or until tender. As the vegetables finish, remove them from the grill with tongs and place in a mixing bowl. Add the vinegar and cilantro to the mixing bowl, toss to coat, and cover with plastic wrap. Let the vegetables sit for 10 minutes before assembling the tortas.

Meanwhile, toast the focaccia on the grill until heated through. Remove and spread each piece of focaccia with the chilled pesto. Divide the grilled vegetables among 4 of the pieces of focaccia, then top each sandwich with another piece of the focaccia.

SERVES 4

Vegetable Cake Sandwich with Tri-Color Potato Chips

This sandwich makes a great alternative to a hamburger, and with the potato chips, it gets even closer. However, it also makes a wonderful dish as a vegetable cake, without the bread. If you would like to go in another direction, mix some salad greens with the relish and serve with the vegetable cake on top.

1 carrot, peeled and grated
1 jicama (about 10 ounces), peeled and grated
1 zucchini, washed and grated
1 yellow squash, washed and grated
2 jalapeño chiles, seeded and minced
1 red bell pepper, seeded and diced
2 tablespoons chopped fresh cilantro leaves
2 large eggs, lightly beaten
3 tablespoons fresh bread crumbs
2 teaspoons salt
1/4 cup corn oil
8 slices rustic whole-wheat bread
1/2 cup Cherry Tomato-Mozzarella Relish (page 36)
Tri-Color Potato Chips (page 83)

Place the grated carrot, jicama, zucchini, and squash in the center of a clean kitchen towel. Gather the towel at the corners and twist to squeeze out any excess moisture. Transfer to a mixing bowl and add the jalapeños, bell pepper, cilantro, eggs, bread crumbs, and salt. Mix thoroughly and set aside.

Preheat the oven to 200°F.

In a nonstick skillet over medium heat, heat 2 tablespoons of the oil until lightly smoking. Using a 1/2-cup measure, form the vegetable mixture into 8 cakes and place 4 of the cakes in the skillet. Cook for 3 minutes per side, or until golden brown on both sides. Transfer to a cookie sheet lined with paper towels and place in the oven to keep warm. Repeat for the remaining vegetable cakes.

Toast the bread and place 2 cakes on each of 4 slices of bread. Top with the relish and the remaining 4 slices of bread. Cut each sandwich in half and serve with the chips.

SERVES 4

Pickled Vegetable and Deviled Egg Salad Torta

Deviled egg sandwiches were another favorite of mine growing up, and my mother made them to perfection. Pickling is one of my favorite preparations for vegetables because it adds such depth of flavor. Most cuisines around the world have pickles of some sort, and this recipe draws its inspiration from the escabeches of Mexico. These pickled vegetables can be used with other sandwiches whenever you would use cucumber pickles. Note that the spice mixture for pickling the vegetables needs to marinate for at least 6 hours and preferably overnight; then, after the vegetables are added, allow 1 to 2 hours for them to marinate.

FOR THE PICKLED VEGETABLES

1 small white baking potato (about 8 ounces)

1 small sweet potato (about 12 ounces)

1 red bell pepper, roasted, peeled, and seeded (page 204)

1 yellow bell pepper, roasted, peeled, and seeded (page 204)

1 small onion, cut into 1/2-inch slices

2 jalapeño chiles, sliced into 1/4-inch rounds

2 oranges, zested, halved, and juiced

1/2 cup olive oil

2 cups white wine vinegar

3 allspice berries

1 cinnamon stick

2 tablespoons lightly toasted cumin seeds (page 211)

1 teaspoon black peppercorns

1 dried bay leaf

4 sprigs of fresh thyme

1 tablespoon kosher salt

1 tablespoon sugar

FOR THE DEVILED EGG SALAD

10 large eggs, hard-boiled, shelled, and chopped

1 garlic clove, finely minced

2 serrano chiles, seeded and minced

1/2 cup Mayonnaise (page 212) or store-bought

1 teaspoon freshly squeezed lemon juice

2 teaspoons dried mustard powder

1/4 teaspoon cayenne

1/4 teaspoon pure red chile powder

1/4 teaspoon paprika

1/2 teaspoon salt

1 teaspoon chopped fresh cilantro leaves

1 teaspoon sliced fresh chives

8 1/2-inch-thick slices Chipotle Brioche (page 180)

In a saucepan of boiling salted water, boil the baking potato and sweet potato together until tender but firm, about 25 to 30 minutes. Let cool to room temperature. Peel the potatoes and cut into 1/4-inch slices. Cut the roasted bell peppers in half lengthwise and then crosswise, and transfer to a large bowl. Add the cooled potatoes, onion, and jalapeños.

Place the orange zest and juice in a saucepan and add 1/4 cup of the olive oil. Add the vinegar, allspice, cinnamon, cumin, peppercorns, bay leaf, thyme, salt, and sugar and combine. Bring to a boil and simmer for 5 minutes. Remove from the heat and let stand for at least 6 hours (and preferably overnight).

Return the reserved liquid to a boil and pour over the prepared vegetables. Let stand to marinate for 1 to 2 hours.

To prepare the egg salad, place the eggs, garlic, chiles, mayonnaise, lemon juice, mustard, cayenne, chile powder, paprika, and salt in a mixing bowl and mash together. Stir in the cilantro and chives and keep refrigerated.

Preheat the oven to 350°F.

Brush the slices of brioche with the remaining 1/4 cup of olive oil. Place on a cookie sheet and toast in the oven for 2 to 3 minutes. Spread 2 tablespoons of the egg salad on each of the brioche slices. Place an assortment of the pickled vegetables on top of the salad on 4 of the slices and then top each with another slice of the brioche.

SERVES 4

Eggplant Parmesan Torta with Oven-Dried Tomato Mayonnaise

Eggplant Parmesan was one of my favorite dishes growing up, and it seemed quite exotic to a West Texas boy like me. Little did I know then that it would inspire this dish. The mayo is very versatile and can be used for other sandwiches or even whisked into a simple vinaigrette to make an unusual dressing. The process of salting the eggplant and letting it stand helps eliminate any bitterness it may have, but if it is immature, it may not need it. Consider serving the torta with Carrot-Jicama Slaw with Ancho Chiles (page 53), Bread and Butter Pickles (page 17), or potato chips. *(photograph opposite)*

FOR THE OVEN-DRIED TOMATO MAYONNAISE

- ¼ cup minced oven-dried tomatoes (page 205) or sun-dried tomatoes packed in oil
- ¼ cup minced onion
- ¼ cup Mayonnaise (page 212) or store-bought
- 1 teaspoon minced lemon zest
- 2 teaspoons freshly squeezed lemon juice

Salt and freshly ground black pepper to taste

FOR THE EGGPLANT PARMESAN TORTA

- 1 eggplant (about 12 ounces), ends sliced off
- 1 teaspoon salt
- 1 large egg
- 2 tablespoons milk
- 2½ cups grated Parmesan cheese

Vegetable oil

- 4 Fresh and Dried Coriander Bolillos (page 185)
- 2 ripe tomatoes, ends sliced off and each tomato cut into 4 slices
- 1 cup shredded romaine lettuce

To prepare the mayonnaise, combine the oven-dried tomatoes, onion, mayonnaise, lemon zest, lemon juice, and salt and pepper in a mixing bowl and refrigerate.

To prepare the torta, cut the eggplant in half crosswise and cut each half lengthwise into ¼-inch slices. Place the eggplant slices on a baking sheet lined with paper towels, sprinkle both sides with the salt, and let sit for 20 minutes. Transfer the eggplant to a colander, rinse briefly under cold water to remove the salt, and pat dry thoroughly with paper towels.

Preheat the oven to 250°F.

Beat the egg and milk together in a bowl and place the cheese on a plate. Dip the eggplant in the egg wash and dredge in the Parmesan, patting gently to make sure the slices are completely coated.

Pour enough vegetable oil into a large heavy skillet to come ½ inch up the sides and heat until lightly smoking. Add the eggplant slices in a single layer (cook the slices in batches) and sauté over medium-high heat for 1 minute on each side. Remove from the pan with tongs and drain on paper towels. Transfer the eggplant to a baking sheet and keep warm in the oven.

Heat the bolillos in the oven for 3 minutes to warm through. Remove from the oven, cut in half, and spread some of the oven-dried tomato mayonnaise on both halves. Place 2 or 3 slices of eggplant on one half of each bolillo, top with 2 slices of tomato and ¼ cup of the shredded lettuce, and cover with the top half of the bolillo. Cut the bolillo in half crosswise and serve.

SERVES 4

Vegetarian Club on Ancho Focaccia

One of the standards by which I judge hotels is the quality of their club sandwich. The correlation almost never fails! Here's one that I would love to find somewhere on my travels. It incorporates some of my favorite vegetables and it has a nice chewiness because of the focaccia. I couldn't imagine a club sandwich without bacon or poultry until I tasted this one. If you wish, before assembling the sandwich, lightly brush the focaccia with olive oil and toast in a 325°F oven for 2 or 3 minutes.

4 large portobello mushroom caps
¼ cup olive oil
1 tablespoon minced garlic
¼ cup Vegetable Stock (page 211) or store-bought, white wine, or water
2 tablespoons corn oil
1 large onion, sliced
8 portions (about 4 inches square) Ancho Focaccia (page 176) or store-bought
½ cup Mayonnaise (page 212) or store-bought
4 bunches of watercress
4 large avocados, cut in half and pitted
2 beefsteak tomatoes, ends cut off, each tomato cut into 4 slices
Tri-Color Potato Chips (page 83)

Preheat the oven to 350°F.

Brush the mushrooms with the olive oil and place in a roasting pan. Sprinkle the garlic over the mushrooms, add the stock to the pan, and roast for 10 minutes, or until soft. Remove from the oven and slice each mushroom cap into 8 to 10 slices. Set aside.

In a sauté pan, heat the corn oil, add the onion, and sauté over high heat for about 4 minutes, stirring occasionally. Reduce the heat to medium and continue cooking until the onions are light brown, about 5 minutes longer. Set aside. Cut the focaccia in half crosswise and spread each slice with ½ tablespoon of the mayonnaise. Place 4 or 5 slices of mushroom and ½ bunch of the watercress on the 8 bottom halves of the bread and top with the caramelized onions.

With a spoon, scoop out the flesh of each avocado half in 1 piece and place, flat-side down, on a cutting board. Cut each half into 4 or 5 slices and place on top of the onions. Place a tomato slice over the avocado. Cover with the top halves of the focaccia and cut each sandwich in half on the diagonal. Serve with the potato chips.

SERVES 8

Smoked Tomato Pizza with Basil and Queso Fresco

This recipe holds special memories as it was on the opening menu at Star Canyon in Dallas. It proved a very popular dish at the bar. You can save some time by roasting or blackening the tomatoes rather than smoking them. The only things this pizza needs are a good salad— try the Egg-Free Southwestern Caesar Salad with Herbed Ricotta (page 56)—and a tasty glass of red wine.

FOR THE PIZZA CRUST
- 1 cup warm water (110° to 115°F.)
- 1 package active dry yeast
- 2½ to 3 cups all-purpose flour
- 2 tablespoons Red Chile-Canela Oil (page 26) or store-bought red chile oil
- ½ teaspoon salt

FOR THE TOPPING
- 4 Roma tomatoes, cut into ¼-inch slices
- ¼ cup cornmeal
- 3 tablespoons chopped fresh basil leaves
- ½ cup grated *queso fresco* or Monterey Jack cheese
- 2 tablespoons olive oil (optional)
- Salt and freshly ground black pepper to taste

To prepare the pizza crust, combine the water, yeast, and 1½ cups of the flour in the bowl of an electric mixer fitted with a paddle attachment. Mix well on low speed. Replace the paddle attachment with a dough hook and turn the machine to low. Add the oil, salt, and the remaining 1 cup of flour (add up to ½ cup more flour if the dough does not readily form a ball). After the mixture forms a ball, run the machine for 5 minutes on low speed. The dough should be smooth and elastic; if not, run for 1 minute longer. Transfer the dough to a lightly oiled glass mixing bowl and cover with plastic wrap or a dampened towel. Let rise in a warm place for 1 hour, or until the dough has doubled in volume.

Meanwhile, prepare the smoker (see page 209). Preheat the oven to 500°F. and place baking stones inside if you have them.

When the dough has risen, punch it down and cut it into 2 equal pieces. Form each piece into a ball and let rest, covered with a damp towel, for 10 to 15 minutes.

Place the tomatoes in the smoker and smoke for 8 to 10 minutes. Remove and let cool.

Flatten each ball of dough on a lightly floured work surface and shape into 12-inch pizza crusts about ¼ inch thick. Brush the tops with a little more oil.

Liberally dust the back of a cookie sheet with half of the cornmeal. Place a pizza crust over the cornmeal and top with half the tomatoes, half the basil, and half of the cheese. Drizzle half of the olive oil, if desired, over the pizza and season with salt and pepper. Place the first pizza in the oven and repeat the process for the second pizza.

Cook each pizza for 10 to 15 minutes, or until the crust is golden brown. Remove from the oven and cut each pizza into 8 or 10 slices.

SERVES 6 TO 8

Vegetarian BLT

Here's a new BLT, deliciously simple and big on flavor, with blue cheese taking the place of bacon. Blue cheese and tomatoes have long been a favorite pairing of mine and the red onion only adds to this classic combination. Try the Tri-Color Potato Chips (page 83) or the Bread and Butter Pickles (page 17) with this sandwich if you would like an accompaniment.

1 red onion, very finely sliced
1/3 cup red wine vinegar
4 to 8 slices rustic bread, such as whole-wheat or multi-grain
1/4 cup Mayonnaise (page 212) or store-bought
1 head of Bibb lettuce, outer leaves discarded
2 vine-ripened tomatoes, each cut into 4 slices
1/2 cup crumbled blue cheese

In a small bowl, place the onions, add the vinegar, and refrigerate for 1 hour.

Preheat the broiler.

Place the bread on a cookie sheet, spread an even layer of the mayonnaise on each slice of bread, and top with 2 or 3 leaves of Bibb lettuce. Drain the onions with a slotted spoon and evenly divide on top of the lettuce. Add 2 slices of tomato to each sandwich and sprinkle the blue cheese on top. Place under the broiler for 2 to 3 minutes, or until the cheese is just melted. Serve open-faced or top with another piece of bread if desired.

SERVES 4

Clayudas with Cilantro-Walnut Pesto and Cheese

I discovered clayudas in Oaxaca when we were filming for one of my television shows. They are much like pizzas and use oversize white corn tortillas as their base. There in southern Mexico, the tortillas are pressed very thin, crisped in a wood-fired oven, then removed and spread with cheese and any number of toppings. Next they're put back in the oven to heat through and are served as a tasty appetizer; typically, they are hand-held when eaten.

(photograph opposite)

2 tablespoons (1/4 stick) butter
1 large white onion, thinly sliced
Salt and freshly ground black pepper to taste
1 pound Mexican chorizo sausage meat (or hot Italian sausage) (optional)
4 large Flour Tortillas (12 to 14 inches) (page 184)
1 cup Cilantro-Walnut Pesto (page 20)
8 ounces grated *queso de Oaxaca, queso fresco,* or Monterey Jack cheese

Preheat the oven to 350°F.

To prepare the clayudas, melt the butter in a sauté pan over medium-high heat. Add the onion and sauté for about 7 minutes, until browned and caramelized. Season with salt and pepper, remove from the pan, and set aside. Add the chorizo, if using, to the pan, breaking up the meat with a fork as it cooks.

Meanwhile, place the tortillas in the oven and bake until crisp and light brown, about 5 minutes. Spread a thin layer of Cilantro-Walnut Pesto on each tortilla and top with the onions and chorizo. Sprinkle with the cheese and return to the oven until the cheese melts and the edges brown slightly, about 10 minutes.

SERVES 4

Tortilla Vegetable Napoleon

This may seem like a complicated, time-consuming recipe, but the outcome is a vegetarian dream. It's a delicious dish that proves what complex flavors vegetables alone can produce. Traditionally, Napoleons are rectangular desserts made with layers of puff pastry and a pastry cream filling, but there is nothing to stop you from making innovative and arresting savory Napoleons like these. You can save some time by substituting mayonnaise or another dressing for the Smoked Tomato Aioli.

FOR THE WHITE BEAN PUREE
- 1 cup cooked white beans (page 213)
- 1 tablespoon white sesame seeds, toasted and ground (page 211)
- 1 teaspoon cumin seeds, toasted and ground (page 211)
- 1/4 onion, chopped
- 1 1/2 cups Vegetable Stock (page 211) or store-bought
- 1/3 cup roasted garlic puree (page 203)

Salt to taste

FOR THE NAPOLEONS
- 2 eggplants (about 10 ounces each), ends sliced off

Salt to taste
- 3 large carrots, peeled
- 4 new potatoes (about 3 ounces each), sliced
- 3 tablespoons chopped fresh cilantro leaves
- 3 tablespoons chopped fresh basil leaves
- 1 tablespoon chopped fresh rosemary leaves
- 2 tablespoons chopped fresh thyme leaves
- 1/4 cup roasted garlic puree (page 203)
- 1/4 cup Red Chile-Canela Oil (page 26)
- 2 small zucchini, ends sliced off and each zucchini cut lengthwise into 4 "planks"
- 1 red bell pepper, seeded and cut lengthwise into quarters

To prepare the bean puree, place the beans, sesame seeds, cumin seeds, onion, and stock in a saucepan and bring to a boil. Reduce the heat and simmer for 20 to 30 minutes, until very soft.

Strain the beans, reserving the liquid. Transfer the beans to a food processor, and add the garlic and just enough of the reserved bean liquid to make pureeing possible. Puree until smooth and season with salt. If the beans seem too thin, place in a small saucepan over high heat, stirring constantly, until they thicken.

Preheat the oven to 400°F.

To prepare the Napoleons, cut the eggplants in half lengthwise and then cut crosswise into 1/2-inch slices. Place on a baking sheet lined with paper towels, sprinkle both sides with salt, and let sit for 20 minutes. Transfer the eggplant to a colander, rinse briefly under cold water to remove the salt, and pat dry thoroughly with paper towels.

Cut the carrots in half lengthwise and then cut crosswise into 2-inch slices. Place in a large mixing bowl, add the potatoes and eggplant, season with salt, and combine. Mix the cilantro, basil, rosemary, and thyme in a small bowl and add one quarter of the mixture to the vegetables. Add 1 tablespoon of the roasted garlic and 1 tablespoon of the red chile oil. Transfer the mixture to a baking sheet and roast in the oven for 10 minutes. Remove from the oven and reduce the oven temperature to 325°F. In a bowl, combine the zucchini, bell peppers, poblano, tomatoes, artichokes, and the remaining herbs, garlic, and red chile oil. Season with freshly ground black pepper and add to the baking sheet. Roast the vegetables for 30 minutes longer, until tender. Remove from the oven, sprinkle the olives over the vegetables, and set aside.

1 yellow bell pepper, seeded and cut lengthwise into quarters
1 poblano chile, seeded and cut lengthwise into quarters
3 large ripe tomatoes (about 6 ounces each), cut into 1/2-inch slices
3 artichoke bottoms, blanched and sliced (page 205)
Freshly ground black pepper to taste
1/2 cup chopped pitted black olives

3 cups vegetable oil, for frying
18 Corn Tortillas (6 inches across) (page 182)
1 cup Smoked Tomato Aioli (page 25)

Meanwhile, in a saucepan over high heat, heat the vegetable oil until lightly smoking. Cut each tortilla into 3-inch squares and fry them in the oil until crispy, about 3 minutes. Remove from the oil, drain on paper towels, and season with salt.

Spread about 1½ tablespoons of the white bean puree evenly over 6 of the tortilla squares. Cover the puree with the mixed, roasted vegetables. Repeat this for 6 more tortillas and place them in a layer on top of each of the first 6 tortilla squares. Place the remaining 6 tortilla squares on top to create a Napoleon. Serve with the aioli.

SERVES 6

CHAPTER ELEVEN
ONE-DISH
MAIN COURSES

Three-Bean Cassoulet with Roasted Garlic

Along with coq au vin, cassoulet was one of the French dishes that fascinated me most and drew me to cooking on a professional level. I once sped along an autoroute in the south of France at over 100 miles per hour with fellow gastronomes Madeleine Kamman and Michael Bauer to reach the medieval town of Carcassonne in time for cassoulet! Although this version contains no pork or duck, it maintains the integrity of the original recipe with its hearty, soulful flavors. To save time, use regular, unsmoked onions in this recipe.

FOR THE CASSOULET

- 7 cups boiling Vegetable Stock (page 211) or store-bought
- 3 tablespoons olive oil
- 2 onions, diced and smoked (page 209)
- 1 jalapeño chile, seeded and diced
- 1 carrot, peeled and diced
- 1 celery stalk, diced
- 2 red bell peppers, seeded and diced
- 1 cup dried white beans, soaked overnight and drained
- 1 cup pinto or kidney beans, soaked overnight and drained
- 1 cup black-eyed peas, soaked overnight and drained
- 4 Roma tomatoes, blanched, peeled, seeded, and diced (page 203)
- 2 tablespoons ancho chile puree (page 206)
- 1/3 cup roasted garlic puree (page 203)
- 1 tablespoon chopped fresh thyme leaves
- 1 teaspoon chopped fresh sage leaves
- 1 teaspoon chopped fresh oregano leaves
- 2 slices day-old bread
- 2 tablespoons (1/4 stick) unsalted butter
- Salt and freshly ground black pepper to taste

Preheat the oven to 350°F.

To prepare the cassoulet, bring the stock to a boil in a stockpot, and then reduce to a simmer. Meanwhile, in a Dutch oven or oven-proof casserole, heat the olive oil over high heat until lightly smoking. Add the onions, jalapeño, carrot, and celery and sauté for 3 minutes, or until the onions are translucent. Add the bell peppers and sauté for 1 minute longer. Add the white and red beans and the black-eyed peas to the pan. Pour in 5 cups of the stock, keeping the remaining 2 cups hot.

Cover the pan and transfer to the oven. Check the beans every 20 minutes and add additional stock to keep the liquid level with the top of the beans. After 30 minutes of cooking time, stir in the tomatoes, ancho puree, roasted garlic puree, thyme, sage, and oregano. Continue cooking for 45 minutes longer, checking the liquid and adding more stock as needed.

Meanwhile, place the bread on a cookie sheet and toast in the oven for 20 minutes, or until it begins to turn brown. Remove from the oven and let cool. Roughly break up the bread, transfer to a food processor, and pulse for 1 minute, until well broken up. Continue pulsing for 2 to 3 minutes, or until the crumbs are of an even consistency (you will need 1/2 cup of bread crumbs). Fold the bread crumbs and the butter into the bean mixture and cook for 15 minutes longer, or until the beans are tender. Remove from the oven and let sit for 10 minutes at room temperature. Season with salt and pepper and serve.

SERVES 4 TO 6

Roasted Vegetable Sakowil with Griddled Tomato-Chipotle Salsa

The sakowil is a gargantuan tamale indigenous to the Gulf state of Veracruz in Mexico. It is usually prepared for fiestas, large family gatherings, and traditional holidays such as the Day of the Dead. Typically, everything from turkey to duck to pork is hidden in rich masa dough and covered with huge banana leaves, wrapped in chicken wire, and cooked in a communal adobe oven somewhere in the village. This version is just as flavorful, even without all the protein. This recipe also makes a festive dish for a buffet.

FOR THE FILLING

- ¼ cup extra-virgin olive oil
- 2 tablespoons roasted garlic puree (page 203)
- 2 tablespoons pure red chile powder
- 1 teaspoon ground cumin
- ¼ teaspoon cayenne
- 2 tablespoons chopped fresh oregano
- 2 tablespoons chopped fresh cilantro leaves
- 2 purple Peruvian potatoes (about 6 ounces each), diced
- 2 small red-skinned potatoes (about 3 ounces each), diced
- 1 sweet potato (about 1 pound), peeled and diced
- 1 carrot, peeled and diced
- Salt to taste
- 1 red onion, diced
- 1 zucchini, diced
- 1 yellow squash, diced
- 1 eggplant (10 to 12 ounces), diced
- 1 red bell pepper, seeded and diced
- 1 yellow bell pepper, seeded and diced
- 1 poblano chile, seeded and diced

Preheat the oven to 350°F.

In a bowl, combine the olive oil, garlic puree, chile powder, cumin, cayenne, oregano, and cilantro. Whisk together and set aside. In a large mixing bowl, combine the three types of potatoes and the carrot, pour in half of the oil and garlic mixture, and toss to coat. Season with salt and transfer the potatoes and carrot to a large cookie sheet. Bake in the oven for 30 minutes, stirring after 15 minutes. Remove from the oven and keep refrigerated until cool.

In the same large mixing bowl, combine the onion, zucchini, yellow squash, eggplant, bell peppers, and poblano. Pour the remaining half of the oil and garlic mixture over the vegetables and toss to coat. Season with salt and transfer to a large cookie sheet. Bake in the oven for 25 minutes, stirring after 15 minutes. Remove from the oven and keep refrigerated.

To prepare the masa dough, place the masa harina in the bowl of an electric mixer fitted with a paddle attachment. With the machine on low speed, add the hot water in a slow, steady stream until the dough forms a ball. Increase the speed to medium and continue mixing for 5 minutes. Transfer the dough to a clean bowl and refrigerate for 1 hour.

Return the masa to the bowl of the electric mixer and beat for 5 minutes on high speed. With the machine running, slowly add the shortening 2 tablespoons at a time. Continue mixing for 5 minutes longer, until the dough is smooth and light. Stop the mixer and scrape down the sides of the bowl with a spatula. Reduce the speed to low and continue beating.

FOR THE MASA DOUGH

3¹/₂ cups masa harina

2¹/₂ cups hot water

1¹/₄ cups chilled vegetable
shortening

1 tablespoon salt

2 teaspoons baking powder

¹/₂ cup chilled Vegetable Stock
(page 211) or store-bought

3 large banana leaves (12 by
24 inches)

4 cups Griddled Tomato-
Chipotle Salsa (page 32)

While the dough is mixing, combine the salt, baking powder, and stock in a small mixing bowl. Slowly add the stock mixture to the masa in a steady stream and continue mixing until thoroughly combined. Increase the speed to high and mix for 5 minutes longer. Fold in the cooled vegetables and set aside.

Reheat the oven to 275°F.

Holding the banana leaves with tongs, wilt the leaves over a gas or electric burner until soft and pliable but not brittle; take care not to tear the leaves during this process. Place the leaves on a work surface and make a six-pointed star, with the centers of the leaves overlapping. Place the vegetable masa in the center and form into a 3-inch-thick circle. Carefully fold the leaves over in order and tuck them underneath the bottom; the masa should be completely enclosed. Carefully transfer to a rack and place the rack in a large roasting pan. Pour in enough water to cover the bottom of the roasting pan but not touching the sakowil. Cover loosely with foil and bake for 2 hours, or until a long skewer inserted in the center comes out clean.

Carefully transfer the sakowil to a large serving platter, cut an X in the top with a sharp knife, and pull back the leaves. Serve with the Griddled Tomato-Chipotle Salsa.

SERVES 6 TO 8

Southwestern Vegetable Paella

Paella is the classic Spanish dish containing rice flavored and colored with saffron, shellfish, meats, and vegetables. It's named after the special large pan in which authentic paella is cooked and served. Some visitors to Spain are surprised that it's hard to find paella for dinner; there, it is normally considered a lunch dish. Jambalaya, the delicious dish from our "next door neighbors" in Louisiana, is a derivative of paella, and this version gives the Spanish original a Southwestern twist with the addition of fresh and dried chiles.

(photograph opposite)

2	tablespoons olive oil
1	onion, diced
4	garlic cloves, minced
1	teaspoon paprika
1	cup freshly shelled peas
1/2	cup green beans, cut into 1/2-inch lengths
1/2	cup fresh corn kernels
1/2	cup diced carrots
1	red bell pepper, seeded and diced
1	poblano chile, seeded and diced
2	Roma tomatoes, blanched, peeled, seeded, and diced (page 203)
1	tablespoon chipotle chile puree (page 206)
2	dried bay leaves
2 1/2	cups long-grain white rice
12	saffron threads, very finely minced with a knife
6	cups boiling Vegetable Stock (page 211) or store-bought
2	tablespoons chopped fresh parsley leaves
1	tablespoon chopped fresh thyme leaves
6	artichoke bottoms, blanched and sliced (page 205)
	Salt and freshly ground black pepper to taste
2	lemons, cut into wedges
8	sprigs of parsley

In a paella pan or large sauté pan, heat the olive oil over high heat until lightly smoking. Add the onion and sauté for 4 minutes, or until the onion just starts to brown. Add the garlic and sauté for 1 minute longer. Add the paprika, peas, beans, corn, carrots, bell pepper, poblano, and tomatoes and cook for 4 minutes, or until the vegetables just start to soften and release their juices. Add the chipotle puree, bay leaves, rice, and saffron and stir to combine. Bring the stock to a boil, add to the pan, and reduce the heat to a simmer. Stir again, cover, and simmer for 20 minutes.

Stir in the parsley, thyme, and artichokes. Season with salt and pepper and cook for 5 minutes longer, or until the rice is tender but not mushy. Serve in the pan, garnished with lemon wedges and parsley sprigs.

SERVES 4 TO 6

Vegetable–Pinto Bean Chili with Pico Sour Cream

I grew up in west Texas in an extended family where all the men knew how to prepare excellent spicy chili. Each crowned himself the chili king of the world, such was the passion and pride involved. Now, this vegetarian version might not pass muster with some of those die-hard chili aficionados, but to my palate, this vegetarian recipe yields results that are every bit as satisfying as chili made with meat.

FOR THE PICO SOUR CREAM

- 2 small ripe Roma tomatoes, seeded and chopped
- 1/2 tablespoon chopped fresh cilantro leaves
- 1 small garlic clove, minced
- 3 tablespoons minced onion
- 2 teaspoons freshly squeezed lime juice
- 1 small jalapeño chile, seeded and minced
- 1/2 cup sour cream

FOR THE CHILI

- 2 tablespoons olive oil
- 1 onion, diced
- 4 garlic cloves, minced
- 2 teaspoons ground cumin
- 1 poblano chile, seeded and diced
- 1 jalapeño chile, seeded and diced
- 2 red bell peppers, seeded and diced
- 1/4 cup ancho chile puree (page 206)
- 2 canned chipotle chiles in adobo sauce, chopped
- 4 tomatoes, blanched, peeled, seeded, and diced (page 203)
- 4 cups Vegetable Stock (page 211) or store-bought
- 1 12-ounce bottle dark beer
- 2 cups dried pinto beans, soaked overnight and drained
- 2 tablespoons masa harina
- 1 tablespoon chopped fresh cilantro leaves
- 1 tablespoon chopped fresh oregano leaves

To prepare the Pico Sour Cream, place the tomatoes, cilantro, garlic, onion, lime juice, chile, and sour cream in a mixing bowl, add salt to taste, and stir to combine. Keep refrigerated (this will keep in the refrigerator for up to 3 days).

To prepare the chili, heat the olive oil in a large saucepan over high heat until lightly smoking. Add the onion and sauté for about 4 minutes, or until the onion begins to brown. Add the garlic and cumin and sauté for 1 minute longer, or until the cumin is fragrant. Add the poblano, jalapeño, and bell peppers and sauté for 2 minutes longer. Add the ancho puree, chipotles, tomatoes, stock, beer, and beans, bring to a boil, and then reduce the heat to a simmer. Cook for 1 1/2 to 2 hours, stirring occasionally, or until the beans are tender. Add more stock as necessary throughout the cooking process to keep the beans covered.

Gently whisk in the masa harina, cilantro, and oregano, cook for 5 minutes longer, and then season with salt to taste. Serve with a generous spoonful of Pico Sour Cream over each serving.

SERVES 4

Eggplant–Roasted Garlic Curry with Lentils

Curry is derived from the Indian word for "sauce," *kari,* and it refers to any number of stews made with curry powder. Authentic Indian curry powder is ground daily and the mix of spices varies from region to region, as well as from cook to cook. Although up to twenty ingredients can be pulverized together to make curry powder, a good representation would include cardamom, cinnamon, cloves, mace, tamarind, dried chiles, turmeric, coriander, cumin, and fennel seed. Use good-quality curry powder and try to make sure it is fresh by purchasing it from a store with high turnover (the same is true for the lentils). Serve this dish with long-grain rice, preferably the aromatic Indian basmati variety.

2 large eggplants (10 to 12 ounces each), ends sliced off
1 teaspoon salt
1 teaspoon ground turmeric
6 tablespoons vegetable oil
1/2 onion, diced
1 carrot, diced
1 celery stalk, diced
1 jalapeño chile, seeded and diced
1 tablespoon curry powder
1/2 cup Marsala wine
1/2 cup dried red lentils, picked through and rinsed
1 1/2 cups Vegetable Stock (page 211) or store-bought
1/4 cup roasted garlic puree (page 203)
1/2 cup canned unsweetened coconut milk
1 cup Pineapple–Green Chile Chutney (page 39)

Cut the eggplants into 1-inch cubes, place in a mixing bowl, and sprinkle with the salt and turmeric. In a large saucepan, heat 4 tablespoons of the vegetable oil until lightly smoking. Add the seasoned eggplant to the pan and sauté over medium-high heat for 10 minutes, stirring occasionally. Remove from the heat and transfer the eggplant to a cookie sheet lined with paper towels. Set aside.

Meanwhile, in another large saucepan, heat the remaining 2 tablespoons of oil until lightly smoking. Add the onion, carrot, celery, and jalapeño and sauté for 4 minutes. Add the curry powder and sauté for 2 minutes longer, or until fragrant. Add the Marsala and reduce for 3 minutes, or until the mixture is almost dry. Add the lentils and stock and bring to a boil. Reduce the heat to a simmer and cook for 15 minutes, or until the lentils are tender.

Stir in the roasted garlic, coconut milk, and the reserved eggplant. Cook for 5 minutes, or until the eggplant is warmed through. Season with salt and top with the Pineapple–Green Chile Chutney.

SERVES 4

Sweet Potato Chilaquiles with Griddled Salsa Roja

Chilaquiles, the ever-popular Mexican casserole, was created to use up stale tortillas. Made with a good sauce, the tortillas come back to life, take on all the flavors, and provide a wonderful textural contrast. Although chilaquiles are usually prepared casserole style, I have seen them made to order with scrambled eggs and chorizo. I particularly enjoy chilaquiles as a brunch item served with margaritas, chilled Mexican beer, or a hearty sangria.

(photograph opposite)

2 small onions
¼ cup red wine vinegar or fruit vinegar
1½ cups sour cream
½ cup whole milk
Vegetable oil, for frying
12 Corn Tortillas (page 182)
1½ cups Vegetable Stock (page 211) or store-bought
8 tomatillos, husked, rinsed, and quartered
2 jalapeño chiles, seeded and chopped
1 garlic clove, chopped
½ cup chopped fresh cilantro leaves
Salt to taste
1 tablespoon vegetable shortening or vegetable oil
1 sweet potato (about 12 ounces), peeled and finely diced
½ cup grated Monterey Jack cheese
2 poblano chiles, roasted, peeled, seeded, and diced
1 cup Griddled Tomato-Chipotle Salsa (page 32)

Slice one onion into very thin strips. Combine with the vinegar in a bowl and set aside. Chop the other onion coarsely and set aside. In a mixing bowl, whisk the sour cream and milk together.

In a large skillet, pour enough vegetable oil to come ¼ inch up the sides. Heat the oil over medium heat until lightly smoking. Fry the tortillas, 1 or 2 at a time (or as many as will fit in the pan), just until crisp, about 1 minute. (You may need to add a little more oil for the last few tortillas.) Drain on paper towels.

Place the stock in a saucepan and bring to a boil. Add the tomatillos and cook until tender, about 6 minutes; drain, reserving the stock. Place the tomatillos, jalapeños, chopped onion, garlic, and cilantro in a blender or food processor and blend until smooth. Season with salt.

In a large skillet over medium heat, heat the vegetable shortening until lightly smoking. Pour in the tomatillo mixture and stir constantly for about 5 minutes, until thick and dark. Add the reserved stock and bring to a boil. Reduce the heat and simmer for 8 to 10 minutes; the sauce should be thick enough to coat the back of a spoon. Meanwhile, preheat the oven to 350°F.

Add the sweet potato to a saucepan of boiling salted water and blanch for 3 minutes, or until tender. Drain and refresh in ice water to stop the cooking process.

Line an 8-inch square baking pan with 3 tortillas; they will overlap slightly. Pour one quarter of the tomatillo sauce on top, and pour one quarter of the sour cream–milk mixture on top of the sauce. Top with one quarter of the cheese, and place a third of the poblanos and sweet potatoes over the cheese. Repeat the process with the remaining tortillas, sauce, sour cream mixture, and cheese; the top layer will not have poblanos or sweet potato.

Cover the baking pan with foil and bake for 30 minutes, or until the cheese is melted and bubbly. Remove and top with the drained marinated onions. Serve with the salsa.

SERVES 8 TO 10

Sweet-and-Sour Red Cabbage with Apples and Cider Vinegar

Just reading the ingredient list for this recipe makes me long for autumn, probably my favorite season for cooking. The flavors of this dish are particularly complemented by pork, so if you choose not to stick to strict vegetarian recipes, try a couple of slices of diced smoked bacon sautéed with the onion and cabbage. Alternatively, serve this dish with a pork loin or chop, chicken, or even an assertively flavored fish such as salmon.

2 tablespoons olive oil

1 red onion, diced

1 head of red cabbage, outer leaves removed, cabbage cored and julienned

1 jalapeño chile, seeded and julienned

1 red bell pepper, seeded and julienned

1/2 teaspoon ground cumin

1 teaspoon ground coriander

1 cup cider vinegar

1/2 cup light brown sugar, loosely packed

2 green apples, such as Granny Smith or Pippin, peeled, cored, and diced

3 tablespoons chopped fresh cilantro leaves

1 tablespoon chopped fresh oregano leaves

Salt to taste

In a large saucepan, heat the olive oil over high heat until lightly smoking. Add the onion, cabbage, jalapeño, red pepper, cumin, and coriander and sauté for 5 minutes, or until the vegetables begin to release their juices. Add 1/2 cup water and the vinegar, bring to a boil, and reduce the liquid for 5 minutes, or until almost dry. Add the sugar and stir until dissolved. Reduce the heat to medium-low and let simmer for 10 minutes. Add the apples, cilantro, and oregano and cook for 4 minutes longer, or until the apples are just tender. Season with salt and serve.

SERVES 4

Asparagus, Artichokes, and Peppers Sautéed in Red Chile–Canela Oil

This springtime recipe is light and refreshing but delivers a pleasing "afterglow" from the red chile oil. Add some diced black olives to the stir-fry if you like; for an even more complete course, add a sturdy green such as watercress or arugula. Serve this dish on its own, with any grilled fish or chicken, or try it for brunch topped with poached eggs.

2 tablespoons Red Chile–Canela Oil (page 26) or store-bought

8 ounces asparagus, bottoms trimmed by 1 inch and cut on a sharp bias into 1-inch lengths

6 artichoke bottoms, blanched (page 205) and very finely sliced

1 small yellow onion, thinly sliced

2 garlic cloves, minced

1 red bell pepper, seeded and julienned

1 yellow bell pepper, seeded and julienned

1 poblano chile, seeded and julienned

1 tablespoon toasted white sesame seeds (page 211)

1 tablespoon toasted black sesame seeds (page 211)

2 tablespoons chopped fresh cilantro leaves

Minced zest and juice of 1 lemon

Salt to taste

In a wok or saucepan over high heat, heat the oil until lightly smoking. Carefully swirl the oil to coat the wok. Add the asparagus and stir-fry for 2 minutes. Add the artichokes, onion, garlic, red and yellow peppers, and poblanos and stir-fry for 4 to 5 minutes longer. Add the white and black sesame seeds, the cilantro, and the zest and juice of the lemon. Stir to deglaze the pan until the liquid is evaporated. Season with salt and serve immediately.

SERVES 4

Grilled Summer Vegetables with Lemon Zest Aioli

There is something satisfyingly simple about preparing a meal on the backyard grill in the summer. Grilling vegetables produces a rich, smoky flavor that is unique among cooking styles and techniques. I like to take advantage of the effort of preparing a fire in the grill by cooking as much as possible for later use. For example, vegetables, beef, and chicken can be grilled for delicious salads or even reheated in the oven for main meals with much of the same flavor as when they are fresh off the grill.   *(photograph opposite)*

FOR THE LEMON ZEST AIOLI

- 2 cups Mayonnaise (page 212) or store-bought
- 1/4 cup roasted garlic puree (page 203)
- 2 tablespoons minced lemon zest

FOR THE VEGETABLES

- 3 tablespoons freshly squeezed lime juice
- 3 tablespoons extra-virgin olive oil
- 3 tablespoons unsalted butter, melted
- 3 tablespoons chopped fresh cilantro leaves
- 1 tablespoon pure red chile powder
- 1/4 teaspoon cayenne
- 1 red bell pepper, seeded and quartered lengthwise
- 1 yellow bell pepper, seeded and quartered lengthwise
- 1 poblano chile, seeded and quartered lengthwise
- 1 zucchini, cut on the bias into 1/2-inch-thick rounds
- 1 yellow squash, cut on the bias into 1/2-inch-thick rounds
- 1 large red onion, cut into 1/2-inch-thick rounds
- 2 ears of shucked corn, each cut crosswise into 4 rounds
- 1 large eggplant, cut into 1-inch-thick rounds
- 2 large portobello mushrooms, quartered

Prepare the grill. To prepare the aioli, whisk together the mayonnaise, garlic puree, and lemon zest. Keep refrigerated.

To prepare the vegetables, in a mixing bowl, whisk together the lime juice, olive oil, melted butter, cilantro, chile powder, cayenne, and salt and pepper to taste. In a separate large mixing bowl, place the red and yellow peppers, poblano, zucchini, yellow squash, onion, corn, eggplant, and mushrooms and add the lime juice mixture. Toss carefully to coat all of the vegetables.

Place the vegetables on the grill and cook until tender, about 5 to 7 minutes. Season with additional salt as the vegetables come off the grill, if desired. Serve on a large platter; drizzle with the aioli or serve it as a dip.

SERVES 4 TO 6

Glazed Turnips and Bok Choy Scented with Lemongrass

Although turnips are available year-round, they are at their best from October through February. Turnips are closely related to radishes and cabbage, and they were known to have been cultivated by the Greeks and Romans. Bok choy is a mild type of Chinese cabbage that resembles Swiss chard, with large white ribs and flavorful dark green leaves. It takes well to stir-frying. The Asian flavors in this dish are further enhanced by the sesame oil and lemongrass, which is one of the most common seasonings in the cuisines of southeast Asia (and especially Thailand). This dish needs only steamed white rice to make it a full meal.

2 pounds baby turnips (about 30) or regular turnips (about 6), cut into chunks
2 tablespoons sesame oil
1 onion, finely sliced
2 garlic cloves, minced
1 serrano chile, minced, with seeds
1½ pounds bok choy
1 large carrot, peeled and julienned
4 stalks lemongrass, bruised and cut in half
2 tablespoons sugar
¼ cup champagne vinegar or rice wine vinegar
Salt and freshly ground black pepper to taste

Bring a saucepan of salted water to a boil and blanch the turnips for 8 minutes. Drain and set aside.

In a wok over high heat, heat the sesame oil until lightly smoking. Add the onion and sauté for 2 minutes, or until just golden brown. Add the garlic and chile and sauté for 1 more minute. Add the bok choy, carrot, turnips, lemongrass, and sugar and continue to sauté for 6 minutes, or until the sugar begins to turn brown. Add the vinegar and cook for 2 minutes longer, or until the vinegar has almost completely evaporated. Remove the lemongrass and discard. Season with salt and pepper and serve.

SERVES 4

Grilled Eggplant and Fennel with Hazelnut Oil Vinaigrette

Eggplant, botanically a fruit, develops a fuller flavor when grilled. Fennel, a vegetable native to the Mediterranean, is also wonderful grilled because its anise flavors are intensified. Fennel and hazelnuts have a natural affinity for each other, so you will appreciate their complementary flavors. Try the vinaigrette with your favorite greens for an enjoyable salad.

FOR THE EGGPLANT AND FENNEL

- 1 eggplant (10 to 12 ounces), cut into 1/2-inch-thick rounds
- 2 fennel bulbs (tops removed), cut lengthwise into 1/2-inch-thick slices
- 5 tablespoons vegetable oil or olive oil

Salt and freshly ground black pepper to taste

FOR THE HAZELNUT OIL VINAIGRETTE

- 2 tablespoons chopped fresh parsley leaves
- 2 tablespoons chopped fresh basil leaves
- 3 tablespoons sherry vinegar
- 2 tablespoons minced red onion
- 3/4 cup hazelnut oil
- 1 ripe Roma tomato, seeded and finely diced
- 1/2 cup toasted chopped hazelnuts (page 211)

Salt to taste

Prepare the grill.

In a large mixing bowl, place the eggplant and fennel slices and pour in the vegetable oil. Before placing on the grill, sprinkle both sides of the vegetable slices with salt and pepper. Grill over medium heat for about 5 minutes per side for the eggplant and 8 minutes per side for the fennel, or until tender. Remove from the grill and let cool to room temperature.

Meanwhile, to prepare the vinaigrette, combine the parsley, basil, vinegar, and onion in a mixing bowl. While whisking slowly, drizzle in the hazelnut oil. Set aside.

When the eggplant and fennel are cooled, cut into dice and transfer to a mixing bowl. Add the tomato and hazelnuts, and then add the vinaigrette. Toss well to coat the vegetables and season with salt. Serve at room temperature.

SERVES 4

CHAPTER TWELVE
BREAKFAST
AND BRUNCH

Apple-Canela Pancakes with Red Chile Honey

Apples and canela (or cinnamon) is a pairing found around the world (for notes on canela, see page 217). There's another distinctly Southwestern spin put on this dish with the delicious drizzle of red chile honey, which is also wonderful simply poured over fresh fruit such as melons and pineapple. The addition of egg whites makes these pancakes fluffy and light.

FOR THE RED CHILE HONEY

- 1 cup honey
- 1 tablespoon dried red pepper flakes or 1 chile de arbol, crushed

FOR THE PANCAKES

- 1 1/2 cups all-purpose flour
- 2 teaspoons baking powder
- 1 tablespoon ground canela or 1/2 tablespoon cinnamon
- Pinch of salt
- 5 tablespoons unsalted butter
- 1 1/4 cups milk
- 2 large eggs, separated
- 1 teaspoon pure vanilla extract
- 2 Granny Smith apples, peeled, cored, and diced

- 2 cups whipped cream

Combine the honey and red pepper flakes in a saucepan and bring to a boil. Remove from the heat and let sit for at least 1 hour. Pass through a fine-mesh sieve and return to the heat. Serve warm.

To prepare the pancakes, sift together the flour, baking powder, canela, and salt in a mixing bowl. Melt 2 tablespoons of the butter and place in another mixing bowl. Add the milk, egg yolks, and vanilla and whisk together. Add this mixture to the dry ingredients and stir until just combined. Set aside.

In a separate mixing bowl, whip the egg whites until they form stiff peaks. Add one third of the egg whites to the batter and stir in. Fold in the remaining two thirds of the egg whites and gently fold in the apples.

Heat a large nonstick skillet over medium heat. When a drop of water sizzles in the skillet, add 1 tablespoon of the remaining butter. When melted completely, ladle 1/4 cup of batter into the pan. Repeat until the pan is full of pancakes. Cook each pancake until bubbles form and pop on the surface and the edges start to look dry, about 2 minutes. Carefully flip each pancake and cook until browned on the other side, about 1 1/2 minutes longer. Keep warm. Repeat until all of the batter is used. Serve 2 pancakes per person with the Red Chile Honey and whipped cream.

SERVES 4

MAKES 8 PANCAKES

Artichoke–Queso Fresco Omelet

This omelet makes the perfect springtime breakfast or brunch item, especially when served with grilled or roasted seasonal asparagus. I particularly enjoy this dish with the Cherry Tomato–Mozzarella Relish (page 36). Remember, omelets take practice, and you can always serve Artichoke–Queso Fresco Scrambled Eggs rather than omelets and still impress people!

6 artichoke bottoms, blanched and diced (page 205)

4 Roma tomatoes, seeded and diced

$2/3$ cup grated *queso fresco,* or feta cheese

$1/4$ cup chopped fresh chives

Juice of 1 lemon

Salt

8 large eggs

$1/4$ cup heavy cream

$1/4$ cup ($1/2$ stick) unsalted butter

In a mixing bowl, combine the artichokes, tomatoes, cheese, chives, and lemon juice. Season with salt and set aside. In another mixing bowl, whisk together the eggs, cream, and 1 teaspoon salt.

Heat a nonstick 9-inch omelet pan over medium-high heat for 2 minutes. Add 1 tablespoon of the butter and, when it stops bubbling, add one quarter of the egg mixture. Cook for 10 seconds (do not stir). Then swirl the center of the eggs with a heat-resistant spatula, gathering them toward the center of the pan. When the bottom of the omelet is set and the top is still creamy and shiny, add one quarter of the artichoke mixture. Carefully loosen the omelet on one side and tip the pan to a 45-degree angle. With the spatula, flip the omelet in half and carefully transfer to a warm serving plate; keep warm. Repeat for the remaining 3 omelets and serve.

SERVES 4

Three-Tomato–Grilled Onion Omelet

I often use a combination of tomatoes in salsas and salads, as much for visual appeal as for flavor. In this recipe, however, the subtlety of the eggs is the perfect foil to showcase the difference in acidity of the three types of tomato. If grilling is not an option, char the seasoned onions and tomatoes in a hot, dry cast-iron skillet.

2 small red onions, cut into
 ½-inch slices
2 small red tomatoes, cut into
 ½-inch slices
2 small yellow tomatoes, cut into
 ½-inch slices
2 small green tomatoes, cut into
 ½-inch slices
Salt to taste
¼ cup chopped fresh cilantro
 leaves
¼ cup olive oil
8 large eggs
¼ cup heavy cream
¼ cup (½ stick) unsalted butter

Prepare the grill.

Season the onions and the 3 types of tomato with salt and place on the hottest part of the grill. Cook until just tender, removing them once they begin charring, about 3 to 5 minutes. Let cool. Dice the vegetables and transfer to a mixing bowl. Add the cilantro and olive oil and toss to coat. Set aside.

In another mixing bowl, whisk together the eggs, cream, and ½ teaspoon of salt. Heat a nonstick 9-inch omelet pan over medium-high heat for 2 minutes. Add 1 tablespoon of the butter and, when it stops bubbling, add one quarter of the egg mixture. Cook for 10 seconds (do not stir). Then swirl the center of the eggs with a heat-resistant spatula, gathering them toward the center of the pan. When the bottom of the omelet is set and the top is still creamy and shiny, add one quarter of the grilled vegetable mixture. Carefully loosen the omelet on one side and tip the pan to a 45-degree angle. With the spatula, flip the omelet in half and carefully transfer to a warm serving plate; keep warm. Repeat for the remaining 3 omelets and serve.

SERVES 4

Huevos Rancheros with Ancho–Roast Garlic Potatoes

Some mornings in Texas—Sundays in particular—huevos rancheros are a flat-out necessity to get the day started. Ranch-style eggs are a classic Mexican dish, and they have a long history of sustaining ranch hands before they embark on a long and arduous day of ropin' and wranglin'. The rustic potatoes are given a satisfying little kick by the ancho chiles and roasted garlic, and you can use them with all kinds of other dishes. Note that you will have to double the salsa recipe.

(photograph opposite)

FOR THE ANCHO–ROAST GARLIC POTATOES

- 3 baking potatoes (about 1 pound each), peeled and cut into 1-inch dice
- Vegetable oil, for deep-frying
- 1 tablespoon olive oil
- 1 onion, julienned
- 8 cherry tomatoes, cut in half
- 1 tablespoon roasted garlic puree (page 203)
- 1 tablespoon ancho chile puree (page 206)
- 1 tablespoon chopped fresh cilantro leaves
- Salt and freshly ground black pepper to taste

FOR THE HUEVOS RANCHEROS

- 1 cup vegetable oil
- 4 Corn Tortillas (page 182)
- 8 cups Griddled Tomato-Chipotle Salsa (page 32)
- 8 large eggs
- ¼ cup crumbled *queso fresco* or Monterey Jack cheese
- 1 tablespoon chopped fresh cilantro leaves

Preheat the oven to 250°F.

In a large saucepan of boiling water, blanch the potatoes for 15 minutes. Drain well in a colander. In a Dutch oven or large saucepan, pour enough vegetable oil to come 3 inches up the sides and heat to 350°F., or until just smoking. Carefully place the blanched potatoes in the oil and fry over high heat for 4 minutes, or until golden brown. Remove with a slotted spoon and drain on a cookie sheet or platter lined with paper towels. Set aside.

In a large skillet, heat the olive oil until lightly smoking. Add the onion and sauté over medium-high heat for 5 minutes, or until lightly browned and caramelized. Add the tomatoes, garlic, ancho puree, cilantro, and the reserved potatoes and heat through. Season with salt and pepper and keep warm in the oven.

Meanwhile, to prepare the huevos rancheros, pour 1 cup of vegetable oil into a large skillet. Over medium heat, bring the oil to 350°F., or until just smoking. Using tongs, dip each tortilla into the hot oil for 5 seconds, and then drain on a cookie sheet or platter lined with paper towels. Do not stack or overlap the tortillas as they will stick together. Transfer the cookie sheet to the oven to keep the tortillas warm while the eggs are cooking.

In a large sauté pan over medium heat, bring the salsa to a simmer. Crack 4 of the eggs into the salsa and let them sit, undisturbed, for 2 minutes. With a slotted spoon, very carefully turn the eggs over to finish cooking, about 2 minutes. Transfer the eggs to a platter and repeat for the remaining 4 eggs. Carefully return the first 4 eggs to the salsa to reheat slightly.

Arrange a tortilla on each serving plate, place 2 eggs on each tortilla, and top with *queso fresco,* cilantro, and salsa. Serve with the warm potatoes.

SERVES 4

Squash and Green Chile Frittata

Frittatas are an Italian type of omelet in which the ingredients are mixed with the eggs before they are put in the pan rather than being added to the omelet partway during the cooking process. The texture is firmer than that of an omelet as the eggs are cooked longer and more slowly, and because it is finished in the oven or under the broiler. Another difference is that frittatas are round, not half-moon-shaped, as they are not folded over.

6 large eggs
¼ cup half-and-half
Salt
2 tablespoons olive oil
½ onion, diced
2 garlic cloves, minced
1 summer squash or zucchini, cleaned and diced
1 poblano chile, roasted, peeled, seeded, and diced (page 204)
1 red bell pepper, roasted, peeled, seeded, and diced (page 204)
½ cup grated Monterey Jack cheese
1½ cups Tomatillo-Serrano Salsa (page 33)

Preheat the oven to 350°F.

In a mixing bowl, whisk together the eggs, half-and-half, and 2 teaspoons salt. Set aside. In a 12-inch nonstick pan, heat the olive oil until lightly smoking. Add the onion and sauté for 2 minutes. Add the garlic, zucchini, poblano, and bell pepper and sauté for 3 minutes longer. Season with salt and add the egg mixture to the pan, stirring to combine the eggs with the vegetables. Let cook, undisturbed, for 20 seconds. Stir the pan one more time and tilt it to let the uncooked egg mixture cover where the cooked parts have come away from the pan. Sprinkle the cheese over the top and place on the middle rack of the oven. Cook for 5 minutes, or until the top is golden brown and is puffed up slightly.

Remove the pan from the oven and shake vigorously to loosen the frittata (alternatively, carefully loosen on one side and slide a spatula underneath to remove). Slide the frittata onto a warm serving plate and cut like a pizza. Serve immediately with the Tomatillo-Serrano Salsa.

SERVES 4

Homemade Granola with Dried Papaya and Mango

Granola evolved from the so-called hippie health food of the 1960s to very modish mainstream breakfast food during the 1980s as its high-fiber healthfulness became appreciated. Usually consisting of grains, nuts, seeds, and dried fruits, granola is a flavorful and crunchy way to start the day. Homemade is the best way to go, however, as some manufacturers add an excess of sweetener (usually honey) and oil to toast the grain. You can substitute your favorite dried fruit in this recipe, such as dried cherries, bananas, cranberries, or apricots.

2 1/2 cups rolled oats
1/2 cup wheat bran
1/2 cup dried shredded coconut
1/2 cup chopped pecans
1/2 cup sunflower seeds
1/2 cup diced dried papaya
1/2 cup diced dried mango
1/2 cup golden raisins
1 teaspoon minced lime zest
1/4 cup pumpkin seeds
1/4 cup honey
2 teaspoons corn syrup
1/2 cup (1 stick) unsalted butter
1/2 cup light brown sugar, loosely packed
1 vanilla bean, split in half lengthwise and seeds scraped
2 teaspoons ground canela or 1 teaspoon ground cinnamon
1/4 teaspoon grated nutmeg
1/4 teaspoon ground allspice
1/4 teaspoon salt

Preheat the oven to 325°F.

In a large mixing bowl, combine the oats, wheat bran, coconut, pecans, sunflower seeds, papaya, mango, raisins, lime zest, and pumpkin seeds. In a small saucepan, combine the honey, corn syrup, butter, sugar, vanilla bean and seeds, canela, nutmeg, allspice, and salt and bring to a simmer. Remove the vanilla bean and pour the mixture over the dry ingredients in the mixing bowl. Using a wooden spoon, toss the dry ingredients until completely coated with the honey mixture.

Grease a 9 by 12-inch baking dish and add the granola in an even layer. Place in the oven and bake for 30 minutes; every 10 minutes or so, open the oven and stir the granola to ensure even browning. Remove from the oven and return to the mixing bowl. Toss to combine and let cool; the mixture will become crunchy as it cools. Break the granola into bite-size pieces. Serve like cereal or with yogurt and fresh fruit.

SERVES 4 TO 6

Banana-Pecan Waffles with Rum-Raisin Syrup

As anyone from the Caribbean will tell you, rum and bananas are one of the classic flavor combinations. In this recipe, the addition of pecans brings the recipe by way of the South, where some of the very best pecans are grown—especially, of course, in Texas. There is simply something indulgent about eating waffles with lots of butter and syrup for a lazy Sunday morning brunch.

(photograph opposite)

FOR THE RUM-RAISIN SYRUP

½ cup dark rum
¼ cup raisins
¼ cup (½ stick) unsalted butter
2 tablespoons light brown sugar, loosely packed
1 tablespoon dark corn syrup
Pinch of ground allspice
Pinch of salt

FOR THE BANANA-PECAN WAFFLES

2 cups all-purpose flour
2 tablespoons light brown sugar, loosely packed
1 teaspoon baking powder
½ teaspoon ground canela or ¼ teaspoon cinnamon
Pinch of salt
2 cups milk
2 large eggs, separated
¼ cup (½ stick) unsalted butter, softened
½ cup toasted chopped pecans (page 211)
1 banana, peeled and diced

To prepare the syrup, combine the rum and raisins in a small saucepan and bring to a boil. Remove from the heat and let sit for 30 minutes. When ready to serve, return the rum and raisins to a simmer and add ½ cup water, the butter, sugar, corn syrup, allspice, and salt. Whisk to combine, remove from the heat, and serve immediately.

Meanwhile, preheat and lightly butter a waffle iron. In a mixing bowl, whisk together the flour, sugar, baking powder, canela, and salt. Set aside.

In another mixing bowl, whisk together the milk, egg yolks, and butter. Pour into the dry ingredients and stir until just smooth. In a separate bowl, whip the egg whites until they form stiff peaks. Stir one third of the egg whites into the batter and then fold in the remaining egg whites. Gently fold in the pecans and diced banana.

Pour enough batter into the waffle iron to fill the bottom. Close the iron and cook over high heat for about 3 minutes, or until steam stops escaping. Carefully open the waffle iron and check to make sure the waffles are fully cooked and golden brown. Serve with Rum-Raisin Syrup.

SERVES 4

Breakfast Tacos with Black Bean Refrito

Also called *migas* in Texas, these tacos are standard fare on restaurant brunch menus around the state and in many parts of the Southwest. The black bean refrito offers the dish a new dimension, and even though it makes a good addition to almost any vegetarian meal, it is also terrific simply served with chips and salsa.

FOR THE BLACK BEAN REFRITO

- 6 cups Vegetable Stock (page 211) or store-bought
- 1/2 cup red wine, such as Burgundy or Cabernet
- 1 cup black beans, soaked overnight and drained
- 1/2 cup chopped onion
- 2 garlic cloves, minced
- 3 tablespoons olive oil
- 3 Pickled Jalapeños (page 17), seeded and diced

Salt to taste

- 2 tablespoons chopped fresh cilantro leaves

FOR THE BREAKFAST TACOS

- 8 large eggs
- 3/4 teaspoon salt
- 2 tablespoons olive oil
- 1 small onion, diced
- 2 garlic cloves, minced
- 2 poblano chiles, roasted, peeled, seeded, and diced (page 204)
- 1 serrano chile, seeded and diced
- 1 tomato, diced
- 1 tablespoon chopped fresh basil leaves
- 1 teaspoon chopped fresh cilantro leaves
- 8 Flour Tortillas (page 184)
- 1 cup Pico de Gallo (page 31)
- 1/4 cup sour cream

To prepare the refrito, place the stock and wine in a large saucepan and bring to a boil. Add the beans, onion, and garlic and return to a boil. Reduce the heat and simmer for 1 1/2 hours, or until the beans are tender. Drain the beans and transfer the cooking liquid to a clean saucepan. Over high heat, reduce the liquid to 1/2 cup and set aside.

In a skillet over medium-high heat, heat the olive oil until lightly smoking. Add the cooked beans and pickled jalapeños, and mash with the back of a spoon or a potato masher until the beans are roughly pureed. Add the reserved 1/2 cup of cooking liquid and bring to a boil. Reduce the heat and let the beans simmer for 3 to 5 minutes, stirring constantly. Season with salt, add the cilantro, and mix thoroughly. Keep warm; the beans will thicken as they sit.

To prepare the tacos, crack the eggs into a large bowl, add the salt, and beat the eggs thoroughly. Set aside. Heat the olive oil in a skillet over medium heat until lightly smoking. Add the onion and garlic and cook for 3 to 4 minutes, or until the onion is translucent. Add the poblanos, serrano, and tomato and cook for 1 minute longer. Pour the eggs into the skillet, add the basil and cilantro, and scramble the eggs to the desired consistency. Wrap the tortillas in foil and warm in a hot dry skillet or in a low (250°F.) oven. Spread each tortilla with the reserved refrito. Spoon the eggs onto the tortillas and roll up. Garnish with the Pico de Gallo and sour cream.

SERVES 4

Roast Banana–Pumpkin Breakfast Bread

This recipe is a delicious variation on an American favorite, banana-nut bread. Roasting the bananas brings out the absolute essence of their flavor because the sugars caramelize and intensify the flavors. Coconut and banana combine to make an unmistakable tropical flavor and the pumpkin seeds contribute a nutty crunch usually associated with pecans or walnuts.

3/4 cup golden raisins
1/2 cup Myers's dark rum
2 ripe bananas, unpeeled
2 cups cake flour
2 teaspoons baking powder
1/2 teaspoon baking soda
1/4 teaspoon salt
6 tablespoons (3/4 stick) unsalted butter, softened
2/3 cup sugar
2 large eggs
1/2 cup unsweetened coconut milk
1 teaspoon pure vanilla extract
1/2 cup toasted pumpkin seeds (page 211)
Powdered sugar (optional)

Preheat the oven to 325°F.

In a small saucepan, combine the raisins and rum. Bring to a boil over medium heat, remove from the heat, and let stand for 1 hour. Strain the plumped raisins and set aside; discard any remaining liquid.

Place the bananas on a cookie sheet. Bake in the oven for 12 minutes, or until the skins are black and they have started to seep. Remove from the oven, set aside, and let cool.

Sift the flour, baking powder, baking soda, and salt into a mixing bowl. Set aside. In the bowl of an electric mixer fitted with a paddle attachment, cream the butter and sugar on medium speed for about 3 minutes. Turn the machine to low and add 1 egg. Mix until completely incorporated and then add the second egg. Mix again until completely incorporated.

Meanwhile, squeeze the flesh of the bananas out of the skins into a small mixing bowl. Add the coconut milk and vanilla and mash together. Add half of the banana mixture to the electric mixer bowl and blend thoroughly on low speed. Add half of the flour mixture and mix until combined. Add the remaining banana mixture, blend thoroughly, and add the remaining flour mixture; mix just enough to thoroughly blend the ingredients. Fold the pumpkin seeds and the reserved raisins into the batter and pour it into a lightly greased 9 by 5-inch loaf pan.

Bake in the oven for 1 to 1 1/4 hours, or until a toothpick inserted in the center comes out clean. Cool on a rack, slice, and serve warm. Alternately, sprinkle with the powdered sugar and glaze briefly under a preheated broiler.

MAKES 1 LOAF

CHAPTER THIRTEEN

BREADS

Mexican Skillet Corn Bread

This corn bread was an accompaniment to many a favorite meal growing up. While everyone in west Texas has his or her own version of this classic, all recipes seem to have Cheddar cheese and roasted green chiles in common. This is the perfect partner for a big bowl of pinto beans or black beans, most Southwestern dishes, and most grilled foods.

(photograph on page 183)

1 cup yellow cornmeal
1/2 teaspoon baking soda
2/3 teaspoon salt
2 large eggs
1/3 cup vegetable shortening, melted and cooled
2/3 cup buttermilk
3/4 cup fresh corn kernels
1/2 cup heavy cream
2 jalapeño chiles, seeded and minced
1 poblano chile, roasted, peeled, seeded, and diced (page 204)
1 cup grated Cheddar cheese

Preheat the oven to 375°F.

In a mixing bowl, combine the cornmeal, baking soda, and salt. In a separate bowl, lightly whisk the eggs. Add the melted shortening and buttermilk, combine thoroughly, and add to the cornmeal mixture. Fold in the corn, cream, jalapeños, and poblano.

Place a large, dry cast-iron skillet in the oven for 5 minutes to heat through. Carefully remove the skillet and pour in half of the batter. Sprinkle in the cheese and then pour in the remaining mixture. Return the skillet to the oven and bake for 30 to 35 minutes, or until golden brown.

SERVES 8 TO 10

Dried Cherry Scones

Many people think of scones as the quintessential English quick bread, but they originated in Scotland. The batter for scones is similar to that for muffins, only with less liquid. The other popular conception—that scones are staples at the afternoon tea table "across the pond"—is entirely correct. In this country, they are also enjoyed at breakfast and may be sweet or savory. In this recipe, any dried fruit, such as raisins or chopped papaya or mango, may be substituted for the cherries.

(photograph on page 178)

1 cup plus 1 tablespoon all-purpose flour
1 1/2 tablespoons sugar
1 teaspoon baking powder
1 teaspoon baking soda
1 teaspoon salt
1/2 cup (1 stick) cold unsalted butter, diced
1 1/2 tablespoons grated orange zest
3/4 cup dried cherries
1/2 cup plus 2 tablespoons buttermilk
1 large egg

Preheat the oven to 350°F.

In the bowl of an electric mixer fitted with a paddle attachment, place the flour, sugar, baking powder, baking soda, and salt. Add the butter and mix on medium speed until the butter is the size of peas. In a mixing bowl, combine the zest, cherries, buttermilk, and egg and whisk to combine. Pour into the flour mixture and mix on low speed until all of the ingredients just come together.

Using a 4-ounce ice cream scoop or ladle, scoop 12 scones onto a lightly greased cookie sheet and flatten with hands to 1 inch. Bake in the oven for 12 to 15 minutes, or until golden brown. Serve warm or let cool.

MAKES 12 SCONES

Ancho Focaccia

This is a Southwestern variation on an Italian theme. This recipe is inspired by Carol Field, one of the true great bakers of our time. Focaccia has a wonderful chewy texture unlike any other bread, and it exudes a seductive pungency. It makes a great accompaniment with soups and salads, and it also makes terrific sandwiches.   *(photograph on page 183)*

2 teaspoons active dry yeast
1½ cups warm water (105° to 115°F)
4 cups unbleached all-purpose flour
3 tablespoons extra-virgin olive oil
3 tablespoons ancho chile puree (page 206)
2 teaspoons salt
¼ cup Red Chile–Canela Oil (page 26) or store-bought

In the bowl of an electric mixer fitted with a paddle attachment, sprinkle 1 teaspoon of the yeast over ½ cup of the warm water and let stand until creamy in appearance, about 10 minutes. Stir in ¾ cup of the flour. Cover tightly with plastic wrap and let the "sponge" rise until very bubbly and doubled in volume, about 45 minutes.

Sprinkle the remaining 1 teaspoon of yeast over the remaining 1 cup of warm water in a small bowl. Whisk together and let stand until creamy in appearance, about 10 minutes. Add the dissolved yeast, the olive oil, and ancho puree to the sponge and, with the paddle attachment, mix on medium-low speed until well blended. Add the remaining 3¼ cups of flour and 2 teaspoons salt and stir until thoroughly mixed, 1 to 2 minutes. Replace the paddle attachment with a dough hook and knead at medium speed until the dough is soft, velvety, and slightly sticky, 3 to 4 minutes. Transfer the dough to a lightly floured work surface and knead until the dough comes together and forms a ball.

Place the dough in a lightly oiled metal or glass bowl, cover with a damp towel or plastic wrap, and let rise in a warm place until doubled in volume, about 1¼ hours; the dough should be soft and delicate and full of air bubbles.

Flatten the dough on an oiled 11 by 17-inch baking sheet and press it out with moistened or oiled fingertips. Since the dough will be sticky and may not cover the bottom of the sheet, cover it with a damp towel and let it rest for 10 minutes; then stretch it again to fill the baking sheet. Cover with a damp towel and let rise for 30 to 45 minutes longer, or until it is full of air bubbles. Just before baking, dimple the top of the dough vigorously with your fingertips, leaving visible indentations. Drizzle the Red Chile–Canela Oil over the top of the dough and sprinkle with additional salt to taste.

Approximately 30 minutes before you are ready to bake, preheat the oven to 425°F. and put a baking stone inside if you have one. Place the baking sheet holding the focaccia directly on the stone or on the center rack of the oven and spray the floor and walls of the oven with water from a spray bottle 3 times during the first 10 minutes of baking. Bake until the crust is crisp and the top is golden, about 20 to 25 minutes (you may remove the focaccia from the pan and place it directly on the baking stone for the last 10 minutes). Remove from the pan immediately and place on a rack to cool. Serve warm or at room temperature.

MAKES 1 LOAF (ABOUT 12 BY 18 INCHES)

Squash and Cheddar Cheese Muffins

The English and Americans have everything in common, observed Oscar Wilde, except for the language. And, we should add, muffins. Where English muffins are light, airy, plain mini-breads, American muffins are denser, cakelike, and usually flavored with sweet or savory ingredients. They are also one of the easiest types of bread to make. Make these muffins when your zucchini are threatening to overrun the garden in summer!

1 1/2 cups cornmeal
1/2 cup all-purpose flour
2 1/2 teaspoons baking soda
1 1/4 teaspoons salt
1/2 tablespoon pure red chile powder
2 large eggs
1 cup buttermilk
1/4 cup (1/2 stick) unsalted butter, melted
12 ounces zucchini, ends sliced off, and zucchini grated
1 cup grated sharp white Cheddar cheese
2 poblano chiles, roasted, peeled, seeded, and diced (page 204)

Preheat the oven to 350°F.

Place the cornmeal, flour, baking soda, salt, and chile powder in a mixing bowl and stir to combine. In another bowl, whisk together the eggs, buttermilk, and melted butter until well blended. Fold in the zucchini, cheese, and chiles and pour the mixture over the dry ingredients. Stir to combine; do not overmix.

Lightly grease two 6-muffin tins or one 12-muffin tin. Ladle the batter into the tins so that it comes three quarters up the inside of each compartment. Bake in the oven for 25 to 30 minutes, or until a toothpick inserted in the center of a muffin comes out clean. Let cool slightly on a wire rack and then remove. Serve warm.

MAKES 12 MUFFINS

Carrot-Coconut Muffins

Here is an unlikely combination—carrots and coconut—but one that works sublimely well in these sweet-and-savory muffins. The addition of pecans gives them an appealing crunchy texture; walnuts are a fine alternative. It is important not to overmix muffin batter, or they will be too heavy and too full of air. If in doubt, leave the batter a little lumpy.

(photograph opposite)

1 cup all-purpose flour
1/2 cup whole-wheat flour
1 tablespoon baking powder
1/2 teaspoon ground canela or
    1/4 teaspoon cinnamon
Pinch of ground allspice
Pinch of salt
2 large eggs
1/4 cup light brown sugar, loosely
    packed
3/4 cup unsweetened coconut milk
2 tablespoons (1/4 stick) butter,
    melted
3/4 cup grated carrot
1/4 cup dried coconut flakes
1/2 cup toasted chopped pecans
    (page 211)

Preheat the oven to 375°F.

Place both flours, the baking powder, canela, allspice, and salt in a mixing bowl and whisk together to blend.

In the bowl of an electric mixer fitted with a paddle attachment, combine the eggs and brown sugar. Beat on medium-high speed until lighter in color and smooth, about 5 to 7 minutes. With the machine on low speed, add the coconut milk and melted butter. Turn the machine off and add half of the flour mixture. Turn the machine back on and mix until well blended. Add the remaining flour mixture and mix until just blended. Remove the bowl from the machine and fold in the carrot, coconut, and pecans.

Lightly grease two 6-muffin tins or one 12-muffin tin. Ladle the batter into the tins so that it comes three quarters up the inside of each compartment. Bake in the oven for 20 to 25 minutes, or until a toothpick inserted in the center of a muffin comes out clean. Let cool slightly on a wire rack and then remove. Serve warm.

MAKES 12 MUFFINS

Dried Cherry Scones and Carrot-Coconut Muffins

Chipotle Brioche

Brioche is a light and rich bread that originated in Vienna and was then taken to France at the end of the eighteenth century. Within less than a hundred years, it became one of the most popular breads in that country. Classic brioche is baked in a special round fluted pan, and by all means use it if you have one. The chipotle chile gives the brioche a smoky flavor with plenty of picante zing, stamping it as distinctively Southwestern. Note that the dough should rest in the refrigerator overnight.

1 tablespoon active dry yeast
2 tablespoons lukewarm water (about 85°F.)
1½ tablespoons sugar
3½ cups all-purpose flour
6 large eggs
2½ teaspoons salt
7 tablespoons chipotle chile puree (page 206)
¾ cup (1½ sticks) unsalted butter, at room temperature
1 tablespoon milk

In the bowl of an electric mixer fitted with a paddle attachment, combine the yeast, water, and 1 tablespoon of the sugar. Stir to dissolve and let stand for about 5 minutes. Gradually mix in 2 cups of the flour. Add 3 of the eggs and continue beating until smooth.

Combine the salt with the remaining 1½ cups of flour and the remaining ½ tablespoon of sugar in a mixing bowl and gradually add to the dough while beating. Add 2 more eggs and the chipotle puree and beat for about 2 minutes until combined.

Replace the paddle attachment with a dough hook. With the machine running, incorporate the softened butter in 1-tablespoon increments. Beat for 5 to 7 minutes, until smooth and silky and the dough pulls away from the sides of the bowl.

Place the dough in a lightly oiled bowl, cover with a damp towel or plastic wrap, and let rise in a warm place until doubled in volume, about 45 minutes to 1 hour. Punch the dough down and let it rest, covered, in the refrigerator overnight.

Remove the dough from the refrigerator and punch down again. Shape it to fit into a lightly oiled 5 by 9 by 3-inch loaf pan. Let the dough rise, loosely covered with a damp towel or plastic wrap, until it has doubled in volume again, about 45 minutes. Meanwhile, preheat the oven to 425°F.

Beat the remaining egg with the milk and, when the dough has risen, gently brush with the egg wash. Bake in the oven for 15 minutes. Reduce the heat to 375°F. and bake for about 25 minutes longer, or until brown. The bread should sound hollow when tapped on the bottom of the pan. Turn out onto a rack to cool.

MAKES 1 LOAF

Sun-Dried Tomato Spoonbread

This Southern, puddinglike specialty must be one of the most tasty dishes to ever be made from cornmeal. Spoonbread is believed to be derived from the Native American porridge called *suppone*. In this recipe, the sun-dried tomatoes deliver an acidic chewiness that I find most appealing. Here we call for sun-dried tomatoes packed in oil, but you can equally well use dehydrated tomatoes that have been soaked in water.

1 cup Vegetable Stock
   (page 211) or store-bought
1 cup milk or half-and-half
1/2 cup fine yellow cornmeal
3 tablespoons unsalted butter
1 1/2 cups fresh corn kernels
1/2 cup diced onion
1/2 cup diced sun-dried tomatoes,
   packed in oil and drained
1 jalapeño chile, seeded and
   diced
3 large eggs, separated
1/2 teaspoon baking powder
1/4 teaspoon salt
1/3 teaspoon white pepper
1 teaspoon sugar
1/2 cup grated Romano cheese

Preheat the oven to 350°F. and prepare a water bath.

Combine the stock and milk in a saucepan and bring to a boil. Reduce the heat to low. Add the cornmeal slowly, stirring constantly, and cook until thickened, about 2 minutes. Remove from the heat and set aside.

Heat the butter in a skillet over medium heat and add the corn, onion, sun-dried tomatoes, and jalapeño. Cook until softened, about 2 to 3 minutes. Add the cornmeal mixture, let cool slightly, then stir in the egg yolks to combine. Stir in the baking powder, salt, pepper, and sugar.

Place the egg whites in a mixing bowl and whisk until stiff peaks form. With a spatula, fold one third of the whites into the cornmeal mixture. Add 1/4 cup of the Romano cheese and then fold this mixture back into the remaining egg whites.

Lightly grease a 9 by 12-inch baking pan, pour in the batter, and sprinkle the top with the remaining 1/4 cup of Romano cheese. Place in the water bath half filled with water. Transfer to the oven and bake for 45 minutes to 1 hour, or until just set. Keep over hot water in a low oven until ready to serve.

SERVES 6 TO 8

Corn Tortillas

Making corn tortillas requires a little more skill than flour tortillas, but it is well worth the practice involved. Using a tortilla press (available at Hispanic markets) is quite a bit easier than patting the tortillas by hand to the right size and shape, but it can be done that way. Corn tortillas can be cooked in advance, stacked in a towel, and then refrigerated. To reheat, wrap in aluminum foil and warm through in a hot skillet or for 5 minutes in a 350°F. oven.

4 cups masa harina
1¼ teaspoons salt
2½ cups warm water
(105° to 110°F.)

In a large mixing bowl, thoroughly mix the masa harina, salt, and water together with your hands until the dough comes together in a soft ball. Divide the dough into 20 pieces, roll into small balls, and cover with plastic wrap.

Heat a cast-iron skillet over medium-high heat to about 425°F. (a drop of water should sizzle on the skillet).

Meanwhile, open a tortilla press and on it lay a sheet of plastic wrap just large enough to cover the base. Place a ball of dough in the center of the plastic wrap, and cover with a second piece of plastic wrap. Close the tortilla press and squeeze down hard on the handle. Open the press and peel off the top piece of plastic wrap, starting with the side opposite the handle. Pick up the plastic wrap underneath the dough and invert it so that the dough is lying on the palm of your hand. Carefully peel away the plastic wrap.

Gently place the tortilla on the hot, dry skillet. After a few seconds, the dough will begin to dry out at the edges. After 25 to 30 seconds, flip the tortilla and let it cook for another 45 seconds. Turn again and cook for another 30 seconds, until the tortilla is slightly puffed but still pliable.

Repeat with the remaining balls of dough. Stack the tortillas, separated by wax paper or plastic wrap, and cover with a towel or foil to keep warm.

MAKES 20 TORTILLAS

Ancho Focaccia and Mexican Skillet Corn Bread

Flour Tortillas

Tortillas are a mainstay of Texas cooking, and I use them in many of the recipes in this book. It is hard to imagine the food of the region without flour tortillas wrapping burritos, fajitas, or enchiladas. The Spanish introduced wheat to Mexico in the sixteenth century, and wheat flour was then used to make bread in the same style as the traditional corn tortillas that had been a staple in Central America for centuries before that.

2 cups all-purpose flour, plus extra for coating
1/2 tablespoon salt
1/2 tablespoon baking powder
1/4 cup vegetable shortening
3/4 cup warm water (105° to 110°F.)

Sift the flour, salt, and baking powder together into a mixing bowl. Using a fork or your fingers, cut in the shortening and mix until it is evenly distributed and the mixture has the texture of coarse cornmeal. Stir about half of the water into the dry ingredients, enough to form a soft dough. Knead the dough for 15 to 20 seconds and form into a ball. Gradually add all but 2 tablespoons of the remaining water, all the while kneading the dough with your hands. Occasionally dip your fingers into the remaining 2 tablespoons of water and knead for 3 to 5 minutes longer. The texture of the dough should be soft and wet but not sticky.

Divide the dough into 20 equal pieces (about 1 ounce each). Stretch each piece out and then fold the sides inward to adhere and form a round ball about 1 inch in diameter. Place the balls of dough on a baking sheet and cover with plastic wrap. Let rest for 5 to 10 minutes.

Heat a cast-iron skillet over medium-high heat to about 425°F. (a drop of water should sizzle on the skillet). Lightly coat each ball of dough with flour. Using your thumbs, gently stretch each ball into a 2-inch circle. Roll each piece of dough into as thin a circle as possible. One at a time, carefully lift each circle and place on the hot, dry skillet. Cook for 35 to 40 seconds, or until bubbles appear on the tortilla surface. Flip the tortilla with a spatula and cook for an additional 5 to 10 seconds on the other side. Stack the tortillas and wrap in a towel or foil to keep warm.

MAKES 20 TORTILLAS

Fresh and Dried Coriander Bolillos

Bolillos are crisp little Mexican rolls, and authentic bolillos get their wonderful crust from being baked in wood-fired ovens. These are multi-purpose rolls that can also be made into small loaves. I like to use them for sandwiches, such as the Eggplant Parmesan Torta with Oven-Dried Tomato Mayonnaise (page 138). The dough contains both ground dried coriander seed and the fresh leaves of the same plant, which are better known as cilantro. This flavorful combination makes for a delicately aromatic bread.

1 tablespoon active dry yeast
4½ cups all-purpose flour
2 tablespoons sugar
1 teaspoon salt
½ cup plus 1 tablespoon
   vegetable shortening
½ tablespoon ground coriander
¼ cup fresh cilantro leaves,
   chopped
1 large egg
2 tablespoons milk

In the bowl of an electric mixer fitted with a dough hook, combine the yeast, 2 cups of the flour, the sugar, and salt. In a saucepan, gently melt the shortening in 1½ cups of water over low heat. Cool to about 105°F., until just warm to the touch. Add this mixture to the flour mixture and combine.

Add the coriander and the remaining 2½ cups of flour, ½ cup at a time, until a soft dough forms and moves freely in the bowl. Add the cilantro and incorporate. The dough should be soft and elastic but not sticky. Transfer the dough to a lightly oiled bowl and cover with a damp towel. Let the dough rise in a warm place until it doubles in volume, about 2 hours.

Gently punch down the dough and turn out onto a floured surface. Divide the dough into 12 equal pieces (about 3 ounces each) and roll each into an elongated football-like shape, pinching each end into a point. Place on a baking sheet lined with parchment paper and press down on the top of each roll to flatten slightly. Make two parallel slash marks with a sharp knife. Cover loosely with a damp towel and let the dough rise again until it has doubled in volume, 45 minutes to 1 hour.

Preheat the oven to 375°F.

In a bowl, beat the egg with the milk, and when the rolls have risen, gently brush with the egg wash. Bake the rolls in the oven for 15 to 18 minutes, or until the rolls are golden brown. Turn out onto a rack to cool.

MAKES 12 BOLILLOS

CHAPTER FOURTEEN

DESSERTS

Most of the recipes in this chapter were developed by Katherine Clapner, executive pastry chef for all of my restaurants. Note that while each dessert may be complex in its entirety, the components can be served alone. For example, most desserts have an ice cream or sauce in the recipe but can be served without it.

Sweet Potato Flapjacks with Honey-Poached Pear Compote and Chocolate-Orange Sorbet

These pancakes, or flapjacks, may appear "homey," but they are actually quite complex in flavor. Their warm and subtle sweet potato flavor provides a wonderful foil for the honeyed pears and citrusy chocolate sorbet.

FOR THE CHOCOLATE-ORANGE SORBET

- 4 ounces unsweetened chocolate
- 4 ounces bittersweet chocolate, such as Hawaiian Vintage Chocolate
- 2 cups freshly squeezed orange juice
- 1/2 tablespoon Grand Marnier
- 3/4 cup granulated sugar
- 1/2 cup water

FOR THE COMPOTE

- 1 cup honey, preferably wildflower
- Minced zest and juice of 2 lemons
- 1 cinnamon stick
- 3 cups dessert wine, such as Bonny Doon Vin de Glace or Far Niente Dolce
- 4 ripe Anjou pears, peeled, cored, and cut into quarters

FOR THE FLAPJACKS

- 2 small sweet potatoes (about 8 ounces each)
- 1/2 cup all-purpose flour
- 1/4 cup light brown sugar, loosely packed
- 1/4 cup grated orange zest
- 3 large eggs, separated, plus 2 large egg whites
- 1/4 cup heavy cream
- 2 tablespoons Grand Marnier
- 1/2 cup melted butter
- 3 tablespoons unsalted butter

To prepare the sorbet, melt both chocolates together in a double boiler and set aside. In a saucepan, combine the orange juice, Grand Marnier, sugar, and water and bring to a boil. Slowly whisk the orange juice mixture into the chocolate mixture, strain, and let cool completely. Transfer to an ice cream machine and freeze according to the manufacturer's directions.

Preheat the oven to 350°F.

To prepare the compote, place the honey, lemon zest and juice, cinnamon, dessert wine, 1 cup of water, and pears in a saucepan. Cover and cook over medium-low heat for 20 minutes, until the pears are soft but not mushy. Remove the pears and set aside. Continue to reduce the cooking liquid until it reaches a syrupy consistency, about 20 minutes longer. Finely dice the pears and add to the syrup. Keep warm.

To prepare the flapjacks, bake the sweet potatoes in the oven for 1 to 1½ hours, or until tender. Cut in half, scoop out the flesh, and transfer to a blender or food processor. Puree until completely smooth and transfer to the bowl of an electric mixer fitted with a paddle attachment. Add the flour, sugar, and orange zest and beat together on medium speed. In a mixing bowl, beat together the egg yolks, cream, and Grand Marnier and slowly add to the sweet potato mixture while beating. Transfer to a clean mixing bowl. Clean the bowl of the electric mixer, fit with a whisk, and whisk the 5 egg whites to stiff peaks. Using a spatula, gently fold in the sweet potato mixture and the melted butter.

To serve, heat the butter in a nonstick sauté pan over medium heat. Drop 2 tablespoons of the flapjack batter into the pan. When the bottoms of the flapjacks turn brown, about 3 minutes, flip over with a rubber spatula and cook the other side for 2 to 3 minutes longer. Serve 3 flapjacks on the center of each plate and spoon the compote on top; garnish each plate with some of the syrup. Place a scoop of the sorbet on top of the pears.

SERVES 8

Mole Cake with Cherry-Almond Ice Cream, Tamarind Anglaise, and Orange Caramel

The name of this cake derives from the flavors that are reminiscent of the classic mole, an aromatic, delicious chocolaty savory sauce that originated in Puebla, Mexico. I have always thought that dried chiles were a surprisingly good match for chocolate, and with the addition of canela, cloves, and pumpkin seeds, the full mole flavors emerge. For a shortcut, substitute sectioned grapefruit for the orange caramel.

FOR THE ICE CREAM
- 4 ounces cherries, pitted
- 1 cup dry sherry
- 2 cups heavy cream
- 1 cup half-and-half
- 3/4 cup sugar
- 1/2 fresh vanilla bean, split in half lengthwise and seeds scraped
- 1/4 teaspoon almond extract
- 1/2 cup toasted sliced almonds (page 211)
- 8 large egg yolks

FOR THE CAKE
- 11 ounces bittersweet chocolate, such as Hawaiian Vintage Chocolate
- 10 tablespoons (1 1/4 sticks) unsalted butter
- 1/2 dried pasilla chile, seeded
- 1/2 dried ancho chile, seeded
- 10 tablespoons sugar
- 1/2 tablespoon canela or 3/4 teaspoon cinnamon
- 1/4 teaspoon ground cloves
- 2 tablespoons pumpkin seeds
- 9 large eggs
- 1/2 tablespoon pure vanilla extract

Preheat the oven to 300°F.

To prepare the ice cream, place the cherries and sherry in a mixing bowl and let soak for 20 minutes. Place the cream in a saucepan, add the half-and-half, sugar, vanilla bean and seeds, almond extract, almonds, and cherries with their soaking liquid, and bring to a boil. Whisk the egg yolks in a mixing bowl and slowly add the cream mixture while continuing to whisk vigorously. Return to the saucepan and cook over low heat while whisking continuously, until the mixture coats the back of a wooden spoon. Remove from the heat and let cool completely. Strain into an ice cream machine and freeze according to the manufacturer's directions (discard the cherries and almonds).

To prepare the cake, melt the chocolate in a double boiler and keep warm. Meanwhile, in a small saucepan over medium heat, heat the butter until golden brown, 8 to 10 minutes. Set aside.

In the bowl of a food processor, place the chiles, sugar, canela, cloves, and pumpkin seeds and grind until superfine. In the bowl of an electric mixer fitted with a whisk, whisk together the eggs and vanilla extract on low speed. Add the chile mixture and whisk for 10 minutes longer. Add the melted chocolate, whisk to incorporate, and slowly add the butter until combined.

Pour the batter into 8 lightly oiled 4-ounce ramekins and place in a water bath. Transfer to the oven and bake for 13 to 14 minutes; the cakes will feel only slightly firm. Remove the ramekins and keep refrigerated until 1 hour before serving. Cakes are even better slightly warmed in the oven.

FOR THE TAMARIND ANGLAISE

- 1 cup heavy cream
- 3 tablespoons sugar
- 1/4 teaspoon pure vanilla extract
- 1/4 cup tamarind paste
- 2 large egg yolks

FOR THE ORANGE CARAMEL

- 1/2 cup sugar
- 1 3/4 cups freshly squeezed orange juice

To prepare the anglaise, place the cream, sugar, vanilla, and tamarind in a saucepan and slowly bring to a boil, breaking up the tamarind with a wooden spoon. Whisk the egg yolks in a mixing bowl and slowly add the cream mixture while whisking vigorously. Return to the saucepan and cook over low heat while whisking continuously, until the mixture coats the back of a wooden spoon. Strain and let cool; keep covered.

To prepare the caramel, heat the sugar and 1 cup of water in a heavy saucepan over high heat. When the sugar turns from golden brown to amber, turn off the heat and slowly whisk in the orange juice; the caramel may turn hard but it will melt again when reheated. Turn the heat back on to medium and cook for 20 minutes, stirring occasionally. Let cool completely.

To serve, place the ramekins in a shallow pan of very hot water for 1 minute. Invert the ramekins and tap on the bottom to turn out the cakes. Transfer to serving plates and bring to room temperature. Top with a scoop of the ice cream and spoon the anglaise and caramel around the cakes.

SERVES 8

Griddled Sweet Mascarpone Polenta with Roasted Nectarines and Blackberry-Swirled Buttermilk Ice Cream

Since mascarpone is a rich cow's-milk cheese originating in the Lombardy region and polenta is also a staple of northern Italy, it would appear that this recipe has its roots firmly established there. However, the grilling technique and the buttermilk-blackberry ice cream make this an American dessert. The roasted nectarines bring a perfect balance to create a dish of complex flavors. The mascarpone I use comes from the Mozzarella Company in Dallas; remember that the better your source for fresh mascarpone, the better your dessert will be.

(photograph on page 191)

(continued on next page)

FOR THE BLACKBERRY-SWIRLED BUTTERMILK ICE CREAM

8 ounces fresh blackberries
9 tablespoons granulated sugar
Juice of ½ lemon
2 cups buttermilk
1 cup heavy cream
Zest of ½ orange
½ vanilla bean, split in half lengthwise and seeds scraped
6 large egg yolks

FOR THE ROASTED NECTARINES

3 cups pure maple syrup
Minced zest of 2 oranges
6 ripe nectarines, cut in half from top to bottom and pitted
½ cup water

FOR THE MASCARPONE POLENTA

5 cups milk
1 teaspoon salt
½ tablespoon pure vanilla extract
½ vanilla bean, split in half lengthwise and seeds scraped
1 tablespoon ground canela or ½ tablespoon ground cinnamon
1 cup granulated sugar
2 cups coarse cornmeal
8 ounces mascarpone cheese

FOR THE BLUEBERRY SAUCE

1½ cups port
½ cup granulated sugar
Juice of 1 lime
8 ounces fresh blueberries

½ cup powdered sugar, for dusting
2 tablespoons (¼ stick) unsalted butter, for griddling

To prepare the ice cream, place the blackberries, 3 tablespoons of the sugar, and lemon juice in a saucepan, cover, and bring to a boil over medium heat. Reduce the liquid by one third, remove from the heat, and set aside. Place the buttermilk, cream, the remaining 6 tablespoons of sugar, orange zest, and vanilla seeds (but not the bean) in a saucepan and bring to a boil. Whisk the egg yolks in a mixing bowl and slowly add the cream mixture while whisking vigorously. Return to the saucepan and cook over low heat while whisking continuously, until the mixture coats the back of a wooden spoon. Remove from the heat and let cool completely. Transfer to an ice cream machine and freeze according to the manufacturer's directions. Once the ice cream is frozen, carefully fold in the blackberry mixture, forming swirls. Keep frozen until ready to serve.

Preheat the oven to 300°F.

To prepare the nectarines, combine the maple syrup, orange zest, and ½ cup water in a baking dish. Place the nectarines, cut-side down, in the dish. Cover with foil and bake for 15 minutes. Remove from the oven, take off the foil, and set aside at room temperature.

To prepare the polenta, place the milk, salt, vanilla extract, vanilla bean and seeds, canela, and sugar in a saucepan and bring to a boil. Slowly whisk in the cornmeal and, stirring with a wooden spoon, cook the mixture over medium-low heat for about 10 minutes, until the polenta no longer has a grainy texture and firms up when you spoon it onto a plate. Remove the pan from the heat and stir in the mascarpone. Pour into a 6 by 9-inch baking tray, smooth out with a spatula, and let cool completely.

To prepare the sauce, place the port, sugar, and lime juice in a saucepan and bring to a boil. Continue to boil for 8 minutes. Add the blueberries, toss together, and keep warm.

To serve, cut the cooled polenta into 1½-inch squares and dust each side with powdered sugar. In a nonstick sauté pan set over medium heat, heat the butter, add the polenta squares, and griddle for 3 minutes on each side. Place 6 of the nectarine halves on serving plates and cover each with a polenta square, keeping them as level as possible. Stack with another nectarine and a second polenta square. Garnish with a scoop of the ice cream and spoon the blueberry sauce around each dessert.

SERVES 6

Griddled Sweet Mascarpone Polenta with Roasted Nectarines and Blackberry-Swirled Buttermilk Ice Cream

Banana Fritters with Pecan Ice Cream, Warm Cajeta Sauce, Candied Pecans, and Mexican Chocolate Fudge Sauce

Developed for Taqueria Cañonita, a new concept of mine in Las Vegas, Nevada, this recipe is a little Creole, with the fritter batter reminiscent of the famous beignets of New Orleans, but also more than a little Mexican. The combination of bananas, pecans, and caramel is a tried-and-true one, and cajeta, made from goat's milk, is the most delicious caramel imaginable. For a shortcut, omit the chocolate fudge sauce.

FOR THE PECAN ICE CREAM
- 2 cups milk
- 6 tablespoons granulated sugar
- 1 cup chopped pecans
- 1/2 vanilla bean, split in half lengthwise and seeds scraped
- 6 large egg yolks
- 6 1/2 tablespoons crème fraîche

FOR THE CANDIED PECANS
- 1/2 cup egg whites
- 1 1/2 cups chopped pecans
- 1 cup granulated sugar

FOR THE MEXICAN CHOCOLATE FUDGE SAUCE
- 8 ounces Ibarra chocolate, chopped
- 2 tablespoons light corn syrup
- 1/2 cup heavy cream

FOR THE CAJETA SAUCE
- 3/4 cup granulated sugar
- 1 cup goat's milk
- 1 cup cow's milk
- 1/2 teaspoon cornstarch
- Pinch of baking soda

To prepare the ice cream, place the milk, sugar, pecans, and vanilla bean and seeds in a saucepan, cover, and bring to a boil over medium heat. Remove from the heat and let steep for 30 minutes. Return the mixture to a boil. Whisk the egg yolks in a mixing bowl and slowly add the cream mixture while whisking vigorously. Return to the saucepan and cook over low heat while whisking continuously, until the mixture coats the back of a wooden spoon. Remove from the heat and let cool completely. Whisk in the crème fraîche. Strain into an ice cream machine and freeze according to the manufacturer's directions.

Preheat the oven to 300°F.

To prepare the pecans, whisk the egg whites in a mixing bowl until they form stiff peaks. Add the pecans and toss together. Place the sugar in a bowl, remove the pecans from the egg whites with a slotted spoon, and toss them in the sugar. Transfer to a cookie sheet and toast in the oven for 5 minutes. Stir the nuts and toast for 3 minutes longer. Let cool.

To prepare the chocolate fudge sauce, place the chocolate and corn syrup in a double boiler and let melt. Bring the cream to a boil in a saucepan and then whisk into the chocolate mixture. Strain and set aside; warm just before serving.

FOR THE BANANA FRITTERS

10 tablespoons bread flour
7 large eggs
1/2 tablespoon pure vanilla extract
1/2 teaspoon ground allspice
1/2 cup egg whites
1/4 cup granulated sugar
4 cups vegetable oil
6 ripe bananas, peeled and ends sliced off
1/2 cup powdered sugar, for dusting

To prepare the cajeta sauce, place 6 tablespoons of the sugar in a small skillet and melt over medium heat for 5 or 6 minutes, stirring continuously, until golden brown and free of lumps. Remove from the heat. Combine the goat's milk and cow's milk in a mixing bowl and pour one quarter (about 1/2 cup) of the mixture into another bowl. Add the cornstarch and baking soda and set aside. Place the remaining 1 1/2 cups of milk and the remaining 6 tablespoons of sugar in a saucepan set over medium heat. Stirring occasionally, bring just to a boil and add the caramelized sugar all at once while stirring vigorously. Add the reserved milk and cornstarch mixture and stir well. Reduce the heat to low and simmer for 45 to 50 minutes, stirring occasionally. The cajeta will thicken during the last 10 to 15 minutes of cooking time; stir more frequently to prevent sticking. Keep warm.

To prepare the fritters, place the flour, eggs, and vanilla in a mixing bowl and whisk together. Slowly add 1 tablespoon of water and the allspice while whisking. In another mixing bowl, whip the egg whites until slightly stiff. Add the sugar and continue whipping until stiff peaks are formed. Gently fold the egg white mixture into the batter.

In a small but deep saucepan, heat the oil until just smoking. Cut each banana lengthwise into 3 "planks" and dip each piece into the batter. Deep-fry until golden brown, about 5 minutes. Place 1/4 cup of the warm chocolate sauce in the center of each serving plate and place the bananas on top of the sauce. Place a scoop of the ice cream in the center of the bananas. Drizzle with the cajeta sauce and dust with the powdered sugar.

SERVES 6

Sangria-Soaked Lemon Pudding Cake Topped with Cinnamon Blood Oranges and Ginger Cream

The flavors of sangria, the refreshing wine and fruit juice drink, are so redolent of Spain, and here it delivers an incredible richness to an otherwise subtle and simple lemon pudding cake. The flavors of sangria are further enhanced by the cinnamon-spiked blood oranges. If blood oranges with their vivid red pulp are not available, feel free to use regular oranges— but remember, the word *sangria* comes from the Spanish word for *blood*. *(photograph opposite)*

FOR THE SANGRIA SYRUP
- 2 cups red wine
- 1/2 cup brandy
- 1/2 cup freshly squeezed orange juice
- 8 ounces fresh raspberries

FOR THE PUDDING CAKE
- 1/2 cup (1 stick) unsalted butter, at room temperature
- 1 1/4 cups sugar
- 8 large egg yolks
- 3/4 cup all-purpose flour
- 1/4 teaspoon salt
- Grated zest and juice of 4 lemons
- 2 cups milk

FOR THE CINNAMON BLOOD ORANGES
- 2 cups cinnamon schnapps
- 1/2 cup sugar
- 8 blood oranges (or regular oranges), peeled and sectioned

FOR THE GINGER CREAM
- 7 large egg yolks
- 1/2 cup plus 2 tablespoons sugar
- 1 cup brandy
- 1/4 cup peeled grated fresh ginger
- 2 cups heavy cream

- 8 ounces fresh raspberries, for garnish
- 6 brandy snaps, for garnish (optional)

To prepare the syrup, place the wine, brandy, orange juice, and raspberries in a saucepan and bring to a boil. Continue to boil for 10 minutes. Remove from the heat, transfer to a bowl, and let cool.

Preheat the oven to 325°F.

To prepare the pudding cake, cream the butter and sugar together in a mixing bowl until light and fluffy, about 4 minutes. Slowly add the yolks while whisking and fold in the flour, salt, and lemon zest and juice. Slowly stir in the milk. Butter and lightly flour 6 individual round 6-ounce cake pans and pour in the batter. Bake in the oven for 1 hour. Remove the pans and let cool; after 30 minutes, remove the pudding cakes from the pans.

To prepare the blood oranges, place the schnapps, sugar, and 1/2 cup of water in a saucepan and bring to a boil. Continue to boil for 5 minutes. Add the oranges and cook for 5 minutes longer, stirring occasionally. Set aside.

To prepare the ginger cream, whisk together the egg yolks, sugar, brandy, and ginger in a double boiler. Continue to cook, while whisking, until very thick and shiny, about 10 minutes. Remove from the heat and cool over an ice bath. When cool, fold in the cream and keep refrigerated until using.

To serve, warm the cakes in the oven for 5 minutes. Place each cake on serving plates and drizzle 1/4 cup sangria syrup over each. Garnish with the raspberries and brandy snaps.

SERVES 6

Double Chocolate Soufflé Tart with Mango-Rum Coulis and White Chocolate Mousse

This dessert is based on Mexican chocolate, which is a delightful blend of dark, rich chocolate, vanilla, almonds, and canela. Some of the best types come from Oaxaca, but many towns throughout Mexico are famous for their blends. In the United States, it is available at Hispanic markets. Don't be put off by the grainy texture of Mexican chocolate, which comes from the minimal blending of the granulated sugar. The coulis provides the perfect balance to the richness of the chocolate. Note that the mousse is optional, which helps if you are short of time.

FOR THE TART DOUGH

- 8 ounces bittersweet chocolate, such as Hawaiian Vintage Chocolate
- 3/4 cup (1 1/2 sticks) unsalted butter, softened
- 1 1/2 cups sugar
- 3 large eggs
- 4 cups all-purpose flour
- 2 teaspoons baking soda
- 3/4 teaspoon baking powder
- 2 tablespoons milk
- 1/2 tablespoon pure vanilla extract

FOR THE MANGO-RUM COULIS

- 3 ripe mangos, peeled, pitted, and chopped
- 1/2 cup Myers's dark rum
- 1/2 cup sugar

FOR THE WHITE CHOCOLATE MOUSSE (OPTIONAL)

- 8 ounces white chocolate
- 7 large egg yolks
- 1 cup plus 2 tablespoons sugar
- 1 cup Amaretto liqueur
- 2 cups heavy cream, whipped

To prepare the tart dough, melt the chocolate in a double boiler and set aside. By hand, cream together the butter and 1/2 cup of the sugar in a mixing bowl and add the melted chocolate. Slowly add the eggs while mixing. In a separate bowl, combine the flour, baking soda, and baking powder and add to the chocolate mixture. Slowly add the milk and vanilla and mix until it is smooth and totally incorporated. Wrap the dough in plastic and refrigerate for 30 minutes.

Unwrap the dough and roll out on a floured work surface to a thickness of 1/4 inch. Lightly butter eight 6-inch ramekins and sprinkle generously with sugar. Cut the dough into circles 1 inch larger than the ramekins, line the ramekins with the dough, and set aside.

To prepare the coulis, place the mangos, rum, and sugar in a saucepan and cook over low heat for 10 minutes. Transfer to a blender, strain, and let cool.

To prepare the mousse, melt the chocolate in a double boiler and keep warm. In another double boiler, combine the egg yolks, sugar, and liqueur and cook, while whisking over medium heat, until very thick and shiny, about 10 minutes. Remove from the heat, fold in the chocolate, and whisk until cool. Fold in the whipped cream and keep refrigerated.

FOR THE DOUBLE CHOCOLATE SOUFFLÉ TARTS

  4 cups milk
  7 tablespoons unsalted butter
  ¹/₂ cup bread flour
  ¹/₂ cup all-purpose flour
  ¹/₄ cup sifted cocoa powder
 16 large egg yolks (1¹/₂ cups)
 10 ounces Mexican chocolate,
       such as Ibarra, chopped
 10 egg whites
 1¹/₂ cups sugar

Preheat the oven to 375°F.

To prepare the soufflé tarts, combine the milk and butter in a saucepan and bring to a boil. In a mixing bowl, combine the bread flour, all-purpose flour, and cocoa and add to the saucepan. Continue to cook over medium heat until the mixture forms a shiny ball, 8 to 10 minutes. Transfer to the bowl of an electric mixer fitted with a paddle attachment and slowly add the egg yolks and the Mexican chocolate; continue to mix until cool. Transfer to a large bowl and set aside.

Clean the bowl of the electric mixer and fit with a whisk attachment. Add the egg whites and whisk on high speed until they form soft peaks. Slowly add the sugar and continue to whisk until they form stiff peaks. Fold two thirds of the egg white mixture into the batter, a little at a time. Spoon into the prepared dough-lined ramekins and bake for 26 minutes.

Remove the soufflés from the oven and run a knife around the inside of each ramekin. Using an oven mitt, turn each ramekin over and invert the soufflé into a clean kitchen towel in your other hand. Transfer, right-side up, onto a serving plate. Repeat for the remaining soufflés. Spoon the coulis next to the soufflés and add 2 tablespoons of the mousse on top of the tart.

SERVES 8

Texas Tornado

This rich, chocolaty dessert is rather complex, but it will be a surefire showstopper at your next dinner party. Chocolate and cherries are one of my favorite combinations and the two are paired twice, both in the parfait and in the sauces. While the spun sugar "tornado" and the chocolate barbed wire definitely make a unique presentation, the dish is equally delicious without them and quite a bit of time and effort can be saved by foregoing the process. If you are going to make the spun sugar tornado, note that you will need a wire whisk that you are prepared to sacrifice for this purpose, two 18-inch wooden dowel rods preferably with a 1/2-inch diameter, 2 trash cans, and plenty of newspaper. *(photograph opposite)*

FOR THE PARFAIT BASE

- 8 large egg yolks
- 1 cup fresh cherries, pitted
- 1/2 cup Kahlúa
- 1 tablespoon pure vanilla extract
- 1/2 tablespoon almond extract
- 1 cup plus 2 tablespoons granulated sugar
- 8 ounces bittersweet chocolate, preferably Hawaiian Vintage Chocolate, melted
- 3 cups heavy cream

FOR THE CANDIED CHOCOLATE BARBED WIRE

- 1 pound bittersweet chocolate, preferably Hawaiian Vintage Chocolate
- 3/4 cup light corn syrup

FOR THE CHERRY COMPOTE

- 1 cup packed light brown sugar
- 1 cinnamon stick
- 1/4 cup Kirschwasser liqueur (or Cherry Heering)
- 1 pound fresh cherries, cut in half and pitted

FOR THE SPUN SUGAR TORNADOES

- 2 pounds granulated sugar

Mexican Chocolate Fudge Sauce (page 192)

To prepare the parfait base, place the egg yolks, cherries, Kahlúa, vanilla extract, and almond extract in the bowl of an electric mixer fitted with a whisk attachment. Begin mixing on low speed. Meanwhile, in a small saucepan, combine the sugar and 1 cup of water and bring to a boil. Cook to the "soft ball" stage, about 10 minutes; this is reached when some of the mixture is dropped into ice-cold water and you are able to form soft balls between your fingers. Slowly add this mixture to the egg mixture and increase the speed to medium. While whisking, add the melted chocolate. Continue to whisk until the mixture is cool, about 5 minutes. Whip the cream into soft peaks and fold into the mixture. Pour into lightly greased 6-ounce Dixie cone cups or other individual molds. Transfer to the freezer and freeze overnight.

To prepare the barbed wire, melt the chocolate in a double boiler and transfer to an electric mixer fitted with a paddle attachment. Place the corn syrup and 5 teaspoons of water in a saucepan and bring to a boil. Slowly add to the chocolate while mixing on low speed. Continue to mix for 4 minutes. Remove the "dough" and pat off any excess oil. Working the dough like Silly Putty, roll out the dough into long, thin 1/4-inch tubes and cut them into 4-inch lengths. Roll out more pieces, half the thickness of the first pieces, and cut into 1/2-inch lengths. Wrap around the thicker lengths and twist to resemble barbed wire. Keep in an airtight container; do not refrigerate.

To prepare the cherry compote, place the brown sugar and 1/2 cup of water in a saucepan and cook over high heat until amber colored and caramelized, about 20 minutes. Add the cinnamon and slowly add the liqueur. Cook for 3 minutes, add the cherries, and cook for 5 minutes longer. Keep warm.

(continued on next page)

To prepare the spun sugar tornadoes, assemble the following items: a wire whisk clipped off at the loop end to resemble a metal broom, 2 wooden dowel rods 18 inches long, 2 kitchen trash cans of equal height, and plenty of newspaper. Place the sugar and 4 cups of water in a saucepan and heat over high heat. Frequently brush down any traces of crystallized sugar on the inside of the saucepan with a pastry brush; keep the brush in a cup of hot water close by for this purpose. When the sugar turns an amber color, remove the pan from the heat and let cool for 10 minutes.

Place the trash cans side by side 1 foot apart and balance the dowels on either side of the top of the trash cans, connecting them like a bridge. Line the floor underneath with the newspapers. Using the wire whisk, dip the cut ends in the cooled sugar mixture and lift above the dowels. Flip the whisk away from you (to avoid getting any on yourself); as the sugar cools in the air, it will fall in glass-type threads over the dowels. Continue until all the sugar mixture is used. Store the threads in an airtight container until ready to use.

To serve, dip the parfait molds in hot water and invert so they fall out. Place in the center of serving plates. Spoon the fudge sauce next to the parfaits and garnish the sauce with the compote. Using dry hands, wrap the sugar threads in spirals around the parfait to resemble a tornado. Garnish each plate with 2 strips of the chocolate barbed wire.

SERVES 8

Tropical Fruit Bars with Passion Fruit–Coconut Salsa

This recipe was developed by our former pastry chef at Star Canyon in Dallas, Katherine Tuason. She named this dessert "Taste of the Tropics" for reasons that become apparent after just one bite. Feel free to experiment with other fruits in this recipe, but don't forgo the passion fruit–coconut salsa, which is also terrific with a host of other desserts, especially anything with chocolate.

FOR THE PASSION FRUIT– COCONUT SALSA

- 1 cup finely grated coconut
- 1 kiwi fruit, finely diced (about ½ cup)
- 5 strawberries, finely diced (about ½ cup)
- ½ papaya, seeded and finely diced (about ½ cup)
- ½ mango, peeled, pitted, and finely diced (about ½ cup)
- ½ cup finely diced pineapple
- 2 tablespoons passion fruit puree
- 2 tablespoons Myers's dark rum
- ¼ cup thinly sliced fresh mint leaves

FOR THE BASE

- 2 cups all-purpose flour
- Pinch of salt
- 1 teaspoon ground dried ginger
- ½ cup (1 stick) unsalted butter, softened
- ¾ cup packed light brown sugar
- 1 teaspoon pure vanilla extract

FOR THE TOPPING

- 3 large eggs
- ¾ cup packed light brown sugar
- 1 teaspoon pure vanilla extract
- 1 teaspoon salt
- 1¾ cups coconut flakes
- ¾ cup chopped dried pineapple
- ¾ cup chopped dried mango
- ¾ cup chopped dried papaya
- 1 cup chopped macadamia nuts

Preheat the oven to 350°F.

To prepare the salsa, place the coconut on a cookie sheet and bake in the oven for 2½ minutes. Remove the sheet and toss the coconut to mix well. Return to the oven and bake for about 2 minutes longer, until golden brown. Set aside and let cool. Place the kiwi, strawberries, papaya, mango, and pineapple in a mixing bowl and toss to combine. Sprinkle the mixture with the passion fruit puree and rum and toss again. Just before serving, add the mint strips and cooled coconut and toss to combine.

To prepare the base, lightly grease a 13 by 9-inch baking pan and line with aluminum foil, allowing a 2-inch overhang along each side. Lightly grease the foil. In a mixing bowl, sift together the flour, salt, and ginger. In a separate mixing bowl, cream together by hand the butter and sugar until light and fluffy. Add the vanilla. With a wooden spoon, stir in the flour mixture and mix until a crumbly dough forms. Using your fingers, lightly knead portions of the dough together and press into the greased pan, covering the bottom with an even layer of dough. Prick the dough with a fork. Transfer to the oven and bake for 15 to 20 minutes, or until very lightly browned. Let cool. Keep the oven on at 350°F.

To prepare the topping, whisk together in a mixing bowl the eggs, sugar, vanilla, and salt until smooth, about 2 minutes. Stir in the coconut, pineapple, mango, papaya, and macadamia nuts. Pour the mixture over the baked crust and spread evenly with a spatula. Bake for 20 to 25 minutes, until the topping is lightly browned. Transfer to a rack and let cool completely. Cut into 24 portions (4 sections along the short side by 6 sections along the long side) and serve with the salsa.

SERVES 24

CHAPTER FIFTEEN
BASIC RECIPES

Roasted Garlic Puree

Preheat the oven to 350°F.

Cut each head of garlic in half and place, cut-side up, in a roasting pan. Pour 1 teaspoon of olive oil over each half head of garlic. Sprinkle the pan with 2 to 3 tablespoons of water, cover tightly with foil, and bake for 30 to 40 minutes.

Uncover the pan and continue baking for 5 to 7 minutes longer, until the garlic is golden brown. Remove the garlic from the pan and let it cool. Squeeze the softened garlic into a blender and discard the skin. Add just enough olive oil to make pureeing possible.

Alternatively, peel individual cloves from 1 or more heads of garlic with a paring knife. Place the cloves on a baking sheet or in a roasting pan. Pour 1/2 to 1 tablespoon of olive oil over each head of cloves and toss to coat thoroughly. Sprinkle with water, cover with foil, and roast in the oven at 350°F. for 30 minutes. Remove the foil and roast for 5 to 7 minutes longer, until brown.

3 HEADS OF GARLIC YIELDS ABOUT 1/3 CUP OF PUREE

Peeling and Seeding Tomatoes

Have a large bowl of ice water ready. Bring a large saucepan of water (about 4 inches deep) to a rapid boil.

With a sharp knife, mark an X 1/4 inch deep in the bottom of each tomato. Plunge the tomatoes into the boiling water and cook for 20 seconds, making sure they stay covered with water. Remove with a slotted spoon and place in the ice water.

When cool, peel the tomatoes, cut in half, and squeeze gently. Remove any remaining seeds with a blunt knife, spoon, or with your fingers and discard the seeds.

To prepare tomatoes that are not watery but still have their skins on (for Pico de Gallo, for example), remove just the outer flesh from each tomato with a sharp paring knife, as you would remove the peel from an orange. Discard the pulp and seeds or use for sauces or soups. Dice the flesh into the size desired.

Roasting Corn

Preheat the oven to 400°F.

Remove the outer layers of husks from ears of corn, leaving 1 or 2 inner layers intact. Pull these remaining husks back, exposing the kernels. Remove the strands of corn silk, spread butter or olive oil over the kernels, and sprinkle with a little salt. Replace the husks over the kernels, place the ears on a cookie sheet, and roast in the oven for 30 minutes. Remove from the oven and, when cool enough to handle, remove the husks. Holding each ear of corn upright, cut off the kernels with a sharp knife.

Roasting Fresh Chiles and Bell Peppers

This technique concentrates the natural sugars of chiles and peppers (which botanically are also chiles), intensifying their flavors and adding a delicious smokiness. Roasting also makes peeling very easy; this is desirable as the skin of fresh chiles and peppers can be tough and bitter tasting. The roasting process blisters and blackens the skin on all sides without burning the flesh.

Chiles and peppers should be roasted quickly and turned frequently, and there are several methods you can use. They can be roasted on a hot grill, broiled, or set on a wire rack over an open flame on top of the stove. After roasting, transfer the chiles or peppers to a large bowl and cover with plastic wrap; alternatively, you can put them in a large paper bag and twist the top to secure. Let them "steam" for about 20 minutes until cool. Then you can peel them using the tip of a sharp knife. Split the chiles or peppers open with a knife and remove the seeds, internal ribs, and the stem.

If the main purpose is to peel the chiles or peppers rather than provide flavor (preferable for chile rellenos, for example), you can dip them in a pan of vegetable oil heated to 375°F. until the skin blisters. Remove and set in a bowl of ice water, and when cool enough, peel with a sharp knife.

Chiles and bell peppers can be roasted ahead of time and stored in the refrigerator for 2 or 3 days.

Oven Drying Cherry Tomatoes

Oven drying, like sun drying and roasting, accentuates and intensifies the flavors and sweetness of tomatoes, as with corn.

Preheat the oven to 200°F.

Slice each red cherry tomato (or a combination of yellow and red) in half, place, cut-side up, on a baking sheet, and salt lightly. Place the sheet in the oven and check every 45 minutes, turning the pan to ensure that the heat is evenly distributed. When the tomatoes are free of moisture, in 4 to 5 hours, remove from the oven and let cool. If not using immediately, the tomatoes can be stored in vegetable oil or olive oil in an airtight container.

MAKES 8 PINTS (ABOUT 2 CUPS)

Preparing and Blanching Artichoke Bottoms

1/3 cup all-purpose flour
2 quarts cold water
1/2 teaspoon salt
4 lemons, cut in half
6 large artichokes

In a large saucepan, place the flour and gradually whisk in 1 quart of the water. Bring to a boil and then reduce the heat to a simmer, whisking constantly to get rid of any lumps. Whisk in the remaining quart of water and the salt. Squeeze the juice from 3 of the lemons into the water. Remove from the heat.

Break the stems from the artichokes so that any fibers are pulled out. With a large knife, cut off the top one third of the artichokes. Remove and discard all of the outer leaves to expose the bottoms. Rub the bottoms with the 2 remaining lemon halves to prevent discoloration. Cut off the remaining inner leaves just above the artichoke bottoms.

With a paring knife, trim all the green parts of the artichoke bottoms to expose the white flesh around the bottoms and leaf ends. Rub with lemon and drop into the water and flour mixture. Bring the water to a boil, reduce the heat, and simmer for 30 to 40 minutes, until the artichokes are tender when pierced with a knife. Keep them submerged while cooking (place a wet towel or plate on top of the water, if necessary).

Remove the artichokes from the pan, allow them to cool, and keep refrigerated until needed. Just before serving, scoop out the choke and discard.

SERVES 6

Home Canning and Bottling

When canning and bottling, it is best to use standard-size canning jars or glasses with matching lids that ensure an airtight seal. The components, including the rubber rings, should be washed and rinsed before sterilizing and the jars or glasses must be hot when they are filled. Place the jars, lids, and rings in a large saucepan or stockpot, cover with water, and bring to a boil. Remove from the heat and keep hot and sterile until ready to fill.

The hot jars should be filled to within ¼ inch of the top with the contents to be canned. Seal quickly and securely with the ring and the lid.

Paraffin can be used to seal the top of glasses to keep the air out. Melt bars of paraffin in a double boiler; never melt over direct heat in a saucepan as paraffin is highly flammable. Seal one glass at a time by pouring or spooning the melted paraffin over the contents in the glass until they are completely covered° with a thin layer of paraffin.

If there are not enough contents to fill a jar or glass to within ¼ inch of the top, do not seal. Instead, cool, cover, and keep the jar refrigerated. Use as quickly as possible.

Pureeing Dried Chiles

Wash and thoroughly dry the chiles. Cut off the stems and slit open the chiles with a knife to remove the seeds.

Heat the oven to 450°F. Place the chiles in a single layer on a baking sheet and roast for 1 minute. Alternatively, dry-roast the chiles over high heat in a dry skillet until they puff up, about 30 seconds to 2 minutes, depending on the heat of the skillet.

Transfer the roasted chiles to a bowl, cover with warm water, and keep the chiles submerged with a plate or other heavy object for 30 minutes to rehydrate.

Strain the chiles, reserving the liquid, and place them in a blender. Puree the chiles, adding just enough of the soaking liquid to make pureeing possible; you should have a thick paste. The puree can be passed through a medium- or fine-mesh strainer at this point, or strained with the sauce or final product.

Pureed Dried Chiles

Preparing the Grill

Grilling food over a fire is the oldest form of cooking. A modern grill cooks food both by direct heat and by heat transferred through the metal bars of the grill.

Build a fire in a grill using natural, lump charcoal or charcoal briquettes. Lump charcoal, processed from hard wood such as hickory, mesquite, cherry, maple, or pecan, is preferred, as it does not contain additives. Briquettes, which are more readily available, are composed of charcoal, coal, starch, and some chemical additives to enhance lighting and burning. Note that mesquite charcoal, which burns the hottest and lasts the longest, throws out showers of sparks and requires special care.

To start the fire in the grill, use wood kindling or an electric starter. The electric starter is an electric coil similar to those fitted in ovens. You will need an electric outlet to use it, of course. I have strong feelings against using lighter fuel, which imparts unpleasant flavors in the smoke and can taint the flavor of the food being grilled.

Lump charcoal (or briquettes) should be stacked in a pyramid over kindling or an electric starter. Light the kindling or turn on the electric starter. Let the coals burn down until they are covered by a uniform, whitish-gray ash, 20 to 30 minutes. Spread out the coals. The grill should be hot. Test for the hottest part of the grill by carefully holding your hand about 2 inches over the fire.

At this stage, before placing any food on the grill, you can add to the fire 6 to 8 hardwood chunks or chips (such as hickory, almond, cherry, apple, orange, or pecan) that have been soaked in water for 20 minutes. This procedure will give an extra smoky flavor to the food.

It is important to scrub the metal bars of the grill with a wire brush and then oil them with a towel or rag before and after use; doing this will help prevent the food from sticking to the grill. For best results, bring the food to be grilled to room temperature before cooking. At room temperature, the heat can penetrate the food more quickly without burning the outside.

While gas grills seem to be more common today than those requiring charcoal or wood, they simply will not impart the same flavor to foods. If you are using a gas grill, the same timing and technique here will generally apply. A gas grill set on high will radiate the same heat as a medium to medium-hot charcoal fire.

Preparing the Smoker

Smoking, like grilling, is one of the oldest cooking methods and was a means of preserving food long before the advent of refrigeration. Now it is used most often to add flavor to meats, poultry, and fish dishes, as well as other ingredients, such as vegetables. In the nineteenth century, large-scale smoking was brought to Texas by German immigrants who introduced smokehouses for sausage making. The practice has been an important part of the Texas culinary tradition and culture ever since. I started to experiment with smoking vegetables in the early 1980s and began a trend that is now widespread. I like to think this is my legacy not only to Texas cuisine, but to a far broader audience as well.

Home smokers are available from specialty hardware stores and mail-order sources; they are relatively inexpensive, so they are well worth the investment. It is also possible to adapt a barbecue grill, as described below. The method of smoking is as follows:

Soak 6 to 8 chunks of aromatic hardwood, such as hickory, mesquite, or apple, in water for 20 minutes. Place a pan of water in the bottom of the smoker. Build a fire in the smoker with hardwood lump charcoal, charcoal briquettes, or kindling and an electric starter (see Preparing the Grill, opposite, for notes on charcoal and starter). Let the charcoal burn down until it is covered by a uniform, whitish-gray ash, 20 to 30 minutes. Spread out the coals. Add the soaked hardwood chunks and let them smoke for 5 minutes. Place the ingredients to be smoked on the grill over the water pan and cover with the top of the smoker. Stoke the fire every 30 minutes, adding more charcoal and soaked wood chunks as necessary.

You can also adapt a standard barbecue grill by placing a pan of water in the bottom beneath the coals, sealing all but one of the vents in the lid, and following the method described above.

As a general guide, smoking at a temperature of 250°F., tomatoes will take about 20 minutes and chiles, bell peppers, and onions will take 20 to 25 minutes.

Sectioning Citrus Fruit

Peel the citrus fruit with a small, sharp knife, removing the white pith and membranes. Cut both sides of each section's membrane and let the fruit slip out into a small bowl. Remove all seeds.

Toasting Seeds and Nuts

This is a technique that brings out the full, rich flavors of seeds and nuts.

For seeds, place in a hot, dry skillet over medium-high heat for 2 to 3 minutes, stirring occasionally with a wooden spoon, until the seeds are lightly browned and fragrant.

For nuts, place in a hot, dry skillet over medium-high heat for 5 to 7 minutes, stirring occasionally with a wooden spoon, until the nuts are lightly browned. Smaller nuts, such as pine nuts, will take 3 to 5 minutes.

Vegetable Stock

I use this building block for many recipes in this book. A spicier variation, Creole Vegetable Stock, follows this recipe. The stock will keep for 1 week in the refrigerator and up to 2 months frozen.

1 tablespoon olive oil
1 head of celery, chopped
2 carrots, peeled and chopped
3 onions, chopped
2 heads of garlic (unpeeled), crushed
1/2 teaspoon black peppercorns
2 dried bay leaves
4 tablespoons chopped fresh thyme leaves

In a large stockpot, heat the oil until lightly smoking. Add the celery, carrots, and onions and sauté for 5 minutes. Add the garlic, peppercorns, bay leaves, thyme, and 3 quarts of water and bring to a boil.

Reduce the heat and simmer, uncovered, for 45 minutes. Strain, pressing very hard with the back of a large spoon to extract all of the liquid. Discard the vegetables and refrigerate the stock until needed.

MAKES ABOUT 3 QUARTS (12 CUPS)

Toasted Seeds and Nuts

Creole Vegetable Stock

For "part-time" vegetarians, use chicken stock instead of water in this recipe. You can also add some chopped bacon.

3 tablespoons olive oil
6 green bell peppers, seeded and chopped
1 head of celery, chopped
2 carrots, peeled and chopped
3 onions, chopped
2 heads of garlic (unpeeled), sliced in half
1/2 teaspoon black peppercorns
1/2 teaspoon cayenne
2 bay leaves
1/4 cup chopped fresh thyme leaves

In a large stockpot, heat the oil until lightly smoking. Add the bell peppers, celery, carrots, onions, garlic, peppercorns, cayenne, bay leaves, and thyme, and sauté for 10 minutes over medium-high heat.

Add 3 quarts of water and bring to a boil. Reduce the heat and simmer, uncovered, for 45 minutes. Strain, pressing very hard with the back of a large spoon to extract all of the liquid. Discard the vegetables and refrigerate the stock until needed.

MAKES ABOUT 3 QUARTS (12 CUPS)

Mayonnaise

You can of course buy store-bought mayo, but there's a world of difference between that and homemade. Be sure to add the oil gradually. This recipe can be stored in the refrigerator, sealed tightly, for 4 or 5 days.

2 large egg yolks
3/4 teaspoon salt
Freshly ground black pepper to taste
1 teaspoon Dijon mustard
1 1/4 cups peanut or safflower oil
1/2 cup extra-virgin olive oil
2 teaspoons freshly squeezed lemon juice

In a mixing bowl, whisk together the egg yolks, salt, pepper, and mustard. Combine the peanut and olive oils and drizzle gradually into the egg mixture while whisking. Continue to whisk until thoroughly incorporated. Whisk in the lemon juice and thin with 1/4 cup water, if desired.

MAKES ABOUT 2 CUPS

Wild Rice

Also called "Indian rice" because it was an important food for Native Americans of the northern plains and Great Lakes region, wild rice is actually the seed of a type of aquatic grass. Its deliciously nutty flavor goes well with many Southwestern dishes. Before preparing the wild rice, it should be thoroughly cleaned.

1 cup wild rice
4 cups Vegetable Stock (page 211) or store-bought, or lightly salted water

Thoroughly rinse the rice and place in a saucepan. Add the stock and bring to a boil. Cook over medium-high heat for 45 to 50 minutes, or until the rice has "opened up" and is still firm but not crunchy. Take care not to overcook. Drain.

MAKES ABOUT 2 CUPS

Black Beans

Black beans, a staple in most parts of Central America and the Caribbean, have a dense and meaty texture. They have enough character to stand up well to assertively flavored foods.

1/2 cup dried black beans, soaked overnight and drained
6 cups Vegetable Stock (page 211) or store-bought, or water
Salt to taste

Rinse the beans and place in a saucepan. Add the vegetable stock or water and salt and bring to a boil over high heat. Reduce the heat and simmer until tender, 45 minutes to 1 hour.

MAKES ABOUT 1 CUP

White Beans

White beans, also called navy beans, are a wonderful medium for carrying other flavors. I use them in several recipes in this book, and I like to have them on hand in the kitchen as a standby.

1/2 cup dried white beans, soaked overnight and drained
6 cups Vegetable Stock (page 211) or store-bought, or water
Salt to taste

Rinse the beans and place in a saucepan. Add the vegetable stock or water and salt and bring to a boil over high heat. Reduce the heat and simmer until tender, 45 minutes to 1 hour.

MAKES ABOUT 1 CUP

Black-Eyed Peas

It comes as a surprise to many visitors to the southern United States and Texas that black-eyed peas are in fact dried beans. It is traditional to serve them on New Year's Eve as a portent of good luck in the year ahead.

½ cup dried black-eyed peas,
    soaked overnight and drained
Salt to taste

Rinse the black-eyed peas and place in a saucepan. Add 6 cups of water and salt and bring to a boil over high heat. Reduce the heat and simmer until tender, about 45 minutes to 1 hour.

MAKES ABOUT 1 CUP

Candied Spiced Pecans

These spiced nuts make a great snack anytime, and make a wonderful gift, wrapped in an attractive jar. They will keep indefinitely if stored in an airtight container.

(photograph opposite)

2 tablespoons (¼ stick) unsalted
    butter
3 cups pecans
½ cup light brown sugar, loosely
    packed
½ tablespoon paprika
2 teaspoons pure red chile
    powder
1 tablespoon ground cumin
¼ cup cider vinegar
Salt to taste

Preheat the oven to 350°F.

In a large skillet over medium heat, melt the butter. Add the pecans and sauté for 3 minutes, or until lightly browned. Add the brown sugar and cook until lightly caramelized. Stir in the paprika, chile powder, and cumin. Add the vinegar and cook until the liquid has just evaporated. Season with salt and spread out in an even layer on a cookie sheet. Bake for 4 or 5 minutes, or until crisp.

MAKES ABOUT 3 CUPS

Glossary

Ancho chiles The dried ripe form of the poblano chile. Deep red in color with mellow heat, sweet and smoky flavor tones that include chocolate, coffee, and raisins. The ancho is the most commonly used dried chile in Texas and Mexico. Buy anchos in Latin markets; to ensure freshness, make sure they are supple and aromatic rather than brittle and therefore old.

Annatto The brick-red seeds of the tropical annatto tree are usually ground into a paste (also known as achiote) and added to dishes in Mexico and parts of the Caribbean as a seasoning or coloring. It is also used commercially in the United States to dye dairy products (butter, cheese, etc.) a more intense yellow color. It has a slightly acidic, earthy flavor similar to that of green olives, with a slight iodine aftertaste. (See also recipe introductions, page 25 and page 48.)

Arborio rice A short-grain Italian rice typically used in risottos for the creamy texture it provides, due to its high starch content.

Asiago cheese A semisoft Italian cow's-milk cheese with a rich and slightly tart flavor. Parmesan or Monterey Jack make good substitutes.

Avocado A buttery-textured fruit indigenous to Mexico and Central America. Ripe avocados are mild and slightly nutty in flavor, rich in minerals, and high in unsaturated fat. Two types are commonly available: the dark-green or purplish, bumpy-skinned Haas, and the larger, smooth-skinned Fuerte. I prefer the more common Haas. Once cut, avocados need to be used right away, as they will turn dark quickly.

Banana leaves Used extensively in South and Central America like premodern plastic wrap for everything from tamales to fish. These leaves not only seal in moisture but also impart a tropical and herbaceous quality to the food they wrap. The leaves can be bought fresh in Latin markets or frozen in Asian markets. If using fresh, derib first and then wilt over an open flame or electric burner before using.

Basil This versatile herb—a member of the mint family that originated in the Middle East—has licorice and clove overtones that combine well with the flavors of Texas. Basil is highly perishable and should not be cut until you are ready to use it. Look for bright green, unwilted leaves.

Beans Beans have been cultivated for thousands of years in the Americas, and the varieties are endless. Their popularity should come as no surprise; in addition to their flavor, they are rich in protein and high in minerals such as calcium, iron, and phosphorus. Always sort beans carefully for dirt, twigs, and rocks before cooking. To shorten cooking time, soak beans overnight.

Bell peppers Members of the chile family, bell peppers (also called sweet peppers) can add a crisp texture and color to dishes as well as a mild, sweet, vegetable flavor. They come in green, red, yellow, and orange. They should always be seeded before use; for instructions on roasting and peeling, see page 204.

Blue corn Usually ground into meal to make breads. It has a slightly sweeter taste than yellow corn. It is traditionally used for celebrations in Mexico.

Cactus leaves and cactus pears Also known as *nopales* and *tunas*, respectively, in Mexico. The "leaves" of the prickly pear cactus are spiny, paddle-like hands that dot the landscape of West Texas and Hill

Country. Their flavor is similar to that of green beans or asparagus, but with the texture of okra. To use cactus leaves, remove all the thin spines with a paring knife (wearing thick leather gloves while doing this is a good idea). Julienne the leaves and boil them twice with tomatillo husks (see below) to minimize their sliminess. Raw cactus leaves make a great addition to salads and they are wonderful grilled. The barrel-shaped pears, the fruit of the same plant, are yellow or purplish-red on the outside, and bright purple to red on the inside. Buy *tunas* that have smooth, firm flesh and are heavy for their size. After cutting off the outside layer of skin, puree the flesh, which tastes slightly like cherries, and strain.

Canela Also known as "Mexican cinnamon," as it is the form of cinnamon (a tree bark) most commonly used throughout Mexico. Originally native to Sri Lanka, canela has a softer, flakier texture and a lighter color than regular (Malabar) cinnamon, and its flavor is milder and sweeter. Canela is available in Latin markets and gourmet food stores, but if unavailable, use half the amount of regular cinnamon.

Cayenne I often use the bright red powdered cayenne chile as a seasoning to add piquancy to dishes. Cayenne chiles are thin-skinned, pungently hot, and somewhat tartly flavored. Cayenne is related to the Tabasco chile and is used extensively in Cajun and Creole cookery.

Chayote A member of the squash family, also called the vegetable pear, mirliton, or christophene. Light green in color, and similar in shape to a large pear. The flavor of chayote is somewhere between those of cucumber and zucchini. (See also recipe introduction, page 35.)

Chipotle chiles The dried form of fresh jalapeño chiles that have been smoked slowly. Chipotles are a favorite ingredient in Mexico, Texas, and the Southwest. The dried chipotle chile is brown and wrinkled in appearance; it is hot and smoky in flavor, with complex tones. Chipotles are also available canned, packed in a spicy tomato and vinegar-based adobo sauce. I use canned chipotles the most in this book, as they are easier to prepare.

Chocolate Cocoa beans used to be traded and used as currency by the Mayans and Aztecs, and many people today still consider chocolate to be as good as gold. Cocoa beans are harvested, fermented, and dried to create chocolate. Columbus took back to Europe the traditional Mexican drink made with cocoa beans, sugar, cinnamon, and vanilla. Since then, chocolate has never looked back!

Chorizo A fabulous way to make your breakfast eggs a little livelier. This highly spiced, loose Mexican sausage is available at most Hispanic markets, but it should not be confused with the hard, cured, Spanish-style chorizo. Most Mexican markets make their own, but commercial varieties work well too.

Cilantro People seem to either love cilantro (like me) or they will cross the Mississippi to stay away from it. Cilantro is as much an integral part of Texas cooking as beef, and its cooling, pungent flavor fits perfectly with this food. The leaves are the most commonly used part, but don't throw away the stems. Tie them in a bundle and use in soups, sauces, or stocks; remove before serving.

Coconut milk Canned coconut milk is the easiest option, although it is possible to prepare a fresh version using fresh coconut meat pureed with warm water. Be sure to use unsweetened canned coconut milk rather than a sweetened product such as Coco Lopez, which instead is ideal for tropical cocktails.

Coriander A commonly misunderstood spice, coriander is the seed of the cilantro plant, but should not be confused with cilantro itself. Its flavor is slightly citrusy with a touch of sage. It is wonderful toasted and tastes best when ground fresh.

Corn The foundation upon which all of South, Central, and North America's native cuisines are based. Every part and form of an ear of corn is used somehow in Texas cuisine. The husks are used fresh and dried as wrappers for tamales. The fresh kernels are best cut straight from the cob and used immediately. Special large-kerneled, high-starch corn is treated with slaked lime and dried to make posole (called hominy in the South). The cobs can also be used fresh; bring to a boil with water to make a wonderful alternative to chicken stock. I use it in my restaurants as an inexpensive vegetarian stock.

Cumin The seed of a plant in the carrot family. It was brought to the New World by Spanish settlers, and its pungent, earthy flavor and aroma is a key ingredient in many Texas dishes. I prefer to toast cumin seeds and grind them myself, but if you are using preground cumin, be sure to toast it first to bring the essential oils back to life.

De arbol chiles Meaning "of the tree" or "treelike," these chiles get their name from the woody, treelike shape of their branches. Related to cayenne, which can be substituted. They are orange-red in color with a hot, slightly sweet and fruity flavor. I often infuse my plain cooking oils with de arbol chiles.

Dill This feathery-leaved herb that is a member of the parsley family imparts a delicate, refreshing flavor and is used most extensively in Scandinavian and Eastern European cuisines. It particularly complements the delicate flavors of fish. Dried dill loses the character of the fresh, while heating dillseed brings out a more pungent flavor.

Epazote A Mexican herb, also known as wormseed, stinkweed, and pigweed. Epazote is more commonly available in dried form than fresh, but its growing popularity means that fresh epazote is becoming more abundant, especially in Latin markets. It has a uniquely pungent eucalyptus flavor that is particularly suited to bean dishes, especially as it also reduces their explosive quality.

Garlic Texas is a major producer of garlic, which is native to the Mediterranean basin. I often use roasted garlic in recipes (see page 203), as it enhances other Southwestern flavors. If you have to chop garlic, cover it with olive oil to prevent it from oxidizing. Avoid using garlic powder or dried garlic.

Guajillo chiles Orange-red, tapered dried chiles with thin, shiny flesh and medium, sweetish heat and flavor. Guajillos are perfect for making chile powder and purees.

Habanero chiles The hottest of all chiles, with fruity flavors. Habaneros are bell-shaped and come in a variety of colors—green, yellow, orange, or red, depending on their stage of maturity. Use with caution!

Hoja santa A Mexican herb with large, heart-shaped green leaves. I discovered hoja santa years ago in Oaxaca, where it is used extensively in salsas and mole sauces, as well as to wrap fish for steaming. Its flavor is rather like that of root beer.

Huitlacoche A gray or black corn fungus that is a much-prized ingredient in Mexico (in the United States, it is considered a blight). It has an earthy, rich flavor similar to that of wild mushrooms and is available canned in Latin markets. (See also recipe introduction, page 133.)

Ibarra chocolate A type of Mexican dark chocolate containing ground cinnamon, almonds, and vanilla. It is rough in texture. Packaged in bright red and yellow striped boxes, it is available in Latin markets.

Jalapeño chiles Named after the Mexican region of Jalapa, these are the most popular and well-known chiles in North America. Jalapeños were the first chiles to be taken into outer space. Buy jalapeños that have white streaks down the side, indicating their flavor has fully developed.

Jicama A crisp-textured, almost turnip-shaped tuber that has long been indigenous to Mexico, jicama has the texture and somewhat the flavor between an apple and a water chestnut. Inside the brown skin, which should be peeled, the white flesh is slightly sweet in flavor and refreshingly cool and crunchy, making it an excellent ingredient for salsas and relishes. (See also recipe introduction, page 37.)

Lard As one of the very few cooking fats available in the early 1800s, lard became a key player in the development of Texas cuisine. The food police have, for the most part, eradicated lard for purportedly healthier alternatives like vegetable shortening and olive oil; however, the USDA reports that lard has less than half the cholesterol of butter. Unfortunately, few things lend the same flavor to food that lard does. As my mentor and friend, Julia Child, says, "Everything in moderation." I say, use your best judgment and give it a try to rediscover an old Texas taste.

Limes Indispensable as an acidic component in Texas. I recommend that you buy the smaller Mexican limes instead of the larger Persian limes, as Mexican limes produce more—and sweeter—juice.

Mangos A tropical fruit that is native to Asia, where it is considered sacred by some. Ripe mangos are much easier to find in grocery stores now, and they are indispensable in many salsas, drinks, relishes, and sauces. The tropical coolness and fabulous sweetness of mangos make them the perfect foil to the heat of chiles in Texas cuisine. Ripe mangos should have orange-red skin and give slightly when pressed. They should also have a heady, gardenia-like perfume.

Marigold mint Very similar to tarragon, but more heady in flavor with anise tones. This herb goes well in salads and works well with corn and squash too. In Mexico, it is considered a medicinal herb and is drunk as a tea. In addition, the flowers make an attractive garnish.

Marjoram One of many members of the mint family used in Texas cuisine. Marjoram is a highly underutilized herb that is sweeter and more complex than oregano, though many cooks use it interchangeably with oregano. In Mexico, it is called "wild oregano," and it looks very similar to oregano.

Marsala wine A fortified red wine from Sicily. Rich and a little smoky in flavor.

Masa harina Masa is the Mexican word for "corn dough" and harina means "flour." Masa harina is distinctively flavored flour made from specially processed corn (posole), and it is used to make tortilla and tamale dough. You can buy already prepared masa dough from tortilla factories in large cities.

Mascarpone A rich triple-cream soft cow's-milk cheese from Lombardy in Italy. It is most commonly used in desserts, but it can also be used in savory dishes.

Mint A Mediterranean herb that grows throughout Texas and the Southwest. It should always be used in its fresh form, as the active oil, menthol, is present to a far greater degree than when mint is dried. There are many varieties of mint that offer a wide range of pungency, such as the intense, peppery peppermint and the slightly milder spearmint.

New Mexico (Anaheim) green chiles Long medium-green fresh chiles with medium heat (although heat can vary from quite mild to quite hot). A little sweet with a clean flavor, the New Mexico chile is also known as the Anaheim, depending on location. Also available in roasted form and frozen.

Oils My favorite cooking oil is olive oil, as it imparts a unique but subtle flavor to food. Use a quality brand for dressings and such, as its flavor has to stand alone. Peanut and/or canola oils are best for frying, because they withstand high temperatures and are relatively flavorless. Vegetable oil is perfect for cooking delicate food that needs a neutral oil; it is also ideal for blending to tone down a powerful olive oil. Nut oils, such as hazelnut, walnut, and almond, are unique additions to salad dressing, but they spoil easily and should be sealed well after each use.

Onions Surprisingly, onions are members of the lily family. I love to cook with sweet onions grown here in Texas—Noonday and Texas Spring Sweet. They are wonderfully sweet, even when raw. The more common sweet onion, the Vidalia, mostly grown in Georgia, is originally from Texas stock. The standard onion I use for cooking in this book is the yellow onion, which is slightly sweeter than the white variety. Red onions tend to be very mild and used mainly for color. As with shallots, look for dry, papery skins and firm, heavy onions.

Oregano Like cilantro, this intensely flavored herb is a key ingredient to Texas and Mexican cooking. Mexican oregano, which I enjoy, is slightly stronger than its close cousin, Italian oregano. It is one of the most versatile members of the mint family, and it should be used fresh rather than dried when possible.

Papayas Those sold in the United States are grown mostly in Hawaii, Florida, and Mexico. This fruit, not unlike the mango, is best when the skin is yellow-orange and gives slightly when pressed. The seeds in the center are usually discarded, although they are edible. If you buy a papaya that is green and under-ripe, place it in a brown paper bag in a warm place for a couple of days.

Parsley I prefer the flat-leafed or Italian parsley to the typical steakhouse garnish, curly-leafed variety. In most Texas cooking, you will find cilantro in lieu of parsley, but it still has its place in cooking and is great for perking up heavier dishes.

Pasilla chiles Dark-colored dried chilaca chiles. The long, dark, wrinkled pasillas are also known as negro chiles and are most commonly used for sauces (and especially moles). They have a rich, slightly smoky flavor with dried fruit overtones.

Pecans The most widely cultivated nut in the world. The sweet meat of this nut is a minimum 70 percent oil. Pecans are rarely used in mole sauces because of their pronounced flavor and high fat content. I prefer to use them as an accent to salads and meat dishes, where their flavor is a perfect addition. They should be used quickly, as they turn rancid quite fast; keep them frozen in an airtight container if not used within a few weeks.

Pecorino cheese An Italian sheep's-milk cheese, one type of which is Romano. A tangy, hard, grating cheese. (See also recipe introduction on page 67.)

Pectin Naturally occurring in certain fruits and vegetables, pectin is a water-soluble jelling agent used for thickening preserves, jellies, and jams. It is sold either in liquid or powdered form; I prefer the liquid, which usually sets up faster.

Pine nuts Also known as piñon nuts and pignolis, pine nuts are expensive because of the complex hand-processing required. Native varieties are available in New Mexico and Arizona, but the majority of the American supply comes from Asia and the Middle East. I prefer to toast them before I use them.

Poblano chiles Fresh dark green chiles commonly used in Texas and Mexican cuisine, especially for rellenos. In dried form, poblanos are known as ancho chiles (see above). Poblanos are thick-fleshed, fairly hot in flavor, and are best cooked or roasted and then peeled.

Pumpkin seeds Also called pepitas in Texas and Mexican cooking, pumpkin seeds are actually the seeds of a different kind of squash. They have a green hue that is only slightly diminished by roasting, and they are a wonderful low-calorie alternative to nuts. Pumpkin seeds have been an out-of-hand snack for centuries south of the border, where they are most commonly used for mole sauces.

Queso fresco A fresh, moist white Mexican cheese made from partially skimmed milk. It is ideal for crumbling as a garnish, and it has a slightly sharp, salty taste. Depending on the recipe, you can substitute feta, Monterey Jack, or Muenster.

Quinoa A staple grain of the Inca civilization of South America. Highly nutritious, with a crunchy texture when cooked. (See also recipe introduction on page 117.)

Rosemary This rustic-looking evergreen shrub is a member of the mint family. It has a powerful flavor that works best when complementing food as opposed to overpowering it. The piney, lemony flavor is a perfect addition to grilled meat, either as a skewer or thrown directly onto the fire to flavor the smoke.

Saffron It takes 70,000 hand-picked stigmas from the Mediterranean crocus flower to make just one pound of saffron, which explains its extremely high price. Used for its delicate flavor and brilliant yellow color, saffron came to the New World by way of the Spaniards.

Sage Multiple varieties of this subtle herb grow wild in Texas. It is the perfect addition to fowl, game, pork, and that American classic, stuffing. Originally, as with most herbs, it was used medicinally.

Scallions Scallions are young green onions, but at their scallion stage, their peppery-onion flavor is milder. Like onions, garlic, and leeks, scallions are members of the lily family. They are versatile and an indispensable component of Texas cooking.

Serrano chiles Literally "highland" or "mountain," serranos are small green chiles widely available in supermarkets. Intense, clean flavor similar to that of jalapeños but hotter and a little more acidic.

Shallots Another member of the lily family with a flavor somewhere between those of onions and garlic. Buy shallots that have dry, reddish-brown, papery skins and that are heavy for their size.

Sweet potatoes A Southern staple from the morning glory family. Contrary to popular belief, sweet potatoes and yams are not the same thing; they are distinct plants from different families. Named for their relatively high (3 to 6 percent) sugar content, they are my favorite tuber. The smaller sweet potatoes are usually more sweet and tender.

Tamarind The fruit of an evergreen tree native to West Africa but widely grown in Mexico and Asia, tamarind pods are pulped and processed into a bittersweet paste that is popular in Southwestern and Mexican cooking, as it complements chiles well. Tamarind is terrific in glazes and marinades, and is an ingredient in many commercial steak sauces. The paste is available in Latin and Asian markets.

Thyme A multipurpose herb from the ever-present mint family, thyme is widely used in Texas cooking. Its clean, green-peppery flavor enhances stocks, soups, and sauces, as well as meats. Like rosemary, it can be added to the grill to provide a fragrant flavor to meats and vegetables.

Tomatillos Resembling unripe green tomatoes (to which they are related), tomatillos are a staple of Mexican and Southwestern cooking. Tart, acidic, and slightly lemony in flavor. Remove their papery husks and rinse their sticky surface before cooking. (See also recipe introduction on page 40.)

Tomatoes A native to the New World whose name comes from the Aztec language. Use vine-ripened tomatoes when possible. Out-of-season tomatoes are harvested green and exposed to ethylene gas to produce a red flesh, but never attain the same flavor. When tomatoes are out of season, use a high-quality Italian canned product; drain them first and adjust the recipe accordingly.

Turmeric A spice related to ginger with a pungent flavor and aroma. Turmeric is native to Asia but cultivated throughout the Caribbean. It is typically used in curries and also as a dark yellow food coloring.

Vanilla Another Aztec addition to the culinary world, and a member of the orchid family. The best-quality beans are grown in Tahiti, although Mexican Papantla vanilla also is excellent. Use fresh vanilla whenever possible, and choose large, plump, soft beans.

Vinegars There are all kinds of flavored vinegars on the market nowadays, and I recommend keeping a number on hand at all times; I also like to have aged sherry and balsamic vinegars available. As with olive oil, use the best quality vinegars, especially in salads and dishes where vinegar is not cooked.

Walnuts Related to pecans and also part of the hickory family, walnuts have a high fat content too. They are the second most popular nut in the United States. I prefer to soak them overnight in cold water to avoid any bitterness encountered in the skin.

Index